IDLENESS AND AESTHETIC CONSCIOUSNESS, 1815–1900

Charting the failure of the Romantic critique of political economy, Richard Adelman explores the changing significances and the developing concepts of idleness and aesthetic consciousness during the nineteenth century. Through careful analysis of some of the period's most influential thinkers, including John Stuart Mill, George Eliot, John Ruskin and Karl Marx, Adelman weaves together evolving ideas across a range of intellectual discourses – political economy, meditative poetry, the ideology of the 'gospel of work', cultural theory, the gothic and psychoanalysis. In doing so he reconstructs debates over passivity and repose and demonstrates their centrality to the cultural politics of the age. Arguing that hardened conceptions of aesthetic consciousness come into being at moments of civic unrest concerning political representation and that the fin-de-siècle witnesses the demonization of the once revolutionary category of aesthetic consciousness, the book demonstrates that late eighteenth-century positivity around human spirituality is comprehensively dismantled by the beginning of the twentieth century.

Richard Adelman is Senior Lecturer in English at the University of Sussex. His previously published work includes *Idleness, Contemplation and the Aesthetic, 1750–1830* (Cambridge, 2011), *Political Economy, Literature and the Formation of Knowledge* (2018; edited with Catherine Packham), as well as numerous essays on figures including Dante Rossetti, John Ruskin, William Wordsworth, Percy Shelley, John Keats and J. M. Coetzee.

CAMBRIDGE STUDIES IN NINETEENTH-CENTURY
LITERATURE AND CULTURE

General Editor
Gillian Beer, *University of Cambridge*

Editorial Board
Isobel Armstrong, *Birkbeck, University of London*
Kate Flint, *University of Southern California*
Catherine Gallagher, *University of California, Berkeley*
D. A. Miller, *University of California, Berkeley*
J. Hillis Miller, *University of California, Irvine*
Daniel Pick, *Birkbeck, University of London*
Mary Poovey, *New York University*
Sally Shuttleworth, *University of Oxford*
Herbert Tucker, *University of Virginia*

Nineteenth-century British literature and culture have been rich fields for interdisciplinary studies. Since the turn of the twentieth century, scholars and critics have tracked the intersections and tensions between Victorian literature and the visual arts, politics, social organization, economic life, technical innovations, scientific thought – in short, culture in its broadest sense. In recent years, theoretical challenges and historiographical shifts have unsettled the assumptions of previous scholarly synthesis and called into question the terms of older debates. Whereas the tendency in much past literary critical interpretation was to use the metaphor of culture as 'background', feminist, Foucauldian and other analyses have employed more dynamic models that raise questions of power and of circulation. Such developments have reanimated the field. This series aims to accommodate and promote the most interesting work being undertaken on the frontiers of the field of nineteenth-century literary studies: work which intersects fruitfully with other fields of study such as history, or literary theory, or the history of science. Comparative as well as interdisciplinary approaches are welcomed.

A complete list of titles published will be found at the end of the book.

IDLENESS AND AESTHETIC CONSCIOUSNESS, 1815–1900

RICHARD ADELMAN

CAMBRIDGE
UNIVERSITY PRESS

University Printing House, Cambridge CB2 8BS, United Kingdom

One Liberty Plaza, 20th Floor, New York, NY 10006, USA

477 Williamstown Road, Port Melbourne, VIC 3207, Australia

314–321, 3rd Floor, Plot 3, Splendor Forum, Jasola District Centre, New Delhi – 110025, India

79 Anson Road, #06–04/06, Singapore 079906

Cambridge University Press is part of the University of Cambridge.

It furthers the University's mission by disseminating knowledge in the pursuit of education, learning, and research at the highest international levels of excellence.

www.cambridge.org
Information on this title: http://www.cambridge.org/9781108424134
DOI: 10.1017/9781108539791

First published 2018

Printed and bound in Great Britain by Clays Ltd, Elcograf S.p.A.

A catalogue record for this publication is available from the British Library.

Library of Congress Cataloging-in-Publication Data
NAMES: Adelman, Richard, 1982– author.
TITLE: Idleness and aesthetic consciousness, 1815–1900 / Richard Adelman.
DESCRIPTION: New York : Cambridge University Press, [2018] | Series: Cambridge studies in nineteenth-century literature and culture | Includes bibliographical references.
IDENTIFIERS: LCCN 2018006509 | ISBN 9781108424134
SUBJECTS: LCSH: English literature – 19th century – History and criticism. | Aestheticism (Literature) | Aesthetics in literature. | Laziness in literature.
CLASSIFICATION: LCC PR468.A33 A35 2018 | DDC 820.9/357–dc23
LC record available at https://lccn.loc.gov/2018006509

ISBN 978-1-108-42413-4 Hardback

Contents

Acknowledgements		*page* vi
List of Abbreviations		vii
	Introduction	1
1	Idleness, Moral Consciousness and Sociability	13
2	Political Economy and the Logic of Idleness	48
3	The 'Gospel of Work'	81
4	Cultural Theory and Aesthetic Failure	114
5	The Gothicization of Idleness	149
	Conclusion	183
	Epilogue: Substitutive Satisfaction	192
Notes		201
Bibliography		221
Index		231

Acknowledgements

I would like to express my gratitude to John Barrell for his invaluable assistance in the initial formulation of this project, to Peter Kitson for his considerable guidance and advice, again at the project's early stages, and to Norman Vance for his careful reading of the completed manuscript and for his generous and insightful suggestions. I am also indebted to the Leverhulme Trust for the Research Fellowship they awarded me in 2014, which enabled me to undertake the bulk of the research and writing for the project, and to my colleagues at Dundee and then Sussex for their considerable intellectual stimulation during the time I was working on the book.

Parts of Chapter 1 first appeared in a different form in 'Idleness & Vacancy' in Shelley's 'Mont Blanc', *Keats-Shelley Journal*, no. 62 (2013): 62–79 and 'Keats and the Sociability of Idle Contemplation', *Poetica*, no. 82 (2014): 21–38. Material from the first article is reprinted with the permission of the Keats-Shelley Association of America, Inc. I am grateful to the editors of *Poetica* for the permission to use material from the second article.

Abbreviations

'Carmilla'   Sheridan Le Fanu, 'Carmilla', *In a Glass Darkly*,
                         ed. R. Tracy (Oxford: Oxford University Press,
                         1993), pp. 243–319.
'Christabel'   Samuel Taylor Coleridge, 'Christabel', *Coleridge's
                         Poetry and Prose*, eds. N. Halmi, P. Magnuson &
                         R. Modiano (London: W. W. Norton, 2004),
                         pp. 161–79.
Culture   Matthew Arnold, *Culture and Anarchy: An Essay
                         in Political and Social Criticism*, The Complete
                         Prose Works of Matthew Arnold, Volume V, ed.
                         R. H. Super (Ann Arbor, MI: University of
                         Michigan Press, 1965), pp. 85–256.
Dracula   Bram Stoker, *Dracula*, eds. N. Auerbach &
                         D. J. Skal (London: Norton, 1997).
'GC'   Matthew Arnold, 'To a Gipsy Child by the Sea-
                         Shore', *The Poetical Works of Matthew Arnold*, eds.
                         C. B. Tinker & H. F. Lowry (Oxford: Oxford
                         University Press, 1963), pp. 41–3.
Letters   John Keats, *The Letters of John Keats*, ed. Hyder
                         E. Rollins, 2 vols. (Cambridge: Cambridge
                         University Press, 1958).
'LE'   Alfred Tennyson, 'The Lotos-Eaters', *Tennyson's
                         Poetry*, ed. R. W. Hill Jr. (London: Norton, 1999),
                         pp. 76–80.
Malthus, *Principles*   Thomas Malthus, *The Principles of Political
                         Economy*, ed. J. Pullen, 2 vols. (Cambridge:
                         Cambridge University Press, 1989).
'MB'   Percy Shelley, 'Mont Blanc', *The Major Works*,
                         eds. Z. Leader & M. O'Neill (Oxford: Oxford
                         University Press, 2003), pp. 120–4.

Mill, *Principles*	John Stuart Mill, *Principles of Political Economy, Collected Words of John Stuart Mill*, vols. II–III, ed. J. M. Robson (London: Routledge, 1965).
Past	Thomas Carlyle, *Chartism, Past & Present* (London: Chapman & Hall, 1858).
Renaissance	Walter Pater, *The Renaissance: Studies in Art and Poetry*, ed. Donald L. Hill (London: University of California Press, 1980).
Ricardo, *Principles*	David Ricardo, *Principles of Political Economy*, ed. P. Sraffa (Cambridge: Cambridge University Press, 1951).
Sartor	Thomas Carlyle, *Sartor Resartus*, eds. K. McSweeney & P. Sabor (Oxford: Oxford University Press, 1999).
'SG'	Matthew Arnold, 'The Scholar-Gipsy', *The Poetical Works of Matthew Arnold*, eds. C. B. Tinker & H. F. Lowry (Oxford: Oxford University Press, 1963), pp. 255–62.
'SF'	Gerard Manley Hopkins, 'Spring and Fall', *The Major Works*, ed. Catherine Phillips (Oxford: Oxford University Press, 2002), p. 152.
Stones	John Ruskin, *The Stones of Venice*, 3 vols. (London: George Allen & Unwin, 1925).
'SR'	Matthew Arnold, 'The Strayed Reveller', *The Poetical Works of Matthew Arnold*, eds. C. B. Tinker & H. F. Lowry (Oxford: Oxford University Press, 1963), pp. 185–94.
Varney	James Malcolm Rymer, *Varney the Vampyre; or, The Feast of Blood, A Romance* (Berkeley Heights, NJ: Wildside Press, 2000).
WH	Emily Brontë, *Wuthering Heights*, eds. P. Nestor & L. Miller (London: Penguin, 2003).

Introduction

When, in George Eliot's *Middlemarch* of 1871–2, Dorothea and her new husband Edward Casaubon travel to Rome and visit the artist Adolf Naumann's studio with Will Ladislaw, Eliot uses the scene as a meeting point of two opposed conceptions of artistic creativity. On the one hand, there is the rapturous, transcendent view of art Ladislaw represents. In commenting on one of Naumann's works in progress, for example, Ladislaw's admiration is apparently too deep to be expressed verbally. Eliot's narrator records how 'Will vented those adjuring interjections which imply that admiration is too strong for syntax'.[1] On the other hand, there is Casaubon's pejorative judgement of art, in which sitting for a portrait and devoting oneself to aesthetic creativity alike are effectively non-activities. When asked to prolong his posing for Naumann, for instance, Casaubon's reply casts the whole business as a species of 'idleness': '"I am at your service, sir, in this matter," said Mr Casaubon, with polite condescension. "Having given up the interior of my head to idleness, it is as well that the exterior should work in this way"'.[2] It may seem as though Casaubon's association of sitting for his portrait with 'idleness' simply opposes that task to his vocation and monomania, his scholarly research for the *Key to All Mythologies*. But in fact, the term 'idleness' is associated, both in Eliot's novel and in Victorian culture more broadly, with artistic practice itself, and especially with the type of aesthetic consciousness Ladislaw's wordless ecstasy implies. When Ladislaw is first introduced to the novel's action, for example, when he is found sketching in the grounds of Lowick, his penchant for artistic creativity is cast as a tendency towards 'indolence' by Arthur Brooke, as being 'idle' by Dorothea and as a 'dislike to steady application' by Casaubon.[3] These terms serve very clearly as synonyms, at this point in the novel, for a devotion to aesthetic consciousness, because Ladislaw's attitude to the acquirement of knowledge is summarized by Casaubon as the belief that 'there should be some unknown regions preserved as hunting-grounds for the poetic imagination'.[4] Again, the clear opposite to these judgements is the diligent work ethic and the rigorous pursuit of factual knowledge Casaubon sees himself as embodying. In this scene at least, Dorothea and her uncle defer to his perspective.

But Eliot's novel stages a more even debate between these poles of aesthetic passivity and diligent 'application' than these two scenes imply. On several occasions, it might seem as though the novel's balancing of these alternatives even tips entirely against Casaubon. Ladislaw is given his first conquest over Casaubon in this sense later in the novel's Roman scenes, for example, just after the episode in Naumann's studio, when he reveals to Dorothea that his aesthetic passivity also connotes a greater breadth of cultural knowledge than Casaubon. He refers there, in a one-on-one conversation with Dorothea, to the German 'Higher Criticism' that will render Casaubon's life's work obsolete before it is even composed.[5] This reference casts Casaubon himself as an idling amateur, and the professionalized world of German scholarship – which Ladislaw, through Naumann, is more in touch with – as genuinely diligent labour. There is also the striking moment of direct judgement, within the passage where Eliot has her narrator delineate Casaubon's consciousness for the first time, in which a set of priorities that seem to invoke Ladislaw's 'poetic' or artistic 'imagination' are overtly used to critique Casaubon's apparently dry diligence:

> For my part I am very sorry for him. It is an uneasy lot at best, to be what we call highly taught and yet not to enjoy: to be present at this great spectacle of life and never to be liberated from a small hungry shivering self – never to be fully possessed by the glory we behold, never to have our consciousness rapturously transformed into the vividness of a thought, the ardour of a passion, the energy of an action, but always to be scholarly and uninspired, ambitious and timid, scrupulous and dim-sighted.[6]

Because Casaubon is 'uninspired', and never 'rapturously transformed' or 'liberated' from his 'small hungry shivering self', the priorities structuring this scathing judgement would seem to be exactly the transcendent, passionate, arduous style of aesthetic thought that Ladislaw felt, but stumbled over and failed to fully express, in Naumann's studio. This passage also associates aesthetic transcendence with religious ecstasy, through Eliot's use of terms such as 'glory' and 'rapture'. In other words, Eliot's narrator is here throwing his or her lot in with aesthetic consciousness, with transcendent imagination, and quite aggressively deprecating diligent, steady, 'uninspired' 'application'.

Middlemarch's staging of this debate between idle, aesthetic passivity and narrow, industrious labour soon transcends the immediate quarrel between Ladislaw and Casaubon and becomes a matter of broader concern for the community the novel focuses on, and for Victorian society more generally. Ladislaw's aesthetic passivity and the broad intellectual culture that seems to attend on it serve, for instance, as the foundation for his political activities and his support for the first Reform Act. Eliot indeed overtly invokes and links these characteristics at the moment that Brooke's purchase of the *Pioneer*, and Ladislaw's involvement in that publication, is revealed:

> For it seemed that Will was not only at home in all those artistic and literary subjects which Mr Brooke had gone into at one time, but that he was strikingly ready at seizing the points of the political situation, and dealing with them in that large spirit which, aided by adequate memory, lends itself to the quotation and general effectiveness of treatment.[7]

What Casaubon and the opening sections of the novel cast as narrow, solipsistic passivity, is thus, by this midpoint in Eliot's plot, rendered a moral and politically progressive force that has the potential to sway the course of the entire nation. Ladislaw's 'large spirit', fostered by the apparent idleness of aesthetic contemplation, even has him denominated a 'Shelley', by Brooke, just after this quotation, though Brooke makes sure to specify that he is not referring to 'laxities or atheism, or anything of that kind'.[8] This association again demonstrates – contra Casaubon – the power and positive effect that aesthetic passivity can ultimately engender. For in this context Shelley's famous conclusion to his *Defence of Poetry* of 1821 is very clearly invoked: poets, or artists, are 'the unacknowledged legislators of the world'.[9] But we should remember too that Shelley's portrayal of aesthetic inspiration with which that essay begins stresses the poet's extreme passivity and therefore intellectual receptivity: 'Man is an instrument over which a series of external and internal impressions are driven, like the alternations of an ever-changing wind over an Aeolian lyre.'[10] Eliot's interest in Shelley and Coleridge's 'Aeolian harp' motif is demonstrated back in the Lowick sketching scene. There, Ladislaw's first observations of Dorothea include his rapturous thoughts concerning her voice: 'But what a voice! It was like the voice of a soul that had once lived in an Æolian harp.'[11]

This highlighting of Ladislaw's 'large spirit' and its association with both Romantic poetics and political progress is not Eliot's last word on aesthetic creativity and poetic consciousness in *Middlemarch*, however.

Indeed, following Casaubon's death, the novel's narrative perspective might be described as swinging back towards that character's emphasis on diligence and arduous labour, because Eliot's narrator more than once portrays Ladislaw as fundamentally unfocused and unproductive. Once Ladislaw has fully immersed himself in his work for the *Pioneer*, for instance, the actual level of his commitment to politics, and to reform, is made clear:

> It is undeniable that but for the desire to be where Dorothea was, and perhaps the want of knowing what else to do, Will would not at this time have been meditating on the needs of the English people or criticising English statesmanship: he would probably have been rambling in Italy sketching plans for several dramas, trying prose and finding it too jejune, trying verse and finding it too artificial, beginning to copy 'bits' from old pictures, leaving off because they were 'no good', and observing that, after all, self-culture was the principal point; while in politics he would have been sympathizing warmly with liberty and progress in general. Our sense of duty must often wait for some work which shall take the place of dilettantism and make us feel that the quality of our action is not a matter of indifference.[12]

A passage such as this is a critique of aesthetic 'self-culture' as dilettantish, unfocused and immature. It also opposes this aesthetic realm to the 'duty' of 'work' and to 'action' that matters for the world, that 'is not a matter of indifference'. The perspective of this passage thus stands quite close to that espoused by Casaubon in the opening sections of the novel. It also demonstrates the extent to which *Middlemarch* sublimates its debate between Casaubon and Ladislaw, and between aesthetic idleness and diligent application, into the very perspective from which it is narrated.

Eliot should ultimately be understood, however, to invoke in *Middlemarch* a synthesis of Casaubon's arduous application and Ladislaw's aesthetic passivity. The novel's dénouement allows Ladislaw to continue to use his 'large spirit' and sympathy with 'liberty and progress', but to work towards reform in a more focused and committed manner. And it is diligent, arduous and honest work that provides the moral blueprint for this future success. Ladislaw, we are told, becomes an 'ardent public man' who 'work[s] well' towards reform and eventually becomes an MP with the support of Dorothea as his wife.[13] And the novel's touchstone for moral values, Caleb Garth, succeeds, at this same final moment in the narrative, in exerting his positive influence on his future son-in-law Fred Vincy, by inspiring him with his modest and honest work ethic that matches Ladislaw's. The scene in which this triumph is made clear thus demonstrates the necessary supplement to Ladislaw's youthful aesthetic imagination and self-culture: Caleb explains to his daughter, Mary, that honest, diligent 'work' is his 'delight'.[14]

This trajectory in *Middlemarch* towards the synthesis of apparent opposites has of course been noted – in general terms – in the novel's critical reception. Donald Stone, for example, uses the Arnoldian vocabulary of 'Hebraic and Hellenic impulses' to explain this aspect of the novel's design: 'In the persons of the overly self-denying Dorothea Brooke and the benignly hedonistic Will Ladislaw, [Eliot] shows how each gains from contact with the other. Dorothea becomes aware of the value of beauty and of her own sensual needs, while Will learns to apply his scattered energies and talents to a useful vocation.'[15] What is left out of an assessment such as this, however, is the manner in which Eliot renders Ladislaw's Hellenism an issue of 'idleness', passivity, 'indolence' and transcendent consciousness, and the extent to which the real opposite force in the novel for this cluster of ideas is something very like the Carlylean 'gospel of work', which has its locus not simply in the character of Dorothea, in Eliot's design. It is also important to note the level of anachronism latent in Stone's approach. Matthew Arnold's exposition of the terms Hebraism and Hellenism is the fruit of the 1860s, the years just preceding Eliot's composition of *Middlemarch*. But the novel itself is set in what Henry Staten calls 'a carefully realized historical conjuncture, the years 1829–31, when England, in the grip of economic crisis, trembled on the brink of the first great Reform Act'.[16] It is in this 'carefully' historical sense that Eliot has Ladislaw referred to as a 'Shelley' (and indeed elsewhere as a 'Byron'[17]), because her design includes the recreation of historical attitudes and associations in quite exact detail. What this dimension of the novel points us to, and what Stone's assessment of the novel cannot access, is thus that *Middlemarch* invokes the nineteenth century's long history of associating 'idleness' and passivity with aesthetic consciousness. Arnoldian Hellenism is in fact an overt and conscious continuation of this trend, while Shelley's celebration of the poetic imagination in his *Defence* and Coleridge's ruminations on the 'Æolian harp' are two of this tradition's key documents. Eliot's novel thus explores in some detail this tradition of aesthetic passivity by dramatizing its various failings, powers and counterarguments. This focus to *Middlemarch* has remained all but unnoticed because, as Felicia Bonaparte observes, the novel's exploration of the subject of art has been significantly overlooked,[18] and because, according to Joseph Wiesenfarth, Ladislaw's pivotal role in the novel also goes frequently unrecognized.[19] The association of Ladislaw's aesthetic consciousness with idleness, passivity and unworldly dilettantism, and the links –

through Shelley – between that passivity and 'liberty', reform and the 'large spirit' of human progress, thus lie at the heart of Eliot's design for *Middlemarch*. Eliot's novel, in other words, invokes, refers to and explores the centrality of idle, aesthetic consciousness to nineteenth-century culture in the broadest terms.

The present study is an attempt to reconstruct and explore the nineteenth century's many debates over idleness and aesthetic consciousness that stand behind – and that are reflected in – Eliot's novel. For it is by no means simply Shelley, Coleridge and Arnold that consider these categories in detail in the years leading up to the composition of *Middlemarch*. On the contrary, a wide constituency of figures, and a wide variety of discourses, position repose, idleness, contemplation, aesthetic transcendence and several other species of passivity as central to contemporary individual and social life. Nineteenth-century political economy, as one example, pays such attention to the human tendencies towards idleness, repose and contemplative leisure that it often leaves economic activity itself looking like a rare and delicate occurrence. The thought of highly influential figures such as Thomas Carlyle and John Ruskin – to both of whom Eliot is considerably indebted – also returns, again and again, to questions of contemplative passivity and aesthetic transcendence. Even the nineteenth century's most successful mode of populist gothic writing consistently dramatizes contemplative idleness in sustained and visceral detail. This study will chart this complex terrain standing behind Eliot's novel, and will identify and account for the marked transformation in conceptions of idle aesthetic contemplation that takes place across the century. For *Middlemarch*'s overall ambivalence over Ladislaw's idle contemplation marks the novel out as a nuanced reflection of the differing associations and connotations aesthetic consciousness has acquired by the 1870s. Eliot's novel partakes at once, that is to say, of both the early century's marked positivity regarding idle contemplation (that which is contemporary to its action) and of the mid- to late century's distrust – or even vilification – of such passivity, especially when divorced from the ideologies of labour and social amelioration.

This study will thus begin with a consideration of the body of thought that Eliot uses to denote the positive social potential of aesthetic passivity, Percy Shelley and his contemporaries' celebrations of idle contemplation. Chapter 1 will examine the manner in which Shelley and John Keats allude to and extend first-generation Romanticism's analyses of contemplative and aesthetic repose, and specifically the extent to which both poets frame idle contemplation as a matter of moral and social utility. The chapter will touch on Shelley's *Defence of Poetry*, but will initially focus on his 1816 poem, 'Mont Blanc'. It will then consider Keats's correspondence, specifically his accounts of the poetic character, aesthetic democracy and 'negative capability'.

Chapter 2 of the study will survey the discourse of political economy across the first half of the nineteenth century, and examine that body of thought's surprising receptivity to the ideas and concerns espoused by Keats and Shelley. While late eighteenth-century political economy had been markedly limited in the space and standing it gave to human repose, in the nineteenth century David Ricardo, Thomas Malthus and John Stuart Mill all follow a kind of logic of idleness in their political economic writings, and all allow the concerns of human repose to influence their primary conclusions. Because this receptivity increases markedly across the first decades of the century, Mill's 1848 *Principles of Political Economy* represents a significant flowering of positivity surrounding idle contemplation, not just in economic thought, but in the century as a whole.

Chapter 3 will contrast political economy's surprising positivity surrounding idleness with the contemporary ideology of the 'gospel of work'. In order to assess this far-reaching and widespread ideology, this chapter will consider the thought of Thomas Carlyle and Karl Marx in detail, before examining one of the effects of this body of thought, the negativity – from mid-century onwards – around idleness and aesthetic consciousness to be found in that period's contemplative poetry. The 'gospel of work' is not just significant for this study because of its very influential opposition to the earlier, positive conceptions of repose discussed in the previous two chapters. Carlyle's and Marx's formulations of this ideology are also in fact constructed on earlier, eighteenth- and nineteenth-century aesthetic theorizations of idleness itself. The 'gospel of work' is thus a paradoxical and double-edged decree.

After exploring this primary counterforce to positive conceptions of idleness across the century, Chapter 4 will consider high Victorian cultural theory in the form of the writing of Ruskin, Arnold and Walter Pater. These figures all contend – overtly and directly – for the power, and social benefit, of aesthetic consciousness, but do so at the same time as introducing a series of practical hurdles to the widespread adoption of that state. The writings of these figures must also be understood to bear the imprint of Carlyle and his contemporaries' 'gospel of work', because their closely connected theories of culture and human aesthetic capability also professionalize, and significantly elongate, the aesthetic encounter.

Chapter 5, which is the final chapter of the study, draws together all of its strands by considering the tradition of vampire fiction across the breadth of the nineteenth century, and by demonstrating the extent to which that genre addresses aesthetic idleness and its social alternatives. My analysis shows how the very conservative vampire tradition villainizes – and indeed demonizes – the poetic idle contemplator, and by the end of the century, in the hands of Sheridan Le Fanu and Bram Stoker, for instance, dramatizes a kind of total warfare against that figure, and against aesthetic conscious-ness, waged by the Carlylean forces of modernity. This subject forms an appropriate conclusion to the study because this genre's highly focused negativity around aesthetic repose is representative of the fate of this category more broadly by the final years of the century.

The study concludes with a brief epilogue considering the afterlife of these debates over idleness and aesthetic consciousness in Sigmund Freud's *Civilization and Its Discontents* of 1930. While Freud stands in a very different tradition of thought from any of the figures considered in the main body of this study, his conceptions of aesthetic creativity and receptivity nevertheless echo and encapsulate many of the developments in these fields that occurred in Britain across the long nineteenth century. Freud's overt negativity con-cerning the place of aesthetic thought in human life thus allows the British enquiries into this subject to be seen from a new angle and with a new clarity.

By means of these analyses, this study will construct a detailed portrait of the centrality of the categories of idleness and aesthetic consciousness to many nineteenth-century debates, ideologies and discourses. It will also identify the manner in which these categories' reputations and associations develop – and transform – with far-reaching consequences across the century. For the changing status of idle aesthetic contemplation is inti-mately tied, as we will see in detail, to the complex logic of democratic reform, and to that process's many moments of intensity and upheaval. This shift is also bound up with the increasing theorization of such concepts as 'capital' and 'class', and with the increasingly fraught class politics of the second half of the century. To describe and account for the changing significance of idleness and aesthetic consciousness in this period is therefore to consider Victorian cultural politics at once in terms of its broad currents and its local details. And to follow the fall in reputation of idle contemplation is to identify the rise of a significant subject of malaise, loss and nostalgia at the heart of Victorian consciousness.

This study, it should be noted, follows on from my account of the growth of widespread positive conceptions of idleness and aesthetic repose around the turn of the nineteenth century, which was published as *Idleness, Contemplation and the Aesthetic, 1750–1830*, in 2011. This work reconstructed the extensive reaction to the birth of political economy, and to that discourse's considerable emphasis on human labour and extremely limited account of repose and leisure. Such reaction took the form of a series of celebrations – and explanations – of the centrality of idleness and aesthetic consciousness to individual and social life in a diverse range of contexts and registers. After considering the political economy of Adam Smith and Adam Ferguson, this study therefore demonstrated the extent to which philosophies as diverse as Benthamite Utilitarianism and Friedrich Schiller's aesthetic idealism are designed to foster aesthetic repose in highly comparable terms. It then explored the string of first-generation Romantic accounts of idle contemplation – those by William Cowper, Samuel Taylor Coleridge and Mary Wollstonecraft, for example – that also take issue with contemporary political economy's degradation of repose. This study then demonstrated how this poetic body of analysis is ultimately enshrined in Coleridge's more formal cultural analysis in his 1829 *On the Constitution of Church and State*. And my analysis in this work concluded with an epilogue looking ahead to the Victorian reaction to such positive conceptions of idle contemplation, in the form of Charles Kingsley and John Stuart Mill's largely problematic engagement with Romantic accounts of aesthetic consciousness.

The present study should therefore be seen to interlock with, as well as continue from, this previous work. Both books consider elements of the Romantic celebration of idle contemplation, because this field is a clear highpoint within the long nineteenth century's widely varied assessments of aesthetic repose. The previous book thus charted the dramatic rise of this body of thought. The present study maps its decline but also its transformation and modification in the complex currents of nineteenth-century intellectual and political culture. The present study must therefore, by necessity, refer to this earlier work at least in passing in its analyses, not least because both early nineteenth-century and Victorian theorists of idle contemplation see themselves as in conversation with their intellectual forebears who also considered this subject. In one sense this study is therefore an account of the complex ways in which Victorian culture inherited, and reassessed, the intellectual legacy of its early nineteenth-century and late eighteenth-century forefathers – especially because the previous book demonstrated the centrality of idleness and aesthetic contemplation to that legacy. But while unpacking Victorian culture's frequent references to Romanticism in these terms, and to the intellectual culture around that literary phenomenon, the present study also moves beyond such conversations to assess what is new, and what is particularly Victorian, about conceptions of idleness across the later nineteenth century. In this context, the period considered by the present study is significantly marked by the development – and the repeated theorization – of a kind of aesthetics of failure, and of problematic self-consciousness, that first appears in Ruskin's architectural criticism, or in the young Arnold's poetic meditations on contemporary culture's distance from Romanticism, both of which were written around the mid-nineteenth century. This development captures a powerful force in the Victorian psyche, not least because it also anticipates and leads in to the scathing negativity of the early twentieth century around aesthetic consciousness that I address in this study's epilogue. And in this case, as throughout the study, it is my belief that the long view provided by knowledge of Romantic and late eighteenth-century cultural politics enriches, and very usefully contextualizes, the Victorian departures from that thought.

It is necessary to say a word here, too, about the geographical remit of the present analysis. This study concentrates on British thought – and, in the case of Marx, thought engaged with British industrial and political life – rather than attempting to trace a series of shared concerns across European culture. (Freud, who is considered in the study's epilogue, is the primary exception to this, but is included as a way of emblematically gesturing beyond the chronological bounds of the study.) It would have been possible, therefore, to broaden and deepen the study's analysis by reference to the numerous examples of German and French thought dealing with comparable ideas and categories at the same time as their British counterparts. The fact that such works – Arthur Schopenhauer's writing that stands in close proximity to Pater's, or Gustave Flaubert's double-edged explorations of aesthetic consciousness, for example – were also translated into English in this period means that the decision to limit my focus to British thought does cut off a range of important and influential European cross-currents. But boundaries must be drawn somewhere, and an analysis of British thought across the nineteenth century complements the focus of my former book on this subject, and allows me to follow in detail how British intellectual life engaged with the birth and then development of political economy and its related patterns of thought. It is my contention, indeed, that the British engagement with the protean significance of idleness and aesthetic consciousness across the nineteenth century constitutes a tradition in its own right. Connectedly, it is a contention of my first book on this subject that the British Romantic reaction to political economy that pays particular attention to the category of idleness develops without reference to the German idealist tradition. Such claims may seem at odds with the figures cut by Kant, Schiller, Hegel and their countrymen in the recent scholarship of connected ideas to those under consideration here (as my analysis in Chapter 1 will demonstrate). But the present study is an attempt to move behind the standard account of nineteenth-century aesthetics and bring a new cast of figures into play with these ideas. In this new line of analysis, Cowper, Coleridge, Keats and Shelley play the roles most often allotted to the German idealists.[20]

There is another conscious and connected omission from the following analysis that I want to close this introduction by justifying and by briefly exploring. The present study does not pursue the many connections between its nineteenth-century sources and recent theoretical writing, even in cases where recent material has partially informed the critical perspective I take up here. The explanation for this decision is, as above, that this study attempts to follow an unfolding current of thought, in a number of areas of the British nineteenth century, and to reconstruct the shape and movements of that current in terms that are broadly contemporary and, as far as possible, chronological. A theory-driven account of the ideas found in this study would not allow for such reconstruction; but likewise an analysis of this material informed by theory in a step-by-step manner would hamper the study's ability to follow the internal logic of the texts and discourses on which it focuses. The main theoretical body of work that could be brought to bear on an alternative treatment of this subject would be the writing of Jacques Rancière (which I do mention in Chapter 1, but only in passing). Rancière's sustained exploration of the social, political and aesthetic 'distribution of the sensible', for example, deals with the contours of the history this study follows in insightful terms. For Rancière, the Romantic reaction to political economy is an 'aesthetic regime of the arts' that 'disrupts' the reigning 'apportionment' of space, occupation and opportunity.[21] It 'brings to light' – by, for example, challenging the notion that life is primarily labour – 'the distribution of *occupations* that upholds the apportionment of domains of activity'.[22] Rancière also picks out the manner in which nineteenth-century thought pushes back against this 'regime': 'In the nineteenth century, this *suspension* of work's negative value became the assertion of its positive value as the very form of the shared effectivity of thought and community.'[23] These two shifts correspond to the two histories I have attempted to unfold in this study and in my previous book on this subject. The first book explores the development of 'the aesthetic regime of the arts', the second – this study –

that regime's atrophy as it encounters the Victorian 'gospel of work' and the ascendancy of political economy (or a popular conception of political economy) among the human sciences. But again, one should note that Rancière derives his interpretation almost exclusively from continental sources. The writers referred to in the passages I have just quoted from are Schiller, Kant and Marx. Elsewhere in Rancière's thought, Flaubert also looms large. But there lies behind this overview of the long nineteenth century an often unseen British line of inquiry into these same shifts and trends. Thus, I submit, one does not need the German idealists and their legatees to make sense of British intellectual life in this period. And, moreover, a detailed consideration of the parallel British tradition to Schiller, Kant and Marx also usefully complicates Rancière's categories. So while the present study could be described as considering in detail the complex interplay of Romantic aesthetics and Victorian labour-theory in terms that fit Rancière's, the position of Victorian political economy, for example, partakes very significantly, and very problematically – as we will see in Chapter 2 – of Rancière's 'aesthetic regime'. Both Benthamite Utilitarianism and the writing around the 'gospel of work' itself are also comparably Janus-faced in their relationship to aesthetic practice and to Rancière's model of the 'distribution of the sensible'. The terms of the present analysis are therefore intended to go behind – and to consciously avoid – Rancière's, so that the British experience of the convulsions shaking the European mindset in these decades can be seen in its own right. The detailed analysis of the shifting parameters and status of aesthetic consciousness that follows will thus produce a specifically British portrait of cultural politics in the long nineteenth century. And the attention paid to intertextuality in my analysis will serve, I hope, to underline and explore how the texts under consideration here constitute a distinct body of thought.

CHAPTER I

Idleness, Moral Consciousness and Sociability

We must begin this study by exploring the strikingly positive conceptions of idle contemplation and aesthetic consciousness that characterize poetic discourse in the early years of the nineteenth century. The poetic portraits of creative and transcendent repose that were written around this time are numerous, and so interconnected that they share a number of fundamental qualities. First, such portraits are obliquely, but powerfully and earnestly, political. What the nascent political economy of Adam Smith and Adam Ferguson treats as a gap in labour – and thus in life – these portraits treat as an intricate bundle of taxing, pleasurable and highly significant activities. The significance of these activities stems from their tendency to engender the moral consciousness that even these political economists admit is denied to the manual labourer. Their pleasure comes from their creativity and the free play of the imagination they stimulate. Second, however, such accounts are also characterized by their consistent use of irony. Alongside the earnest celebration of idleness's potential and importance is a tendency to back down, to conclude that the boasted attributes of rumination and repose are in fact illusory, or to define the poet's own earnestness as momentary and misplaced. Such irony is connected to the motif of the 'flight of fancy' that structures poetic accounts of idle contemplation. These accounts always involve the poet him or herself, or the poet's imagination, departing from his or her body and considering in detail the object being contemplated. And because this motif is more than metaphorical in this context, because it is consistently deployed as a description of the physical experience of aesthetic contemplation, such accounts are haunted by the possibility that the poet might not return to his or her body, that his or her identity might be reconstituted by, or somehow lost in, the physicality of the objects being contemplated. The irony found in these portraits of idle contemplation is therefore a kind of defence mechanism against this metaphysical danger. It thus signals an ambivalence to the experiences being described that is as necessary to their depiction as the consistent earnestness.

John Keats's and Percy Bysshe Shelley's writing on idle contemplation, which will form the focus of this chapter, conforms to this dichotomy. And because it was primarily William Cowper and Samuel Taylor Coleridge who developed the poetic discourse of idleness in the last decades of the eighteenth century, it is to these poets that Keats and Shelley allude, and from these poets that they depart, in the texts we are going to consider. The analysis that follows will thus chart these intertextualities, and will thereby demonstrate the depth and complexity of the positive discourse of idleness that was taking place by the second decade of the nineteenth century. For, by this time idle contemplation was frequently understood as the central category in human life, as an engagement that would solve the problems attendant on an advanced division of labour – such as alienation and mental stultification – by instantly liberating and moralizing an individual's consciousness. Idle contemplation is thus, for Cowper and for Coleridge, as for many of their contemporaries,[1] a paradoxical species of intense activity. To engage in passive aesthetic contemplation is to be active in a manner that goes beyond the limited and limiting world of mechanical labour, for example. While Shelley and Keats, as we will see now, are both adherents to this line of thinking, both also push this intellectual and political position in new directions. In order to trace these developments, we will begin with Shelley's writing, concentrating first on his 1817 poem 'Mont Blanc'.

Percy Shelley's 'Mont Blanc' was first published at the back of the volume of travel memoirs he coauthored with Mary Shelley, the 1817 *History of a Six Weeks' Tour*. Unannounced on the title page, though briefly described in the final paragraph of its preface, the poem is in some respects an odd presence in the volume. Its apparent immediacy, for instance, described in the preface as 'an undisciplined overflowing of the soul' 'composed under the immediate impression of [. . .] deep and powerful feelings',[2] contrasts strongly with the retrospective calm of many of the volume's prose narratives. Yet Percy Shelley's contribution to the *History* other than 'Mont Blanc', his two long letters from Geneva and Chamonix, are characterized, in part, by a set of concerns to be found in the poem as well. When Shelley first encounters Mont Blanc, for example, the sheer force of the mountain's presence generates a circularity of thought, and a complexity of syntax, that foreshadows the language of the poem:

> Mont Blanc was before us – the Alps, with their innumerable glaciers on high all around, closing in the complicated windings of the single vale –

forests inexpressibly beautiful, but majestic in their beauty – intermingled beech and pine, and oak, overshadowed our road, or receded, whilst lawns of such verdure as I have never seen before occupied these openings, and gradually became darker in their recesses. Mont Blanc was before us, but it was covered with cloud; its base, furrowed with dreadful gaps, was seen above.[3]

The repetition of the phrase 'Mont Blanc was before us' here, containing within its bounds a kaleidoscopic impression of the scene's 'complicated windings', recalls the form of the poem's second section: 'thou, Ravine of Arve – dark, deep Ravine – / Thou many-coloured, many voiced vale, [. . .] thou art there!' ('MB', 12–13, 48). Both descriptions are marked by a tension between the sheer solidity, volume and stillness of the scene, and a simultaneous awareness of its intricacy and movement. Just a few pages on in the *History*, similarly, alongside further observations on the ceaseless movement of this scene's 'vast mass of ice' ('it breaks and bursts for ever'; 'it is never the same'), we find Shelley toying with the possibility of personifying the mountain in much the same vein as the poem: 'One would think that Mont Blanc, like the god of the Stoics, was a vast animal, and that the frozen blood for ever circulated through his stony veins.'[4] Importantly here, Shelley keeps this possibility at arm's length; the phrase 'One would think' stands at a considerable distance from the assertion that this is the case, that the mountain is in some sense alive, or Godlike. Of course, the manner in which the poem both makes and backs down from this gesture has been thoroughly documented.[5]

In addition to these quite direct affinities between Shelley's prose and verse accounts of his encounter with the Ravine of Arve, however, there is another, more tentative idea in his contribution to the *History* that can also be traced in 'Mont Blanc', and that opens up a way of reading the poem that is importantly distinct from its recent critical appreciations (more of which presently). This idea emerges out of Shelley's observations on the problematic tendencies of the idle mind, and is highly reminiscent of a key Coleridgean motif. In his letter from 'Montalegre' over a month before his letter describing Mont Blanc itself, Shelley records an encounter with a young boy in a village called Nerni. Unexceptional in many respects, seeming to offer simply local colour in the scheme of the letter as a whole, this description nevertheless concludes by raising significant doubts about the poet's imaginative powers. Here is the letter's description together with its sceptical coda:

> On returning to the village, we sat on a wall beside the lake, looking at some children who were playing at a game like ninepins. The children here appeared in an extraordinary way deformed and diseased. Most of them were crooked, and with enlarged throats; but one little boy had such exquisite grace in his mien and motions, as I never before saw equalled in a child. His countenance was beautiful for the expression with which it overflowed. There was a mixture of pride and gentleness in his eyes and lips, the indications of sensibility, which his education will probably pervert to misery or seduce to crime; but there was more of gentleness than of pride, and it seemed that the pride was tamed from its original wildness by the habitual exercise of milder feelings. My companion gave him a piece of money, which he took without speaking, with a sweet smile of easy thankfulness, and then with an unembarrassed air turned to his play. All this might scarcely be; but the imagination surely could not forbear to breathe into the most inanimate forms some likeness of its own visions, on such a serene and glowing evening, in this remote and romantic village, beside the calm lake that bore us hither.[6]

The description of this child begins as one of matter of fact. Amongst a group 'in an extraordinary way deformed and diseased', one boy has such 'exquisite grace' that Shelley is certain he has never seen his equal. Further, the apparent objectivity of these observations is corroborated by the poet's companion also being struck by the child's beauty and sensibility. This companion, although his reactions are not specified, gives the boy 'a piece of money' as if also picking him out from his playmates. The 'overflowing' beauty of the child's countenance, the 'pride and gentleness in his eyes and lips', are thus established, in the first section of this paragraph, as accurate, if slightly enigmatic, observations, likely to be remarked by any sensitive observer of this scene. Importantly, however, the final two sentences of this paragraph significantly complicate this sense of objectivity. There, rather, the reality of these observations is thoroughly cast into doubt. That '[a]ll this might scarcely be', that the boy's grace and beauty might be an illusion, is now explained as a possible effect of the imagination's desire to project its own ideas onto the objects it observes. Indeed, Shelley explains that this self-projection on the imagination's part is particularly active, or particularly likely to occur, in scenes of beauty. It would seem to be the serenity, remoteness and romanticism of the situation – depicted here in the soothingly regular rhythm of the paragraph's final three clauses – that has fired the imagination into potentially problematic activity. And it is also worth noting that such projection is likely to occur, according to Shelley, into even 'the most inanimate forms'. Thus, the beauty and grace of the living child might be entirely illusory, if the imagination could 'breathe' its 'likeness' into even inanimate objects.

Before looking at the recurrence of this idea in 'Mont Blanc', it needs to be observed that the idea is also to be found in Coleridge's 'Frost at Midnight'. There, in the poem's first published version from 1798, Coleridge comments on the 'dim sympathies' he detects between his mind and the fluttering film on the grate of the dying fire before him in the following manner:

> Idle thought!
> But still the living spirit in our frame
> That loves not to behold a lifeless thing,
> Transfuses into all its own delights
> Its own volition – sometimes with a deep faith
> And sometimes with fantastic playfulness.[7]

The sense that this poem's poet and this film of soot might be 'companionable'[8] is challenged in this sentence by the observation – almost identical to Shelley's – that the mind can 'transfuse' 'its own delights' into 'all' objects, even if they are 'lifeless'. Further, Coleridge specifies what Shelley leaves open to conjecture, that this act can take place either correctly, 'with a deep faith', or creatively but wrongly, 'with fantastic playfulness'. In both Shelley's and Coleridge's scenes, nevertheless, the contemplative, ruminative mind is seen to act of its own creative accord, regardless of the details of the objects with which it is working.

We should also note, in this sentence from 'Frost at Midnight' and in this idea in Shelley's prose that the identification of the mind's workings in this manner represents a kind of alienation of the mind from itself, or a splitting of individual identity into at least two components. If Coleridge's 'thought' 'loves not to behold a lifeless thing', then this faculty of his mind would seem to be working in separation from the poet as a whole. The latter, indeed, is sceptical about the former's operations. In Shelley's description of the boy at Nerni, similarly, the poet's 'imagination' is endowed with enough subtlety and intricacy of will to be not quite able to 'forbear' breathing 'some likeness of its own visions' into the objects around it. It is as if the poet's own will is not at issue when that of his imagination is so overriding. As in 'Frost at Midnight', therefore, the poet is cast as being in a state of inertia – here, sitting 'on a wall beside the lake' – while his faculties of mind are personified as at play, seemingly without his control. The appearance of passivity masks an intense level of imaginative and 'spiritual' activity. In Coleridge's poem, and indeed in the 'brown study' episode from Cowper's *The Task* which it recreates, this sense of involuntary but creative separation leads to an atmosphere of eerie uncanniness. One part of the mind is set working, while its usual operator, the poet, reposes. Shelley's scene has similar connotations.

Whilst I wish to demonstrate that many of the concerns of 'Frost at Midnight' are shared by Shelley's 'Mont Blanc', and indeed that Shelley's poem in fact belongs to the same sub-genre of poetry as 'Frost at Midnight' and 'The Eolian Harp', in order to see how the latter poem echoes the particular sentence of Coleridge's that we have been considering, and its corresponding idea from the *History*, we must turn first to the poem's final rhetorical question:

> And what were thou, and earth, and stars, and sea,
> If to the human mind's imaginings
> Silence and solitude were vacancy?   ('MB', 142–4)

Addressed here to Mont Blanc itself, this question can be understood to repeat the Nerni and 'Frost at Midnight' problem. If, in scenes of beauty, the imagination can breathe its own likeness into the objects around it, then the qualities one observes in those objects must be cast, to some extent at least, into doubt. Confronted with the immensity of Mont Blanc and the Ravine of Arve, the poem has enumerated the qualities of the scene and the ideas arising from it. In this final question, though, as at Nerni, Shelley adds a sceptical coda. If the 'mind's imaginings' did not operate on 'the most inanimate forms', if '[s]ilence and solitude' were allowed to remain as 'vacancy', uncoloured by the imagination's 'visions', then the possibility of seeing the mountain objectively – and not as these lines imply it has appeared for the duration of the poem – would arise. The question, therefore, would be the same were it addressed to the boy at Nerni: what would you be if the imagination did not breathe its likeness into objects it observes? Alternatively, Coleridge's key sentence in 'Frost at Midnight' could be rephrased in the same manner: what would this film be if thought did not transfuse its own delights into lifeless objects?

The shared motif between Shelley's scene at Nerni, the first version of 'Frost at Midnight', and the closing lines of 'Mont Blanc', is just one of a series of similarities by which Shelley investigates the workings of the idle mind in terms shared by Coleridge. Before looking at more of these moments in detail, however, it should be observed that the identification of such connections serves to question one of the common portraits of the poem that has emerged out of its recent criticism. There the poem is frequently viewed as a collection of fragmented echoes of

Wordsworthian and Coleridgean ideas and phrases, designed to cast doubt – so these readings go – over every idea it alludes to, or to explode every image it borrows. For Jerrold Hogle, for instance, Shelley 'wants to put in question' Wordsworth and Coleridge's '"natural pieties" [and] internal and eternal Absolutes' and the poem is the ideal means to achieve this. Thus, Shelley is seen as 'pull[ing] figures from Wordsworth and Coleridge "back to basics"' in order to demonstrate the unacknowledged motifs of thought standing behind those two poets' ideas. The poem's opening is a clear example of this process, according to Hogle, as Wordsworth and Coleridge's 'hierarchical "codes of fraud and woe"' are there '"repealed" by an exposure of the actual movement underwriting and "flowing through" the world we observe.'[9] For John Rieder, likewise, the poem's reference to 'local poetry' such as 'Tintern Abbey' enables 'Mont Blanc' to stand back from such writing and to 'question [. . .] the very possibility of writing about nature'. For Rieder as for Hogle, therefore, '[t]he situation of the opening lines is that of a tradition being placed in the critical view of a principle'.[10]

The 'Mont Blanc' that will emerge out of its present treatment is one closely tied, both formally and thematically, to 'The Eolian Harp' and 'Frost at Midnight'. It is a poem more sympathetic to the subtlety and ambitions, even if not the theology, of Coleridge's poetry, one that foregrounds and explores the intense workings of the idly contemplative mind in terms inherited from Coleridge. In this context, it is 'The Eolian Harp' and 'Frost at Midnight', rather than Coleridge's 'Hymn before sunrise in the vale of Chamouni', that emerge as the primary intertexts of 'Mont Blanc'.[11] And from this approach, these two former poems of Coleridge's can be seen to be as 'critical', and as self-reflexive, as the 'Mont Blanc' that emerges from Hogle and Rieder's readings.

Let us look, for instance, at the opening of Shelley's poem that Rieder and Hogle find so 'critical' of Coleridge:

> The everlasting universe of things
> Flows through the mind, and rolls its rapid waves,
> Now dark – now glittering – now reflecting gloom –
> Now lending splendour, where from secret springs
> The source of human thought its tribute brings
> Of waters, – with a sound but half its own,
> Such as feeble brook will oft assume
> In the wild woods, among the mountains lone,
> Where waterfalls around it leap forever,

> Where woods and winds contend, and a vast river
> Over its rocks ceaselessly bursts and raves.   ('MB', 1–11)

When Coleridge recalls his previous 'tranquil mus[ing] upon tranquillity' in 'The Eolian Harp', it is in terms that stress the passivity of his mind and the intense activity of the thoughts that are about to be classified as coming from the 'intellectual breeze': 'many idle flitting fantasies / Traverse my indolent and passive brain – / As wild and various as the random gales / That swell or flutter on this subject lute!'[12] In both Coleridge's and Shelley's scenes, the objects or forces that 'flow through the mind' bring with them connotations of subtly powerful control, or even of potential domination. In 'The Eolian Harp', this is achieved by the contrast of the terms 'wild', 'various' and 'random' with the poet's 'indolent and passive brain'. It is as if the 'flitting fantasies' in fact contain the power to quite violently reshape that mind in their own shifting image. In 'Mont Blanc', similarly, the mind's complete lack of control over what flows through it is hinted at by the 'rapid[ly]' fluctuating 'waves' of the 'universe'. Spilling over from the third into the fourth line of the poem, these waves oscillate between 'dark[ness]', 'glittering', 'reflecting gloom' and 'lending splendour'. The range of these alternatives signals the mind's inertia in comparison to this force of nature, and the manner in which the former's will or ability to control itself, much like at Nerni, is simply not at play here. The language of Shelley's opening thus recalls that of Coleridge's 'Eolian Harp' in quite exact terms. Both poems make use of the quotidian but enormous power of natural forces – Shelley in the '[f]low[ing]', 'roll[ing]', 'rapid waves', Coleridge in 'wild' and 'random gales' – and both do so to stress the uncanny combination of passive receptivity and intense, apparently externally imposed mental activity.

Moreover, because the mind was conceived as an inert receptacle of intensely active thought in 'The Eolian Harp', and because that relationship was described there in terms that rendered this dynamic problematic, the opening to Shelley's poem should be seen to draw out and to echo these features, not to undermine them, as Hogle would have it. Coleridge's 'intellectual breeze' is thus formally and thematically similar to Shelley's 'universe of things'. Hogle's claim that 'Mont Blanc' challenges of 'the "one life"' Coleridge 'find[s] "within us and abroad"' is therefore unconvincing.[13] This is especially so as the 'one life' passage was not added to 'The Eolian Harp' until its 1817 publication in *Sibylline Leaves*, where it appeared only in the volume's errata. Whilst the version of 'Mont Blanc' that appeared in the *History* was modified from Shelley's original

1816 'Pont Pelissier' draft after Shelley had ordered *Sibylline Leaves* (which he did on 13 July 1817), its modifications do not point to any engagement whatsoever with the 'one life' passage. Placing 'Mont Blanc' alongside the version of Coleridge's poem with which it is contemporary thus demonstrates the shared concerns of the two poets.

The mind is also rendered problematically inert in Shelley's opening lines by the manner in which 'human thought' is described as only a 'tribute' in comparison to the mass of thought that exists outside the mind in this portrait. The former is as a 'feeble brook' contrasted to the 'wild woods' and the vast 'mountains lone' that surround it. Or, in the poem's reinforcing of this idea, 'human thought' is as a tributary over which 'a vast river' 'ceaselessly bursts and raves'. In the context of Shelley's allusion to Coleridge, these images might be seen to represent a fulfilment of the potential in the earlier poem for the mind to be overcome by the forces around it. The 'ceaseless' raving of the intellectual breeze's river has now overcome the mind to the extent that its banks have been 'burst'. These opening lines thus depict a scene of an almost impossible level of activity flooding into the passively receptive mind, and are in this sense highly problematic. Confronted with the constant, violent, raving movement of the 'universe of things', the mind is all but overcome. The 'feeble brook', as Frances Ferguson notes, would seem to lose its own identity and bounds, when flooded by a 'vast river'.[14] It is as if the exact effect of Coleridge's tranquil scene has been magnified by the vast and sublime object before Shelley. What was threatened in 'The Eolian Harp' – the overwhelming of the mind by external physicality – might be said to take place in 'Mont Blanc'.

The most significant connection between 'The Eolian Harp' and 'Mont Blanc', however, is to be found in the progression of Shelley's poem, and in the manner in which its two opening sections interact. We observed, at Nerni, a seemingly factual description being undermined by the operations of the poet's imagination. What takes place in the first two sections of 'Mont Blanc' is a movement towards the same type of reconsideration. After the first section delineates the apparently correct relationship between the mind and the 'everlasting universe of things', a relationship in which the mind is 'feeble' and the universe's 'flow' all-powerful, the objectivity of this account is problematized by its striking similarity to the actual scene now described in section II. This problem (or that there even is a problem here) is made most clear by considering the more general plot of 'The Eolian Harp'. In that poem, combining his experience of lying in complete repose and his observations on the harp's mode of making music,

Coleridge offers an account, at the poem's midpoint, of the mind's relationship with the world:

> And what if all of animated nature
> Be but organic harps diversely framed,
> That tremble into thought, as o'er them sweeps,
> Plastic and vast, one intellectual breeze,
> At once the soul of each, and God of all?[15]

Again, like the opening of 'Mont Blanc', this image positions human will as nothing in comparison to the force of the universe and the seemingly accidental manner in which one is 'framed'. Importantly, however, this suggestion, tentative as it is, is challenged, in 'The Eolian Harp', forcefully and swiftly by Coleridge's listening wife, Sara. And the basis of Sara's objection as it is reported by Coleridge in the poem is that the world is not necessarily as it appears to the idle, reposing poet. Such 'shapings of the unregenerate mind, / Bubbles that glitter as they rise and break / On vain philosophy's aye-babbling spring'[16] that have made up the poem until this point are not the same, according to Sara, as the priorities of social, active, labouring life. Sara's role in the poem is thus to contend, or to raise the possibility, that the connection between the workings of the harp and the way in which ideas seemed to flow across the reposing poet does not offer an insight into the secret workings of the world. Rather, the image of the harp can be seen to have radically coloured and influenced the poet's understanding. Philosophy's 'spring' is thus defined as 'vain' and 'aye-babbling' by Sara because the poet has seen and heard a beautiful object, and affirmatively built a way of understanding the world around that object. Much like the 'transfusions' of thought in 'Frost at Midnight' and at Nerni, Sara Coleridge raises the possibility that the insight offered by the poem's 'effusion'[17] is actually an effect, and an echo, of the scene in which the poem is set.

Returning to 'Mont Blanc', since that poem alludes to the ideas of 'The Eolian Harp' in its opening section, the exact match between that philosophical portrait of the mind's relationship with the world (section I) and the physicality of the Ravine of Arve now described in section II anticipates something like the same problem recorded at Nerni and by Sara Coleridge. The seemingly factual contents of section I might be prompted, or coloured, by the scene now to be described in section II. This is the case because, while the mind sits idle and inert as the 'universe of things' flows and rolls across it, that exact model of passivity overcome by external activity is likewise stressed in Shelley's description of the Ravine:

> Thus thou, Ravine of Arve – dark, deep Ravine –
> Thou many-coloured, many voiced vale,
> Over whose pines, and crags, and caverns sail
> Fast cloud-shadows and sunbeams: awful scene,
> Where Power in likeness of the Arve comes down
> From the ice-gulfs that gird his secret throne,
> Bursting through these dark mountains like the flame
> Of lightning through the tempest; – thou dost lie,   ('MB', 12–19)

'Thus' is the key word here, because it occurs in a similar context in 'The Eolian Harp' (at l. 34), and because almost every detail in these lines links this portrait with that of section I. The Ravine, personified so as to recall the role of the poet there, 'lie[s]' in extreme inertia as an endless series of activities takes place around and above it. Indeed, the postponement of the clause describing the Ravine's role in this scene – 'thou dost lie' – until the end of the eighth line of its description serves to recreate the imbalance of passivity and powerful surrounding forces found in the poem's opening. The portrait of ceaseless motion to be found in these lines is also formally similar to that of the 'universe of things' in section I. The running-on of line 14 into 15, for instance, following the two previously end-stopped lines, recalls the spilling over of forces in the poem's third and fourth lines. That '[f]ast cloud-shadows and sunbeams' 'sail' over the passive Ravine is thus rendered an act lacking any control or will on the Ravine's part, in exactly the same way that the rolling of things through the poet's mind took on connotations of being, in Coleridge's term, 'uncalled and undetained'.[18] 'Power [...] [b]ursting through' the 'dark mountains' serves similarly to cast the Ravine as utterly inactive, and indeed as powerless to be anything but inactive. Moreover, the language of power here recalls section I's analogy of the mind to the 'feeble brook'; in both instances powerlessness is contrasted with an object that 'bursts' from above.

The Ravine is therefore depicted as a precise image of the poetic mind so in thrall to the physicality around it that it has lost all will and self-control. And in the context of Coleridge's poetry the identification of this similarity would seem to tend in the same direction as the question that ends Shelley's poem. If the portrait the poem offers of the mind's relationship with the world is so similar to the physical image before the poet, then there is the strong possibility, in a poem about the insights available to the contemplative mind, that one has been coloured, or inspired, by the other. Philosophy's 'aye-babbling spring', imaginatively affirming that a scene of beauty offers an insight into the secret workings of the world, could be as active here as it is suggested it might be in 'The Eolian Harp' and in 'Frost at Midnight'.

The generic convention of these poems, however, is to outweigh only one moment of doubt with an otherwise entirely sustained implication that what is being offered by the poem is an insight into the secret workings of things, and into the secret connections between mind and world. Even if such doubts can be retrospectively cast over the entire plot (as Sara Coleridge's objections can be used to critique all the suppositions of 'The Eolian Harp', for example), the primary tone of these poems is one of earnestness. Thus, even though the logic of Nerni, or of the poem's final question, could be used to unpick the connections made in its first and second sections (as I have been moving towards doing in my last few paragraphs), Shelley's poem does not do this. Rather, 'Mont Blanc' names the connection between the Ravine and the mind as one of special significance, in a passage equivalent in its structural role to Coleridge's 'Methinks its motion in this hush of nature ' lines in 'Frost at Midnight':

> – and when I gaze on thee
> I seem as in a trance sublime and strange
> To muse on my own separate phantasy,
> My own, my human mind, which passively
> Now renders and receives fast influencings,
> Holding an unremitting interchange
> With the clear universe of things around;   ('MB', 34–40)

The relationship between the Ravine and the world, in this remote and sublime scene, is identical to that between the poet's mind and the universe in the extreme state of mind this scene engenders. This earnest corroboration thus positions the knowledge contained in the poem as particularly insightful, and as unavailable elsewhere. The poem is uncovering a normally hidden set of correspondences that allow us to peek behind the world's – and the mind's – quotidian veil. In 'The Eolian Harp', likewise, the similarity between the harp and poetic contemplation points towards all entities being 'organic harps'. Or, in 'Frost at Midnight', the companionability of the film on the poet's fire-grate and his mind would mean that there is truthful knowledge to be found in the contemplative workings of the brain in the same way that the film is said to portend a visitor. These lines of Shelley's thus make the connection between the scene and the mind explicit, because such a connection will guarantee, in the primarily earnest mode of this sub-genre of poetry, that the knowledge gleaned in this scene is indeed accurate, or is indeed useful in some sense.

It is no doubt apparent that I am yet to name at all precisely the equivalent knowledge to be found in 'Mont Blanc' to that found in 'The Eolian Harp' or in 'Frost at Midnight'. This is in part because, whilst recent criticism of the poem has not observed the similarity of the poem's generic formula to that of Coleridge's poems, it has very thoroughly identified and explored the main class of knowledge offered in 'Mont Blanc'. It is for this reason that so many recent studies of the poem discuss the details and connotations of the mountain's 'voice'.[19] For it is the burden of the Ravine's silence and the mountain's possession of 'a voice [. . .] to repeal / Large codes of fraud and woe' ('MB', 80–1) that Shelley positions as his poem's equivalent to Coleridge's moral insights into the divine order. Rather than dwell on the area of knowledge that has been the centrepiece of most of the poem's recent scholarship, however, I want instead to pick out another, closely connected type of insight offered by 'Mont Blanc', one made newly visible by the approach I have taken to the poem, and which in fact colours the connotations of the mountain's 'voice' in an important manner. This class of knowledge is connected to the generic identity of the poem I have been arguing for, in that it revolves around the particular workings of the idle, contemplative mind, the mind set at play by objects and scenes of beauty.

We have seen that, in Coleridge's 'Eolian Harp' and in the opening of 'Mont Blanc', the aesthetically contemplative mind approaches a position of problematic passivity. It is a feature of Cowper's brown study and of the two poems of Coleridge's that we have been considering that the eerie uncanniness of such scenes is in part created by the way in which, when the poet ceases consciously to control his mind, the physicality of the objects he is considering threatens to reconstitute that mind in the likeness of its non-human, random and fitful form. In this sense these are poems of the insights, and of the simultaneous dangers, available and courted in the contemplation of aesthetic objects. Shelley's poem fits this pattern. But to observe this similarity could be to miss the fact that 'Mont Blanc', like 'The Eolian Harp' and 'Frost at Midnight', is also an attempt to illustrate, and to contend for the worth of, the powers of the idle mind and of the intense, seemingly externally driven mental activity that occurs in aesthetic contemplation.

In order to see this contention and examination more clearly, let us return to the poem's second section, to Shelley's fleshing out of the 'unremitting interchange' his mind holds, in this scene, with 'the clear universe of things around'. This is Shelley's description of the qualities of the 'universe of things' in this context:

> One legion of wild thoughts, whose wandering wings
> Now float above thy darkness, and now rest
> Where that or thou art no unbidden guest,
> In the still cave of the witch Poesy,
> Seeking among the shadows that pass by,
> Ghosts of all things that are, some shade of thee,
> Some phantom, some faint image; till the breast
> From which they fled recalls them, thou art there!   ('MB', 41–8)

To be mentally prone and inert while the 'everlasting universe of things / Flows through' one's 'mind' is to participate – in these lines as in the opening moments of the poem – in a 'legion' of 'wild' movement. It is to experience a powerfully intensified consciousness. Thus, while the poet is passive, his thoughts, in the imagery of these lines, 'wander' and 'float above' the Ravine's 'darkness'. Thought leaves the mind to join the universe of things. Importantly again, such an excursion on thought's part is in line with the heightened activity sketched out for the idle mind in 'Frost at Midnight'. There, in the second published version of the poem, the version most recently in print when 'Mont Blanc' is composed, Coleridge further classifies the mind's 'transfusions' as 'wild relics of our childish thought, / That flit about, oft go, and oft return / Not uninvited'.[20]

This process is far from unproblematic. Coleridge's thoughts returning '[n]ot uninvited' serves to classify their excursion out of the poet as not entirely willed, wanted or pleasurable. Cowper's brown study and the description of the poet's reverie in 'The Eolian Harp' are similarly poised between the voluntary and involuntary, between pleasure and danger, and between insight and risk. And in 'Mont Blanc', familiarly, the double negative of Coleridge's 'not uninvited' is recalled in the location to which Shelley's thoughts wander: 'Where that or thou art no unbidden guest, / In the still cave of the witch Poesy.' To be a bidden guest in this context, and in this phrasing, would seem to stand at some distance from being an entirely willing guest, because the home to which the poet's thoughts are being summoned holds connotations of significant danger. The 'still cave of the witch Poesy', filled with 'shadows', '[g]hosts' and 'phantom[s]', is also the site to which thought has 'fled'. This is clear gothic terminology. That the figure who presides over the cave is 'Poesy', however, ensures the reestablishment of the careful balance between creativity and danger – between the poetic and the gothic – that is to be found in Coleridge and Cowper's accounts of such paradoxically active contemplation.

It is highly significant for understanding 'Mont Blanc' as a whole that this episode's carefully poised tone, treading the fault-line between intense creativity and metaphysical danger, also stands behind the act of grasping the knowledge that the mountain can offer in the poem. Thus, in its third section, the poet's 'spirit' is 'Driven like a homeless cloud from steep to steep / That vanishes among the viewless gales!' The danger of this engagement with the scene's radical physicality is again signalled as the poet's spirit seems to 'fail' ('MB', 58–9, 57). But yet what is achieved by courting such danger, by letting one's 'spirit' be carried out of oneself in this manner, is the subsequent appearance of, and indeed the retrieval of knowledge from, Mont Blanc. For it is only after the details of such Coleridgean and Cowperian contemplation have been thoroughly set out that 'Mont Blanc appears' in Shelley's poem (at l. 61), and that the mountain's many possible significances can begin to be explored. It is thus by contemplating in this fraught and intense manner, by accessing the secret home of 'Poesy' but by courting the company of its witch and her attendant phantoms, that the moral knowledge offered by the poem can be grasped. What this means is that, in addition to offering the prize of the recognition of the mountain's 'voice' as the object that the poet has seized during the poem, 'Mont Blanc' also offers a set of insights into the manner in which aesthetic contemplation functions, into the intense, active capability of the idly contemplative mind. It also means that the poem contends for the usefulness of such acts. If the mountain has 'a voice [. . .] to repeal / Large codes of fraud and woe', then the repealing can only take place thanks to the risks the poet has taken in that knowledge's retrieval. Much like Coleridge's 'Eolian Harp' and 'Frost at Midnight', 'Mont Blanc' classes the paradoxically intensely active reverie as one of direct utility because of the types of knowledge to which it gives access.

We are now in a position to make two key observations on the status of this knowledge. Firstly, the connections I began by observing between the poem and the scene at Nerni – connections that enabled us to read the poem's final question as a reassertion of the doubts to be found in Coleridge's poetry on this subject – mean that such doubts are also cast over the validity, and the truth, of the knowledge retrieved by the poet at Mont Blanc. If silence and solitude could be left as vacancy, if thought did not transfuse into inanimate objects its own delights, then the pressing similarity between the poet's mind and the Ravine might not have arisen, and the poet's mind might not have been understood to float above its station, or to grasp from Mont Blanc the knowledge that it appears to. The final question cuts to the roots of the poem's action, in other words, suggesting as at Nerni, that 'all this might scarcely be', that both the contemplative plot and the product of the poem's contemplation are in fact illusory. It should also be observed, in this connection, that in comparison to 'Frost at Midnight', these doubts might arguably seem slightly more terminal, positioned as they are at the end, rather than at the beginning of the poem. 'Frost at Midnight' seems to overcome temporary doubts to assert the validity of its final vision. 'Mont Blanc', by contrast, lets its enraptured and sustained vision proceed, before it bathetically considers backing down, in a move that threatens to deflate any and every achievement of the poem. Its form is thus similar to that of 'The Eolian Harp', the doubts of which form the final moment in that poem's plot, but cast a considerable shadow over all its suppositions. In comparison to the *History*, likewise, one should note that the possibility remained, at Nerni, that the poet's observations 'might' be accurate: 'all this might scarcely be'. The final question of 'Mont Blanc', by contrast, seems to leave no doubt that the 'mind's imaginings' were indeed at work: 'what were thou [...] / If to the human mind's imaginings / Silence and solitude were vacancy?' The poem's doubts thus appear to stand troublingly close to being a wholesale rejection of the events of the poem.

The second observation we are now in a position to make concerns the contents, rather than the formal framing of the poem's primary knowledge. The insight gleaned by the poet in 'Frost at Midnight' is that there is an 'eternal language which [...] God / Utters, who from eternity doth teach / Himself in all and all things in Himself'.[21] The vision of the young Hartley Coleridge being educated by this system of natural signs is the poem's equivalent of the visitor's image being foreseen in the flutterings of the film of soot. Coleridge's courting of the dangers of idle contemplation is thus rewarded by an insight into the moral and divine workings of the world. The equivalent to this knowledge in 'Mont Blanc', however, is doubt rather than faith, an ability to repeal rather than to affirm. In comparison to 'Frost at Midnight', therefore, Shelley's poem might be understood as rather hollow. It positions doubt, an ability to repeal and an absence of affirmative knowledge, where Coleridge puts seemingly concrete insight into the workings of the world. The vision offered in 'Mont Blanc' is one of sustained and extended dizzying emptiness, suited in this sense to the nagging doubts which conclude the poem. To say that 'Mont Blanc' belongs to the same sub-genre of poetry as 'The Eolian Harp' and 'Frost at Midnight' then is also to highlight the manner in which it gives more weight to the kind of doubts that were nevertheless present in Coleridge's poems. No longer a cosy and concise vision of the mind reflected everywhere, and of the divine order neatly given to the earnestly contemplative poet, 'Mont Blanc' is a record of the difficulty of stealing useful knowledge from a remote chaos of objects, in this comparison. Shelley's poem, in other words, subtly rebalances the tensions that animate Coleridge's poetry of the idle mind.

The significance of 'Mont Blanc' interacting with Coleridge's thought in this manner is signalled by even glancing elsewhere in Shelley's thought. In *A Defence of Poetry*, for example, composed five years after 'Mont Blanc' in 1821, Shelley again detaches Coleridge's contemplative motifs from their theological framework in order to depict apparently inherent human aesthetic capabilities. Thus, as we saw in the context of *Middlemarch*, '[m]an is an instrument over which a series of external and internal impressions are driven, like the alternations of an ever-changing wind over an Aeolian lyre'.[22] Or 'the mind in creation is as a fading coal which some invisible influence, like an inconstant wind, awakens to transitory brightness'.[23] While these images recall the central, visionary analogies of Coleridge's 'Eolian Harp' and 'Frost at Midnight', respectively, Shelley's repetition of these motifs is also the occasion for their subtle modification. Such images are, firstly, not deployed as a strategy to arrive at the conclusion that to contemplate aesthetically is to come closer to God, as they are – albeit problematically – in Coleridge's poems. Secondly, Shelley reduces the level of intellectual passivity that troubled 'The Eolian Harp' and 'Mont Blanc' by his qualification of the intellectual breeze of the *Defence* as both 'external and internal', in the quotation above. This is a point that Shelley explains at some length:

> But there is a principle within the human being, and perhaps within all sentient beings, which acts otherwise than in the lyre, and produces not melody alone, but harmony, by an internal adjustment of the sounds or motions thus excited to the impressions which excite them. It is as if the lyre could accommodate its chords to the motions of that which strikes them, in a determined proportion of sound; even as the musician can accommodate his voice to the sound of the lyre.[24]

To be blown into life by the intellectual breeze of the *Defence* is thus not to sit passive and inert as the 'universe of things' flows across and fills one's mind. Rather, the 'interchange' between the mind and the world now described as taking place includes a significant contribution from the mind. Again, in other words, Shelley might be seen to be alluding to Coleridge's poetry in order to rebalance its energies. And again, this is a portrait of human intellectual life, and of aesthetic capability, that stresses the centrality of paradoxically active idle contemplation, and in terms directly inherited from Coleridge.

It should also be observed, however, that the idiosyncrasy of Shelley's treatment of this idea in the *Defence* might be complicated by the modifications Coleridge had made to 'The Eolian Harp' around the same time that Shelley was writing 'Mont Blanc', as we saw. For the 'one life' passage that Coleridge added into that poem in the errata of the *Sibylline Leaves* notably defines that life force comparable to the poem's 'intellectual breeze' as both 'within us and abroad', and as a power that 'meets all motion and becomes its soul'.[25] In this context, these lines would seem to situate the impetus of the intellectual breeze as simultaneously inside and outside the individual mind. The subtle difference in Shelley's handling of this Coleridgean motif between the *Defence* and 'Mont Blanc' could therefore be the result of the *Defence*'s detailed engagement with the *Sibylline Leaves*, which we noted that Shelley ordered in July 1817. Because the *Defence* returns to this issue – and subtly restates this allusion – several times,[26] whatever one decides about the origins of its precise observations, the essay must be understood to demonstrate the continued pertinence of the Coleridgean model of idleness for Shelley's thought. Likewise, it would be possible to treat the poem like the 'Hymn to Intellectual Beauty', which is broadly contemporary with 'Mont Blanc', or the 'Ode to the West Wind', written after the *Defence*, in similar terms. Both poems dramatize the 'visit[ations]' of 'some unseen Power',[27] and both allude to, and subtly modify, the motif of the intellectual breeze. In the 'Ode', for instance, the request for the West Wind to 'make' the poet its 'lyre' is just one of a series of possible interactions between that power and the poem's speaker, and thus the poem's closing lines almost frantically explore the aptness of the Coleridgean, idle motif.[28]

If these examples of Shelley's thought represent a sustained fascination with the powers of idle, aesthetic contemplation that operates almost entirely in line with Coleridge's understanding of that activity, then the thought of John Keats, to which we turn now, must be seen to offer a significant extension of Coleridge's paradigm. For Keats's writing challenges the solipsism of a poem such as 'Mont Blanc', and indeed of Coleridge's thought on this subject, by repeatedly understanding idle contemplation as an act that is explicitly, and centrally, social. It is in his correspondence that Keats makes this extension most clearly, and it is in fact by alluding to Cowper's 'brown study' episode of *The Task* – that text that stands behind 'Frost at Midnight' – that Keats advances on Coleridge and Shelley's conceptions of aesthetic contemplation.

Let us look, to begin with, at Keats's famous definition of 'the poetical Character', from his letter to Richard Woodhouse on 27 October 1818:

> A poet is the most unpoetical of any thing in existence; because he has no Identity – he is continually in for – and filling some other Body – The Sun, the Moon, the Sea and Men and Women who are creatures of impulse are poetical and have about them an unchangeable attribute – the poet has none; no identity – he is certainly the most unpoetical of all God's Creatures. [. . .] When I am in a room with People if I ever am free from speculating on creations of my own brain, then not myself goes home to myself: but the identity of every one in the room begins to to [sic] press upon me that, I am in a very little time anhilated [sic] – not only among Men; it would be the same in a Nursery of children[.] (*Letters*, I, 387)

The central idea in this passage is that being a 'poet' is synonymous with having one's own 'identity' 'annihilated', with continually 'filling some other Body' rather than remaining solidly within one's own. The passage, at one level, thus gives a very personal, and a very dramatic, vocabulary to the conventional Romantic figure of the flight of fancy that I referred to at the beginning of this chapter. Yet Keats's version of this motif also celebrates the aspect of this process that is a notable problem for Cowper, for Coleridge and indeed for the Shelley of 'Mont Blanc'. Surpassing the conventional boundaries of one's identity may offer a host of intellectual and spiritual rewards, but that act also threatens to reconstitute the poet's identity in the shadowy physicality of the object being contemplated and visited. Cowper's 'brown study' is the first – and the most influential – expression of this problem in the Romantic tradition. There, a troublingly, gothic, fitful and uncanny 'waking dream', seemingly instigated by the poet's 'fancy', comes to an end when the poet's more quotidian intellectual 'powers' are 'summon[ed] home':

> the freezing blast,
> That sweeps the bolted shutter, summons home
> The recollected powers, and snapping short
> The glassy threads with which the fancy weaves
> Her brittle toys, restores me to myself.[29]

This conclusion to Cowper's waking dream thus classifies the flight of fancy the episode has described as a problematic excursion out of the self. Not only was the poet not himself during this episode, according to the terminology now employed by Cowper, but such non-identity is also now represented as an excursion out of the self on 'glassy threads'. That these threads can be snapped, 'short' of their unknown final destination, and by a 'freezing blast', moreover, renders them, troublingly, both alien and insubstantial. The episode of 'unthinking'[30] that is the brown study thus becomes also an episode of 'unbeing' in its final four lines. And the possibility is sustained, by this description, that the poet's identity might have become 'unrestorable' were it not for the accident of the 'freezing blast', were the progress of fancy's 'glassy threads' not halted.

We saw how Shelley's 'Mont Blanc' contained a similar motif in the poet's 'spirit' seeming to 'fail' as it left his body and visited Mont Blanc. Returning to Keats, therefore, it is clear that what poses a problem for Cowper, Coleridge and Shelley is both expressed more as a simple matter of fact, in the letter to Woodhouse, and is also invoked as a positive mental attribute: '[a poet] has no Identity – he is continually in for – and filling some other Body'. Even though this is a comparison of Keats's theoretical prose description to his contemporaries' nuanced, experiential poetry, the phrasing of this sentence is still conspicuously untroubled. Despite this general tenor, however, one should also note that key elements of Keats's language in the passage from which this quotation is taken seem to fit the tradition of ambivalence over the poet's self-excursion represented by Cowper and Coleridge. The grammar and vocabulary of the following sentence, for instance, are conspicuously negative: 'not myself goes home to myself: but the identity of every one in the room begins to to press upon me that, I am in a very little time anhilated'. If the poet as he is normally understood is 'annihilated' in this process, if the other figures in any room 'press upon' him to such an extent that this annihilation occurs, then 'not [him]self go[ing] home to [him]self' could be understood as, to some extent at least, a violent, confrontational process of destruction and revocation. Identity being 'annihilated' 'in a very little time' would seem to accord with Cowper's description of the poet being taken from himself, stealthily but swiftly, by a process outside of his conscious control. For the plotting of the brown study episode renders fancy's 'glassy threads' only visible when the poet's fit comes to an end, and has 'an hour' passing as if it was a moment.

In comparison to the passage suggested by Hyder Rollins as the dominant allusion of this sentence, therefore, this passage from Cowper's poem, with its language of dangerously destructive identity politics and the withdrawal of contemplative agency, surely represents a more compelling intertext for Keats's letter. Rollins follows the clear echo of *Troilus and Cressida* in Keats's characterization of the 'wordsworthian sublime' [sic] as 'a thing per se [that] stands alone' (Shakespeare's Alexander has 'he is a very man *per se*, / And stands alone'[31]) with the assertion that the phrase 'not myself goes home to myself' refers to Achilles's speech in Act III of the same play (*Letters*, I, 387, nn. 4, 7):

> The beauty that is borne here in the face
> The bearer knows not, but commends itself
> To others' eyes: nor doth the eye itself –
> That most pure spirit of the sense – behold itself,
> Not going from itself; but eye to eye oppos'd
> Salutes each other with each other's form[.][32]

Here, however, the eye's activity which Achilles describes is conspicuously contrary to that imagined in Keats's line. The point being made is that it does not 'go [. . .] from itself', and thus cannot assess its own beauty. Moreover, even though the eye here stands in for the individual's whole 'sense', of which it is apparently the 'spirit', this is still a very different idea from the actual self, the full conglomeration of an individual's identity, returning home, or failing to do so.

The final phrase of Cowper's 'brown study' episode, therefore, describing how the poet is 'restore[d] to himself', how he returns to himself after an excursion from his quotidian identity, would seem to be invoked by Keats's description of the poetical character.[33] More generally, Keats also seems to be interacting, in this letter, with the tradition of thought instigated by Cowper that examines the dangers and rewards of intense aesthetic contemplation. For Keats is not describing a permanent feature of the poet's intellectual life, as some commentators have implied, but rather a temporary state of intense poetic concentration and reverie. It is for this reason that his clause about not going home to himself follows the qualification that this can only occur 'if [he is] ever [. . .] free from speculating on creations of [his] own brain'. In the same way that Cowper's brown study analyses mental states beyond or beneath normal understanding (his scene most suits 'the unthinking mind', the 'soul that does not always think', and he whose 'understanding takes repose' (IV, 279, 285, 296)), Keats is describing the effect of the poetic 'fit', to use the terminology common to Cowper and to Keats's own circle, the style of thought distinct from rational 'speculation'.[34] So where Cowper, Coleridge and Shelley see the individual as courting a kind of metaphysical danger in the process of aesthetic contemplation, Keats's description invokes this tradition in order to embrace its possibilities in a very different spirit. The annihilation of the self, the outcome risked at Mont Blanc, in the brown study and elsewhere, is positioned by Keats as the desirable and inevitable result of full aesthetic contemplation.

Reading Keats's letter in the context of this tradition also makes clear that Keats's depiction of poetic activity departs from those of Cowper, Coleridge and Shelley in terms of its social ramifications. The solitariness of the idly contemplative individual at Mont Blanc is entirely representative of this tradition. Cowper and Coleridge, for instance, also stress the poet's solitude to such an extent that it might seem a condition for the experiences they describe. In Keats's letter, by contrast, the poet is imagined amongst people. And the permeability of the poet's identity, as a consequence, leads directly to an engagement with 'every one in the room'. This connection of the mechanism of idle contemplation inherited from Cowper with the kind of democratic social politics implied by this diffuse, collective model of identity is no accidental occurrence here. It is also a connection Keats makes at much greater length in a letter to John Hamilton Reynolds from 19 February 1818. There, Keats imagines a scenario in which a community of people all engage at the same time in the style of reverie that can be instigated by a 'Page full of Poesy'. Since 'any Man may like a Spider spin from his own inwards his own airy Citadel', this imagined scenario leads to a situation in which, 'doz[ing] upon a Sofa' or 'nap[ping] upon Clover', many men create 'a tapestry empyrean – full of Symbols for [their] spiritual eye[s], of softness for [their] spiritual touch, of space for [their] wandering [and] of distinctness for [their] Luxury' (*Letters*, I, 231–2). Again, it is physical passivity and mental receptiveness that leads to the poetic experience. And again, this portrait of now wide-scale aesthetic contemplation is used by Keats to contend for its social possibilities:

> But the Minds of Mortals are so different and bent on such diverse Journeys that it may at first appear impossible for any common taste and fellowship to exist between two or three under these suppositions – It is however quite the contrary – Minds would leave each other in contrary directions, traverse each other in Numberless points, and all last greet each other at the Journeys end – A old Man and a child would talk together and the old Man be led on his Path, and the child left thinking – Man should not dispute or assert but whisper results to his neighbour, and thus by every germ of Spirit sucking the Sap from mould ethereal every human might become great, and Humanity instead of being a wide heath of Furse and Briars with here or there a remote Oak or Pine, would become a grand democracy of Forest Trees. (*Letters*, I, 232)

This passage thus contains a very similar motif to that found in the 'poetical Character' letter. The contemplative mind, the mind that has weaved itself an 'empyrean' tapestry, is now expressed as voyaging out from its usual confines, as interacting at 'numberless points' with the concerns of others, and as returning, presumably altered, to its home. As with the phrase 'not myself goes home to myself', in other words, identity here is open to modification during its flight from the body. And once again, this process is figured as positive because of the interaction between individuals it facilitates: 'A[n] old Man and a child would talk together and the old Man be led on his Path, and the child left thinking'. Neither figure takes up a position of authority here, despite the different social positions implied by their ages. Both are instead further propelled on their contemplative, passive journeys.

In his recent treatment of this letter, Jacques Rancière argues for the centrality of Keats's 'passivity' to any conception of the poet's politics. In contrast to the egotism of the Wordsworthian walker – who preaches equality by insisting on the 'superiority' of he who can recognize it – Keats's democratic principle is imaged by the poet 'stretched out in a state of indistinction between activity and passivity, perceptions and evocations, waking and sleep, personality and impersonality, life and death'.[35] Keats's equality is thus 'horizontal' rather than 'vertical' for Rancière. It is to be found in the web of thought 'that extends to infinity without recognizing high or low, inverse or converse', and that is thus so impersonal that its poems are 'by "no one"'.[36] But the political ramifications of these motifs are not simply confined to challenging the paradoxical status of 'equality' in Wordsworth's writing, according to Rancière. Keats's effusions are also politically implicated because of the undirected, undetermined mode of being they embody. Alongside 'the limbless heroes of Winckelmann, the "finality without end" of Kant, the activity equal to passivity of Schiller', Keats's poetic repose thus challenges the definition of action as 'the use of the appropriate means to ends'.[37] Undetermined existence, contemplation that is at once active and passive but that is not limited by a projected end-point, should thus be seen as a direct challenge to the quotidian conception of action and personal responsibility.

It is this political economic component of the aesthetic reverie that I have previously drawn out of Cowper and Coleridge's writing,[38] and that is also central to the thought of Shelley and Keats in my view. I am thus in agreement with Rancière's identification of the politics of Keats's model of reverie to this extent. What is lacking from Rancière's subtle and convincing treatment of Keats's writing, however, is an assessment of the poet's individual position in what is actually a wide debate in contemporary English literary circles. So where Rancière draws analogies between Keats's writing and that of Winckelmann, Kant and Schiller, the connections we have already begun to notice between Keats, Cowper, Coleridge and Shelley allow us to position his thought even more precisely. This is not to deny that Keats's handling of the subject of idleness holds affinities with the German tradition Rancière mentions, but to observe that the immediate frame of reference in Keats's writing is Cowper and Coleridge.

Turning back to Keats's letter to Reynolds, then, one should note the manner in which the letter as a whole recreates something very similar to the generic formula imitated by Shelley's 'Mont Blanc'. Coleridge's 'Eolian Harp' tentatively extrapolates from the poet's experience, suggesting that all objects might be 'organic harps', but then backs down from, and ironizes, that possibility in its final moments. Keats's letter, likewise, runs with the possibility that men 'might' benefit from poetic 'wander[ing]' and 'mus[ing]' only to recast this as probably false, in its final paragraph, which thoroughly undermines the potential insight of the letter:

> Now I am sensible all this is a mere sophistication, however it may neighbour to any truths, to excuse my own indolence – so I will not deceive myself that Man should be equal with Jove – but think himself very well off as a sort of scullion-Mercury, or even a humble Bee[.] (*Letters*, I, 233)

What Rancière casts as the revolutionary politics of this letter thus in fact ends up, in Keats's hands, as 'mere sophistication'. The letter's contents might 'neighbour truths', but even if they do so, they are still primarily an excuse for 'indolence'. The letter, like 'The Eolian Harp', has thus been a Promethean event, according to this passage. The sentiment Keats took up seized at the status of Jove, tentatively placing the reposing, poetic individual alongside the King of the Gods. But the bathetic reality of the letter's close may be that even the contemplative man is flattered by the suggestion that he might be 'a sort of scullion-Mercury', a low-ranking messenger figure. The resonance of this analogy, as of the idea of a 'humble Bee', is that man is primarily a worker, rather than a reposer, that what Rancière casts as indolence's political power is in fact illusory.

It is not that this mood, and this stance on its contents, characterizes the letter as a whole, of course. Rather, much like 'Mont Blanc', Keats's letter participates in the generic conventions of the English tradition of poetic enquiry into the parameters and powers of idle, aesthetic contemplation. Just as Cowper closes the 'brown study' episode by casting its action as the poet 'los[ing] an hour' rather than gaining any particular insight, Keats pulls back from his poetic flight to serio-comically cast its conclusions as overblown. When one identifies this motif clearly, however, what Keats achieves in the speculative heart of his letter is made highly visible. Once again envisaging the poetic contemplator amongst people, as in the letter to Woodhouse, Keats renders the idle aesthetic reverie a direct step to contemplative sociability in a manner it had not been in the tradition with which he is interacting. The otherwise undeveloped 'heath of Furse and Briars [. . .] would become a grand democracy of Forest Trees', if each man engaged in poetic contemplation, and if each let his own thoughts be complemented and nourished by those of others. As in the letter to Woodhouse, therefore, Keats is not only recasting the problematic identity politics of Cowper and Coleridge as a positive model of spiritual nourishment. He is also eliminating the solipsism of those poets' idle reveries and replacing it with the possibility of a radical sociability. Such sociability is at once spiritual and political. The former is figured by the idea of growth from a gorse bush to a 'grand' forest tree. The latter, by the fact that the occasional and 'remote Oak or Pine' would be matched by a whole community of such trees.

The economic component that Rancière identifies in Keats's depiction of idleness also bears an important relationship to the poetry of Cowper and Coleridge. The older poets' concentration on the intricate details of idle contemplation served to challenge the portrait of human life, and human capability, put forward by late eighteenth-century political economy. Yet this frame of reference was as latent in Cowper's brown study and Coleridge's 'Eolian Harp' as it is in Shelley's 'Mont Blanc'. Repose and contemplation are not explicitly contrasted to labour in those episodes, even though they are in *The Task* as a whole.[39] In Keats's letter to Reynolds, by contrast, the consideration of contemplative sociability we have already seen leads immediately to a consideration of idleness's relation to labour. The contrast draws out what is at stake in this tradition of thought very clearly:

> It has been an old Comparison for our urging on – the Bee hive – however, it seems to me that we should rather be the flower than the Bee – for it is a false notion that more is gained by receiving than giving – no the receiver and the giver are equal in their benefits – The flower I doubt not receives a fair guerdon from the Bee – its leaves blush deeper in the next spring – and who shall say between Man and Woman which is the most delighted? Now it is more noble to sit like Jove that to fly like Mercury – let us not therefore go hurrying about and collecting honey-bee like, buzzing here and there impatiently from a knowledge of what is to be arrived at: but let us open our leaves like a flower and be passive and receptive – budding patiently under the eye of Apollo and taking hints from every noble insect that favors

us with a visit – sap will be given to us for Meat and dew for drink[.] (*Letters*, I, 232)

Before the ironic backing-down that takes place in the letter's final paragraph, human life can be seen to strive for the condition of the gods, for 'it is more noble to sit like Jove than to fly like Mercury'. Likewise, just as that backing-down will render human life full of work rather than repose by the analogy with Mercury, the comparison of the 'Bee' to the 'flower' here signals the opposite. Passivity is positioned above activity in this passage, and a life of labour – or 'fly[ing]' – is rejected in favour of one of receptive idleness – 'sit[ting]'. Because, as David Bonnell Green observed many years ago, the 'Beehive' as a 'comparison for our urging on' has almost 'countless' parallels, which probably all derive from Aristotle or Pliny, the size of the tradition which Keats's letter is playfully overturning here is vast.[40] To 'weave a tapestry empyrean [. . .] full of symbols for [one's] spiritual eye', to render life contemplative, passive and aesthetically led, is thus an act of significant political philosophy in Keats's hands. The concentration on the intricacies and possibilities of idleness serves as a focused challenge to the whole history of economic thought that has understood man as a worker, as a labouring animal, above all else. And perhaps even more graphically than the 'grand democracy of Forest Trees' image, Keats's 'blush[ing]' flower figures the alternative to a life of labour as one with beauty at its centre. To contemplate is to grow, to blossom and to bud. Keats's ruminations also corroborate this multi-layered judgement by asking a more sensual rhetorical question: 'who shall say between Man and Woman which is the most delighted?' In the context of the passage's classical allusions, it is Tiresias's answer that must spring to mind. The woman, passive here like the flower visited by the bee, will receive more than her active partner.

At the rhetorical centre of this letter to Reynolds, therefore, before the bathetic conclusion characteristic of all English treatments of aesthetic contemplation, Keats makes two connected extensions to the thought of Cowper, Coleridge and Shelley. First, by conceiving of idle contemplation as always social, as always tied to engagement with 'every one in the room' or with a wider community of contemplators, Keats imbues that act with more overt political significance than it held in the writing of his contemporaries. Second, this significance, and the idea of a community connected by its members' intellectual rumination, allows Keats to contrast this scenario with more conventional social bonds. The connections stipulated by the idea of an economy, therefore, the image of men as bees, labouring alike for common ends, can be challenged by Keats's handling of the idea of idle contemplation in a way that Cowper, Coleridge or Shelley's treatments of this idea do not immediately allow.

The tendency of Keats's writing, in his correspondence, to render explicit and factual what is implied or tactically avoided in the poetry of idle contemplation written by Cowper, Coleridge and Shelley also extends to his most famous account of intellectual activity, his writing on 'negative capability'. Yet the manner in which this term is connected to the ideas and intertextualities under consideration here might seem rather obscure. This is because almost all recent writing on 'negative capability' highlights what is dramatic and pragmatic in Keats's explanation of that term at the expense of its more theoretical elements. Li Ou's recent book entirely devoted to the term, *Keats and Negative Capability*, is a case in point. Li's summary definition of 'negative capability', for instance, moves the term very close to 'disinterestedness', the ability to 'let the mind be a thoroughfare for all thoughts' that Keats explores in a letter to his brother and his family in September 1819 (*Letters*, II, 213). At the 'centre' of the negative capability's 'conceptual core', Li finds

> a great poet's capability of remaining 'negative', in the sense of being able to resist the instinctive clinging to certitude, resolution and closure in the firm belief that great poetry is marked by its allowance for a full-scale human experience that is too copious and diverse to be reduced to a neatly unified or conceptualized system. To be negatively capable is to be open to the actual vastness and complexity of experience, and one cannot possess this openness unless one can abandon the comfortable enclosure of doctrinaire knowledge, safely guarding the self's identity, for a more truthful view of the world which is necessarily more disturbing or even agonizing for the self.[41]

Abandoning 'doctrinaire knowledge', identifying that such knowledge normally houses 'the self's identity', believing that 'human experience' is not 'reduc[able] to a neatly unified or conceptualized system', Li's negative capability is entirely concerned with negotiating the opinions of others and with removing thought's association with political ideologies. To be 'negative' is thus to not be involved in systematic thought here, and Keats's 'uncertainties, Mysteries' and 'doubts' that form a key element of his description of negative capability (more of which below) would seem to refer to opinions not yet hardened into political beliefs.

Walter Jackson Bate, who Li identifies as the most influential of Keats – and negative capability – scholars, performs a very similar superimposition. Here is Bate's 'paraphrase' of Keats's negative capability sentences:

In our life of uncertainties, where no one system or formula can explain everything – where even a word is at best, in Bacon's phrase, a 'wager of thought' – what is needed is an imaginative openness of mind and heightened receptivity to reality in its full and diverse concreteness. This, however, involves negating one's own ego. Keats's friend Dilke, as he said later, 'was a Man who cannot feel he has a personal identity unless he has made up his Mind about everything.'[42]

That Bate goes on to quote in full Keats's account of the 'disinterestedness' that Dilke doesn't possess, from the September 1819 letter to George Keats, signals again that negative capability is being read as very close to, if not synonymous with, the opinion-based ability to avoid doctrinaire knowledge. And again, much like Li, Bate has recourse to 'system[s]' of thought in his attempt at paraphrase, situating negative capability firmly in the realm of ideologies and opinions.

But 'uncertainties, Mysteries' and 'doubts' do not have to refer to the opposites of opinions, ideas and thoughts. What I have classed as the tendency towards reading negative capability politically, pragmatically and as concerned with opinion, Steven Knapp denominates the 'ethical' misreading of Keats's term.[43] And in a similar vein to Margaret Ann Fitzpatrick, who finds 'imagination and disinterestedness [. . .] quite distinct' in this example of Keats's writing,[44] Knapp instead explores the manner in which the capacity of negative capability is more properly understood as the capacity for 'aesthetic' thought, as distinct from rational understanding. It suits Knapp's frame of reference and agenda – his reading of Keats occurs in *Literary Interest*, his far-reaching analysis of the phenomenon of the literary – to make this distinction by reference to Kant, the standard recourse of any theoretical analysis of Romantic aesthetics, as we saw in the case of Rancière. Thus Knapp observes that, '[i]n Kantian terms, reaching after fact and reason in Keats's sense is the business of the understanding; it involves an interest in concepts, and the aesthetic is explicitly defined in opposition to conceptual knowledge.'[45] That negative capability and Keatsian 'speculation'[46] in Knapp's analysis are to be understood not as 'ethical' but as 'aesthetic' phenomena, and that I have frequently described the English literary tradition concerned with idle thought that frames this chapter as one examining 'aesthetic contemplation', will point towards the affinity I see between negative capability and Cowper, Coleridge and Shelley's conceptions of idleness. For the tradition in which this chapter is attempting to situate Keats and Shelley is one that I have argued bears a striking affinity with the German idealist tradition in terms of its analysis of aesthetic contemplation, and indeed one that can be seen to laud that state for its individual and social significance before, and without reference to, German idealism.[47] Knapp's connection of Keats and Kant can be supported, in other words, by further reference to the tradition of thought set in motion by Cowper. It will be possible to draw this connection more explicitly by quoting Keats's description of negative capability in full.

The term 'negative capability' is used only once by Keats, in a letter to his brothers George and Tom from December 1817. And the letter, rather problematically, now exists only in a 'very puzzling transcript' made by John Jeffrey in 1845.[48] The key passage, however, so frequently quoted as to be almost ubiquitous in Keats scholarship, runs as follows:

> I had not a dispute but a disquisition with Dilke, on various subjects; several things dovetailed in my mind, & at once it struck me, what quality went to form a Man of Achievement especially in Literature & which Shakespeare possessed so enormously – I mean *Negative Capability*, that is when a man is capable of being in uncertainties, Mysteries, doubts, without any irritable reaching after fact & reason – Coleridge, for instance, would let go by a fine isolated verisimilitude caught from the Penetralium of mystery, from being incapable of remaining content with half knowledge. This pursued through Volumes would perhaps take us no further than this, that with a great poet the sense of Beauty overcomes every other consideration, or rather obliterates all consideration. (*Letters*, I, 193–4)

Let us consider the terminology at the very heart of this description to begin with. The terms 'uncertainties, Mysteries' and 'doubts', when emancipated from their 'ethical' context, can be seen to hold a striking affinity with a key feature of all the texts we have considered in this chapter. Because to engage in aesthetic contemplation, for Cowper, Coleridge and Shelley, is to travel out of one's body and to encounter a shadow-world of dangerous physicality, and of phantom-like figures. And what these mysteries and uncertainties lead to are wholesale metaphysical doubts as to whether the aesthetic experience was in fact as it appeared to be, and whether the object being visited was truly encountered at all. Recall, for instance, Shelley's phrase 'all this might scarcely be', or Sara Coleridge's classification of her husband's reverie in 'The Eolian Harp' as the effect of 'vain philosophy's' intensely affirmative gaze. Thus, if we glance back to Shelley's 'Mont Blanc', to a key passage quoted above, for example, we will find a mental and a physical geography that represents the poetic contemplator plunged into a world of 'uncertainties' and 'mysteries':

One legion of wild thoughts, whose wandering wings
Now float above thy darkness, and now rest
Where that or thou art no unbidden guest,
In the still cave of the witch Poesy,
Seeking among the shadows that pass by,
Ghosts of all things that are, some shade of thee,
Some phantom, some faint image; till the breast
From which they fled recalls them, thou art there!

It is not only the syntax of this passage that renders the encounter with Mont Blanc an engagement with radical uncertainty. Just as the final phrase – 'thou art there' – comes about illogically in grammatical terms, recalling the kaleidoscopic first impression of the mountain Shelley sketched in the *History of a Six Weeks' Tour*, so the 'witch', 'ghosts', 'shadows' and 'phantoms' also serve to cast the poet into a world of dangerous mystery. Mont Blanc as the site of a 'legion of wild thoughts', and of '[g]hosts of all things that are', could thus be described very accurately using Keats's negative capability terminology. And likewise, one could easily point to comparable passages in Cowper's brown study, and in Coleridge's 'Eolian Harp' that depict the act of aesthetic contemplation as an engagement with mysteries, uncertainties and doubts. Think, for instance, of Coleridge's 'wild', 'various' and 'random gales' that represent his 'intellectual breeze', or of Cowper's 'strange visages expressed / In the red cinders',[49] one of the many features of the brown study that render its action mysterious and uncertain.

Negative capability's emphasis on 'being in uncertainties, Mysteries' and 'doubts', then, would seem to fit the manner in which the tradition that stands behind this chapter dramatizes aesthetic contemplation's encounter with the physicality of the natural world. To look further into Keats's description of negative capability from this perspective, furthermore, is to find more significant parallels between these fields. Take, for instance, the final clause of Keats's mysteries and doubts sentence. The capability of experiencing uncertainties is given further precision, in Keats's letter, by the phrase 'without any irritable reaching after fact & reason'. We have already seen Keats's qualification, in his letter to Woodhouse, that 'not [him]self goes home to [him]self' only if he is 'ever free from speculating on creations of [his] own brain'. And we have already noted Cowper's depiction of the brown study episode as exploring thought beneath, or beyond, normal understanding, exploring what Kevis Goodman describes as the 'conscious gaps or syncopes of thought' in John Locke's *Essay Concerning Human Understanding*.[50] Keats's distinguishing of negative capability from the thought that 'reach[es] after fact and reason' thus fits with these characterizations of aesthetic thought as unconcerned with quotidian rationality.

Fact and reason are thus not what is probed by the negatively capable poet, just as the intellectual products of the brown study – that experience during which the poet's 'understanding [. . .] sleeps'[51] – are not to be identified as discrete items of knowledge. To be 'in uncertainties, Mysteries, doubts, without any irritable reaching after fact & reason' is therefore to let one's poetic vision proceed, without needing to take from it rational conclusions. It is not to call off the poetic fit in order to understand it, not to 'let go' 'from being incapable of remaining content with half knowledge'. Strikingly, therefore, Shelley's 'Mont Blanc' proceeds, for almost its entire length, in these terms. The poem's key lines, structurally speaking – those lines that correspond to Coleridge's 'Methinks its motion' sentence in 'Frost at Midnight' – serve to confirm that its speaker's poetic fit is in full flow, for instance: 'and when I gaze on thee / I seem as in a trance sublime and strange / To muse on my own separate phantasy'. Since these lines immediately follow the poem's depiction of the ravine in terms equivalent to its portrait of the mind, Shelley's identification of his 'trance sublime' might be said to signal his exploration of what Keats describes as 'half knowledge'. That the comparison between ravine and mind might raise the same doubts as those that occur at the end of the poem is irrelevant, according to these lines, because what is being accessed in the analogy is distinct from rational knowledge. Shelley's poem is analysing its scene, and its speaker's mind, through the lens of a 'trance', without 'any irritable reaching after fact & reason'. And the terminology of the 'trance', like Keats and Cowper's 'fit' (or, as I have argued elsewhere, like Wordsworth's terminology of 'sleep' in the Lucy cycle[52]), seems to stand in for aesthetic, non-rational vision and comprehension. The lengthy portions of Shelley's poem I have not analysed in this chapter – its long fourth section, for instance – are thus also evidence of the poem's interest in letting its intense vision proceed. For they repeatedly consider the ravine and the mountain in a variety of non-factual terms, and from a variety of imagined, factually unreachable perspectives.

To be 'in uncertainties', therefore, not 'reaching after fact & reason' and not troubled by the kind of 'doubts' that conclude Shelley's 'Mont Blanc', is to undergo the intense aesthetic contemplation that is the preoccupation of the poetic accounts of idle thought that were written in the wake of Cowper's brown study. And because we have seen Keats working in this tradition at the same moment that he renders its political ambitions transparent – in his comparison between poetic 'wandering' and an apian life of labour, for example – it would seem plausible to read the phrase 'negative capability' in a similar vein. Following Rancière's identification of Keatsian passivity as a critique of the category of labour, it does not seem a stretch to define negative capability as the opposite of productive, economic capacity. The terminology of negative capability describes the poetry of idle contemplation so exactly, in other words, that one who is negatively capable would seem to possess the ability to not work and to not produce, but to be idle and to receive. This is why, in the letter to Reynolds from February 1818, poetic 'wandering' is synonymous with 'sucking the Sap from mould ethereal', and the task of rejecting bee-like 'buzzing', towards the end of the letter, is qualified by the reassurance that 'sap will be given to us for Meat and dew for drink'. And this is why, in Keats's closely connected 'Ode on Indolence', composed in spring 1819 (after the letters to Woodhouse and Reynolds, but before the 'negative capability' letter itself), all activity or achievement is rejected under the heads of 'Love', 'Ambition' and 'Poesy'.[53] The nonsaleable, non-material outcomes of aesthetic contemplation paradoxically serve, in Keats's formulations, as the sustenance for its contemplators. Negative, non-economic capability is thus depicted as an alternative organizing principle to the economic. What the letter to Reynolds describes, then, tentatively and before ironizing its contents as absurd, is a negatively capable society, a social idleness that rejects economic exchange.

One obstacle perhaps still remains in this attempt to read negative capability as germane to both the idly contemplative tradition that emerges in the wake of Cowper's *Task* and the often implicit opposition to economic assumptions that animates that writing. This is Keats's use of names in his negative capability letter, specifically his naming of Coleridge as the epitome of a poet who does not possess negative capability, and his naming of Shakespeare as the fully realized, negatively capable poet. For Coleridge holds a key position in the tradition of thought with which I am saying Keats is interacting. Indeed, in the examples of Keats's writing we have considered here, I have suggested almost as many analogies with Coleridge as I have with Shelley's 'Mont Blanc' or with Cowper's brown study. Shakespeare, meanwhile, stands at such a distance from the historical and intertextual cluster that forms this tradition that his presence threatens to complicate the tight-knit analysis of idle contemplation to which I am saying Keats is contributing.

   Far from challenging Keats's place in this tradition, however, the presence of these names in fact tells us something very useful about the ideas under consideration in this chapter as a whole. The deployment of Coleridge's name in a role that seems almost completely at odds with both contemporary and recent appreciations of his writing is most often explained by Keats's limited knowledge of Coleridge's work.[54] Bate, for instance, describes the reference to Coleridge as 'ludicrously inept, though forgivable considering how little Keats had read of him'.[55] But this anomaly also demonstrates that to share the conception of poetic activity espoused by Keats at this historical moment one does not need detailed knowledge of each of the proponents of idle contemplation that emerge in Cowper's wake. On the contrary, the idea that idle, aesthetic contemplation represents the central component of poetic activity, and the idea that this act holds the potential to expose the limitations of political economy's description of human life, are shared by such a broad variety of writers between 1784 and the moment at which Keats is writing that they represent a solid consensus, not a tentative possibility only discoverable by reading Coleridge's poems, for instance, in the right way. Thus, as I have demonstrated elsewhere, Cowper, Coleridge and Wordsworth, as well as Mary Wollstonecraft and Anna Letitia Barbauld, all understand the poetic act in these terms, while figures as distant from this list as Jeremy Bentham and John Howard also conceive of the state of idleness as central to human moral and intellectual capacity.[56] That Keats and Shelley fit this pattern renders the cluster of ideas under consideration here not a narrow set of beliefs, but an intellectual mainstream. Such ideas are not to be encountered only in one or two generically similar or historically connected poetic accounts, but are the norm at this historical moment for a wide variety of economic, political and philosophical reasons. Keats's espousing of what I am loosely referring to as the poetics of Cowper is thus by no means compromised by his rejection of Coleridge in the portrait of negative capability itself.

The case of Shakespeare tends in a similar direction. Although Keats's reference to Shakespeare 'possess[ing]' negative capability 'so enormously' has prompted Li, for instance, to scour *King Lear* for material that fits her conception of Keats's term,[57] the inclusion of Shakespeare's name here does not need to be taken this straightforwardly or this specifically. Because for the poets that form this tradition idle aesthetic contemplation is the condition of all poetic creativity. The texts considered by this chapter, as well as those just referred to in the course of its analysis, are thus not to be understood as attempting to portray a poetry of idleness, or to depict a marginal, optional but interesting human engagement in their account of idle contemplation. Rather, these texts use the figure of paradoxically active idleness in order to depict what they see as the essential, central feature of poetic creation. In their hands, human aesthetic ability is a synthesis of passivity and activity. Poetic creation, idle contemplation or negative capability – however one wants to describe such an engagement – is the most significant of human occupations, according to this tradition. Mentioning Shakespeare in this context thus affirms that what is being described by the term negative capability is not a historically specific version of the poetic act, even though the intertextualities I have explored in this chapter could cause it to appear that way. Rather, Shakespeare's name serves to guarantee the universality of negative capability, the trans-historical accuracy of the Romantic conception of idle aesthetic contemplation. And of course the persistence of Shakespeare's fame, especially at this moment when the playwright still dominates the British stage, also serves to invoke the permanence and the value – both economic and spiritual – of such idle contemplation.

For all its irony, and for all its awareness of its own occasional absurdity, the cluster of ideas we have encountered in this chapter is thus animated by a highly positive conception of idle contemplation. Even when not making the economic relevance of its observations explicit, the poetry of idle contemplation depicts repose, reverie and aesthetic thought as intricate, complex, paradoxical and fully engaging activities. Aesthetic contemplation, at this moment, holds connotations of utter passivity, inertia and even paralysis. But such states are above all means of suspending individual agency in order to open the mind to modes of being and modes of thinking beyond quotidian consciousness. Idle contemplation is thus a species of mental and spiritual activity that surpasses anything else offered by commercial society, for the early nineteenth-century proponents of this discourse. And Keats and Shelley should thus be ranked alongside Cowper, Coleridge, William Wordsworth, Mary Wollstonecraft and others in their consistent advocacy of this intellectual and political position.[58] The poetic contemplator, in the portraits of all these figures, thus courts a host of metaphysical dangers, and risks the dissolution of his identity in a shadow-world of radical physicality, but is subsequently rewarded with a type of moral knowledge otherwise unavailable, or with a direct conduit to an intense sociability denied to active, labouring man. The fact that both Keats's and Shelley's extensions and modifications to the conceptions of idle contemplation they inherit from first-generation Romanticism are so subtle and technical should also be understood to demonstrate the very high pitch that accounts of aesthetic consciousness have reached by this historical moment. We might say that negative, non-economic capability is the subject of an intricate and sophisticated discourse in its own right, by the first decades of the nineteenth century, and that idleness is conceived at this moment as a psychological category of central importance to human life. It is to the question of the influence of these ideas outside of poetry and poetics that I want to turn now. And perhaps surprisingly, the first place to register this influence after Romanticism is in the very discourse that inspired the Romantic conception of creative idleness by its extreme negativity to human repose. It is early nineteenth-century political economy that we will examine next.

CHAPTER 2

Political Economy and the Logic of Idleness

Keats's juxtaposition of idleness's paradoxical and powerful sociability with the more conventional interactions of the worker sets economic activity against aesthetic inactivity in no uncertain terms. A society built on economic relations is cast as limiting in terms of the interactions between individuals it allows for and the individual development it promotes. In the case of Keats, this opposition between the economic and the aesthetic clearly extends to matters of style. The poet's impressionistic and associative letters – which often ignore precise syntax and correct spelling – could be opposed, in a number of ways, to the discourse of political economy, the contemporary science of economic activity and relations. The former might be described as teasing out the intellectual and spiritual content of idle contemplation; the latter – in the hands of Keats's contemporary David Ricardo, for instance – strives to pin down the laws of development and production with mathematical and systematic accuracy. And yet to consider early nineteenth-century political economy in detail, as we are to do now, is in fact to find this opposition not just complicated, but thoroughly challenged. Political economy from Adam Smith to Ricardo might fit such a crude sketch of its ambitions, and might be placed in opposition to Keats, or indeed Shelley, in quite definite terms. But in the nineteenth century economic science in fact departs from its earlier forthright negation of idleness and contemplative creativity, and by mid-century pays very significant attention to the style of thinking about society that Keats's letters exemplify. What we will see in the present chapter is therefore not a series of refutations of the Romantic notion of powerful and socially useful idleness, as the nineteenth century progresses. Neither will we find a disciplinary ignorance of the politics of idleness as it is set out by both generations of Romantics. Instead, the development of political economy in these decades is in fact characterized by an accommodation of positive notions of idleness within its workings. The very discourse that inflected and motivated the development of Cowper and Coleridge's model of idleness, and that did so by its apparent negation of repose, of contemplation, and of anything other than work, must thus be seen to take on board later versions of those ideas, and to place them at the heart of its systems.[1] What we will see in this chapter thus represents the powerful and far-reaching influence of the early nineteenth-century positive conception of idle aesthetic contemplation espoused by Keats and Shelley. This influence is so marked that it can even effect a profound change of principle in a largely ideologically consistent discourse like political economy.

Let us start with Ricardo himself, so as to delineate the style of economic thought with which Keats is engaging and to begin our examination of the discourse's ambivalence around questions of repose. Ricardo's *On the Principles of Political Economy and Taxation* of 1817 represents in one sense a temporary narrowing of political economy's remit. For, whereas Smith's *Inquiry into the Nature and Causes of the Wealth of Nations* of 1776 repeatedly tackles fundamental questions of human motivation and ambition, strenuously making the case that man is a labouring and trading animal above and before all else, Ricardo's work largely ignores questions of human nature in favour of technical analysis. The relative absence of such human considerations has been frequently noted in critical accounts of Ricardo's thought. In Catherine Gallagher's terms, Ricardo is 'extremely sparing with the language of sensation', in comparison with his contemporaries; the term 'happiness' being used only twice in the *Principles*, for instance.[2] Philip Connell, similarly, describes the difference in style between Ricardo and Smith as an 'abandon[ment]' of 'the conventional, polite prose of *The Wealth of Nations* [. . .] in favour of dense, closely argued, and logically structured treatises'.[3] This path away from questions of human nature is one not taken by Ricardo's most notable successors, Thomas Malthus and John Stuart Mill (both of whom we will consider shortly). Ricardo's *Principles* are as a consequence significantly drier than the works of his contemporaries, as well as less concerned with human repose and its social pertinence.

The scientific technicality of Ricardo's *Principles* which stands behind this style consists, in Maxine Berg's terms, of his 'formulation' of 'a strict model' of human society and his tightly logical enumeration of that model's workings.[4] 'The Ricardian model', again according to Berg, 'assumed that land was limited, that there was no technological improvement, and no international trade'. These abstractions were useful, to Ricardo, in that they allowed for a separation of the 'effects' of 'the growth of capital, the rise of population, and the extension of this population to less fertile lands'.[5] Ricardo's treatise thus concentrates much more than any political economy written before him on questions of distribution (a trend that we will see Mill continue). As Pedro Schwartz expresses it, Ricardo 'was no longer content to operate with *rates*, he needed to compare distributive *shares*'.[6] A representative sample of Ricardo's analysis from his *Principles*, here from the chapter 'On Rent', thus reduces human agents to something close to counters, or ciphers, participating in a logic that is beyond their influence:

> It is only, then, because land is not unlimited in quantity and uniform in quality, and because in the progress of population, land of an inferior quality, or less advantageously situated, is called into cultivation, that rent is ever paid for the use of it. When in the progress of society, land of the second degree of fertility is taken into cultivation, rent immediately commences on that of the first quality, and the amount of that rent will depend on the difference in the quality of these two portions of land. (Ricardo, *Principles*, I, 70)

Phrases like 'rent immediately commences' here gloss over the idiosyncratic possibilities of human agency, morality or custom. Ricardo's analysis is thus a species of game theory that does not concern itself – for the most part – with the kind of perspectives that stress human variety found in nascent political economy in the mid-eighteenth century. Adam Ferguson, for instance, foregrounded in his 1767 *Essay on Civil Society* the features of human life that work against economic calculation: 'Even while the head is occupied with projects of interest, the heart is often seduced into friendship; and while business proceeds on the maxims of self-preservation, the careless hour is employed in generosity and kindness.'[7] Ricardo's more mathematical, model-based approach to political economy has an ultimately 'negative purpose', according to Berg. It is 'a counterfactual, set up precisely in order to emphasise the significance of the factors from which Ricardo abstract[s] – free trade and technological improvement'.[8] Ricardo's treatise thus follows the consequences of its model as they lead towards 'successive reductions in the rate of profit' and, ultimately, a 'stationary state' in which 'there would be no further incentive for investment'. But it does so in order to stress the considerable extent to which trade and technology can retard progress towards that state.[9] If this prospect of the cessation of economic growth sounds theoretical, abstract or in the far distant future, it is worth observing that Ricardo's thought is directly engaged with contemporary political debates. Commentators such as Mark Blaug and Maurice Dobb have contended that Ricardo's treatise must be read in relation to the Corn Laws and their prohibitive import duties,[10] not least because in the later stages of the *Principles* Ricardo develops a comparative theory of international trade that advocates thorough specialization in national manufacturing and agriculture.[11]

With this summary of Ricardo's aims and methods in mind, and with some appreciation of the ways in which Ricardo's *Principles* are normally discussed, we can now turn to his specific relevance for the present study, and we can now develop an alternative account of some of the preoccupations found in his treatise. Because despite its overall tendency to sidestep – or go beyond – questions of human nature, and to reduce human agents to mathematical counters, Ricardo's *Principles* nevertheless contain the trace of a mode of thinking about idleness – inherited primarily from the Scottish Enlightenment's model of stadial history and its attendant proto-anthropology of so-called barbarous societies[12] – that momentarily transforms economic activity into a problematic imposition on the individual. Such moments are of interest for the present study because they are considerably built upon, and amplified, in Malthus and Mill, but also because they expose the contradictions even in the narrowest form of early nineteenth-century political economy that Keats's analysis exploits.

And yet such moments can be hard to identify in Ricardo's work. If one was reading the final, 1821 third edition of the *Principles*, for example, the most significant of these moments, occurring in the chapter 'On Wages', would be traceable only as a brief and suggestive aside of just two short sentences. These sentences, which are thorny and interesting in themselves, are in fact the rewriting of a much longer and more problematic passage from the work's first edition that threatens to undermine the thrust of Ricardo's entire analysis. Let us first look at the reworking of this moment:

> The friends of humanity cannot but wish that in all countries the labouring classes should have a taste for comforts and enjoyments, and that they should be stimulated by all legal means in their exertions to procure them. There cannot be a better security against a superabundant population. (Ricardo, *Principles*, I, 100)

This passage is quoted by Schwartz as a direct expression of one of the main theses of Malthus's second edition of his *Essay on Population* (from 1803), which Ricardo builds into his *Principles*. The thesis is that there is, in Schwartz's terms, a 'culturally determined subsistence minimum' that the labouring population will not allow themselves to fall below.[13] Thus, culturally acquired 'tastes' protect against 'superabundant population'. But this perspective leaves the key ideas of this passage untouched. The passage refers, for example, through the term 'friends of humanity', to George Canning's attack on Robert Southey's soft-headed humanitarianism in the second number of *The Anti-Jacobin* from 1797.[14] Beyond this, the formulation of the first sentence of the quotation is also notably double edged. A 'taste for comforts and enjoyments' is equated with the pluralistic morality of 'humanity' at the very same moment that its existence is portrayed as not innate but as imposed upon a population. Further tensions are to be found in the fact that the 'exertions to procure' such 'comforts and enjoyments' are in need of 'stimulat[ion] by all legal means'. This notion implies that either the exertions themselves, or the policies and practices that promote them, clash with and rub up against social justice and the rule of law. To be a 'friend of humanity' here, or to be one of the unnamed agents of all the 'stimulation' which the law allows, is therefore to consider 'humanity' in a narrow and local sense. This passage advocates support for economic man, in other words, while simultaneously figuring that man as an ongoing and potentially problematic construction.

If this pulling apart of the logic of this moment seems unfair, or overblown at all, a consideration of the fuller passage that stood in its place in the *Principles'* first edition in 1817 demonstrates that such issues are entirely germane. The original passage makes what Berg calls the characteristic 'appeal to anthropology' of late eighteenth- and nineteenth-century political economy, a 'way of writing' which generates 'a more scientific posture', but which also opens up 'a definite analogy [. . .] between the savage and the poor and unemployed':[15]

> In some countries of Europe, and many of Asia, as well as in the islands in the South Seas, the people are miserable, either from a vicious government or from habits of indolence, which make them prefer present ease and inactivity, though without security against want, to a moderate degree of exertion, with plenty of food and necessaries. By diminishing their population, no relief would be afforded, for productions would diminish in as great, or even in a greater, proportion. The remedy for the evils under which Poland and Ireland suffer, which are similar to those experienced in the South Seas, is to stimulate exertion, to create new wants, and to implant new tastes; for those countries must accumulate a much larger amount of capital, before the diminished rate of production will render the progress of capital necessarily less rapid than the progress of population. The facility with which the wants of the Irish are supplied, permits that people to pass a great part of their time in idleness: if the population were diminished, this evil would increase, because wages would rise, and therefore the labourer would be enabled, in exchange for a still less portion of his labour, to obtain all that his moderate wants require. (Ricardo, *Principles*, I, 100, n. 1)

The fact that the examples in this paragraph come from across Europe, Asia and the 'South Seas' does more than just tie Ricardo's analysis to contemporary state-of-the-art anthropology. It also serves to indicate that the 'evil' of idleness being discussed here is not an isolated anomaly, but a widespread condition of human life outside of the commercial societies of Western Europe. The problematically narrow notion of 'humanity' in the previous quotation is an echo of this issue. The colonial project implied in this account is therefore one of eliminating idleness and 'implanting' the 'new wants' and the 'new tastes' that must 'stimulate exertion'. This passage, consequently, illustrates a notable ambivalence surrounding the category of idleness in Ricardo's writing. Its language and perspective recognize the arduousness of labour and the greater desirability of 'present ease and inactivity'. It thus portrays a life of even 'moderate' labour as an imposition on the individual who has previously made a conscious and logical choice to avoid that labour. (One should note that this leaves the notoriously time-consuming and hard labour of the nineteenth-century English working classes looking like a tortuous burden.) The passage also depicts a world in which a large number of societies and individuals have chosen the pleasures of idleness, and in which the natural resources of many countries give the lie to this choice. 'The facility with which the wants of the Irish are supplied', for instance, 'permits that people to pass a great part of their time in idleness'. But despite these manifold and powerful admissions, the gist of the passage is still that it would be beneficial to those societies mentioned 'to create new wants, and to implant new tastes' in their members. Even those who have been 'permitted' by natural abundance to 'pass [. . .] their time in idleness' cannot be allowed to do so by the dictates of 'humanity', when that term is equated with political economy's visions of life and progress. The people being described are therefore in paradoxical need of 'relief' from their own 'preference' for 'ease'. The oscillation of Ricardo's vocabulary here between the morally pejorative 'indolence' in the first instance and the subsequently more neutral – or even positive – terms, 'ease', 'inactivity' and 'idleness', thus embodies a wholesale ambivalence around the category of repose.

In many other political economists both before and after Ricardo, a version of this transformation – of inactivity and inertia into exertion motivated by consumption – underpins so much of their analysis that the logic of idleness repeatedly surfaces in their treatises, even when it runs counter to their stated arguments. We will soon explore the many instances of this undercurrent in detail in Malthus and Mill, for example.[16] Ricardo's *Principles* are unusual, though, in that his narrower, more technical mode of political economy largely forestalls the problems and ambiguities of idleness as they occur in this passage. Even this moment, as we have seen, is covered over and played down by the time of the work's second and third editions – from 1819 onwards, in other words. A reader of any but the work's first edition could not therefore discover that it is the globally pervasive tendency to idleness that stands behind the issue of creating new wants. Neither could he or she detect the moral ambiguity surrounding passivity after the terms 'indolence' and 'ease' are removed. And of course, the entire problem is presented as one of the economics of population by Ricardo, and one relating to the controversy of Malthus's *Essay*, after the first edition; the issue is not one of human nature or colonial imposition at all.

Ricardo does write of labour, elsewhere in the *Principles*, in such a way that it could seem precariously sustained in the face of the pleasures of inactivity. He records, for example, that '[n]o man produces, but with a view to consume or to sell, and he never sells, but with an intention to purchase some other commodity' (Ricardo, *Principles*, 290). In the light of the South Seas passage, if one was reading this statement in the work's first edition, for instance, one might consider it as delimiting the narrow conditions which motivate labour, as if the tendency of human life is not to produce. Connectedly, there are occasions on which Ricardo depicts even commercial life as leading towards indigence and inactivity, as if a life filled with labour is only a temporary consequence of economic growth, and as if the more permanent condition of human life is one of inertia. In his reconsideration of 'the substitution of machinery for human labour' in Chapter XXXI, for instance, he admits the following: 'the same cause which may increase the net revenue of the country, may at the same time render the population redundant, and deteriorate the condition of the labourer' (Ricardo, *Principles*, I, 388). Ultimately, however, these are brief and undeveloped moments of possibility in Ricardo's work, rather than wholesale engagements with the idea of human repose. Elsewhere, more characteristically, Ricardo expresses even aesthetic, contemplative and therefore 'inactive' pursuits as economic activities. The value of artworks figures in his analysis, for example, as liable to absurd inflation by the development of civilization:

> Those peculiar wines, which are produced in very limited quantity, and those works of art, which from their excellence or rarity, have acquired a fanciful value, will be exchanged for a very different quantity of the produce of ordinary labour, according as the society is rich or poor, as it

possesses abundance or scarcity of such produce, or as it may be in a rude or polished state. (Ricardo, *Principles*, I, 250)

The values of art and wine can be described as 'fanciful' because manual exertion – 'ordinary labour' – is consistently privileged by this mode of political economy. The contemplative, reposeful consideration of artworks is thus invisible in this passage, even though it has been anticipated in the ideas of 'present ease' and of course 'new wants'. Ricardo's *Principles* directly play down the categories of activity and repose that emerge in its consideration of idleness, therefore. The work is in tension between reducing non-economic activity – and easy activity – to an irrelevance and allowing those species of idleness to threaten all of its tenets and conclusions. And because of the modifications made to the work's second edition, these tensions can be picked out as a source of concern to Ricardo.[17] The *Principles* are therefore notably Janus-faced around the category of inactivity, but only momentarily in comparison to what we will see of Malthus and Mill's texts. Ricardo conspicuously limits and clamps down on the logic of idleness after the work's first edition.

Thomas Malthus's primary work of political economy – which is titled *Principles of Political Economy, Considered With a View to Their Practical Application*, published in 1820 – may stand in the shadow today, as it did in the nineteenth century, of his notorious 1798 *Essay on Population*.[18] But the later work is in fact an important document in the development of nineteenth-century political economy, not least because it develops a much fuller consideration of human nature both within and outside commercial society than Ricardo's *Principles* do, and thereby engages extremely thoroughly with the logic of idleness. This change of emphasis is a function of the fact that Malthus writes political economy in a mode closely related to that of Adam Smith, positioning himself as a philosopher of human life, rather than just a scientific analyst of the laws of the market. The concerns surrounding the imposition of new wants and the pervasive tendency towards present ease that we traced in Ricardo are thus writ relatively large in Malthus's *Principles*. And Malthus's work develops the implications of these considerations directly and thoroughly.

The consanguinity between Malthus's *Principles* and the *Wealth of Nations* is no surprise given that the former work, according to John Pullen, 'had its origins in a long-standing but unsuccessful proposal to publish a work on Adam Smith'.[19] Malthus's notion of political economy, connectedly, was for many years fundamentally tied to Smith's text, as demonstrated by the fact that his syllabus at the East India College, where he lectured from 1806, consisted largely of 'detailed analysis of the *Wealth of Nations*'.[20] Yet Malthus's *Principles* must also be thought of as in dialogue with Ricardo, following the friendship and detailed correspondence that developed between the two men from 1811.[21] Between June of that year and the publication of Malthus's *Principles* in April 1820, 134 letters were exchanged between the two, covering many of the same ideas and issues dealt with in their publications.[22] Malthus's treatise is thus in part an engagement with, and an attempted 'refutation' of, some of Ricardo's ideas. This closeness between Malthus's and Ricardo's concerns and writings, however, should not lead one to see Malthus's *Principles* as a parallel project to Ricardo's. Because while Ricardo's *Principles*, as we saw, are a tightly logical and systematic treatise, Malthus's work is in fact much more disparate, and unsystematic, in design. Malthus's work was nearly titled a series of 'essays' or 'tracts', and even after being titled *Principles*, it still announces itself as a slightly motley discussion of some of the 'disputed areas' of political economy since 'the æra' of 'the Economists and Adam Smith' (Malthus, *Principles*, I, 3):

> Among these [subjects on which 'there are still great differences of opinion'] may be reckoned – The definitions of wealth and of productive labour – The nature and measures of value – The nature and extent of the principles of demand and supply – The origin and progress of rent – The causes which determine the wages of labour and the profits of stock – The causes which practically retard and limit the progress of wealth – The level of the precious metals in different countries – The principles of taxation, &c. (Malthus, *Principles*, I, 3–4)

Many of these subjects may be central to the identity of political economy itself, but their arrangement and selection still fall short of Ricardo or Smith's design for their works. For all its difference in style from Ricardo's *Principles*, in other words, Malthus's work should not be seen as a whole new mode of political economy.

Malthus's role as disputant, and as synthesizer of the debates of 'the last twenty or thirty years' (Malthus, *Principles*, I, 3), is perhaps connected to his ability to see the kind of logical inconsistencies that we observed in Ricardo's work. He positions himself, from his very first paragraph, as open to the wider, human perspective of someone like Ferguson, that we saw Ricardo reject:

> [W]e should fall into a serious error if we were to suppose that any propositions, the practical results of which depend upon the agency of so variable a being as man, and the qualities of so variable compound as the

soil, can ever admit of the same kinds of proof, or lead to the same certain conclusions, as those which relate to figure and number. (Malthus, *Principles*, I, 1)

This statement sets the tone for an approach that considers the human subject much more in the round than Ricardo's cipher. It also leads to a style of political economic thought that stresses its 'resembl[ance]' to 'morals and politics founded upon the known passions and propensities of human nature' (Malthus, *Principles*, I, 1–2). When Malthus writes of human labour, consequently, he is much more inclined than Ricardo to stress its arduousness and its undesirability. A passage concerning the relation between technological advancement and manual labour is representative of this tendency:

> If manufactured commodities, by the gradations of machinery supposed by Mr. Ricardo, were to yield a rent, man, as he observes, would do more by the sweat of his brow; and supposing him still to obtain the same quantity of commodities, (which, however, he would not,) the increase of his labour would be in proportion to the greatness of the rent so created. But the surplus, which a given quantity of land yields in the shape of rent, is totally different. Instead of being a measure of the increase of labour, which is necessary altogether to produce the quantity of corn which the land can yield, it is finally an exact measure of the *relief* from labour in the production of food granted to him by a kind of Providence. (Malthus, *Principles*, I, 229)

The phrase 'the sweat of his brow' is Malthus's addition here, rather than being found in the Ricardian idea he is challenging. In this passage this phrase anticipates, and complements, the idea of the '*relief* from labour' (these are Malthus's italics too) by graphically picturing labour as hard, taxing and liable to be given up as soon as the opportunity arises. Thus, not only is this passage arguing against the notion that technological advancement immediately engenders increased productivity, it is doing so by keeping in mind the human experience of labour. There is consequently a kind of implicit tendency to idleness here, even though it is not picked out by Malthus on this occasion. The assumption of the passage is that not labouring is the natural and predominant condition of human life. The notion of 'Providence', connectedly, echoes Smith's 'invisible hand' to construct a portrait of human life in which the distribution of the obligation to labour and the relief from that obligation is a matter beyond human control.

If the tendency to idleness goes unnamed in this passage, there are nevertheless many points in Malthus's *Principles* where such concerns surface more overtly. The work's criticism of Ricardo in his chapter 'On the Immediate Causes of the Progress of Wealth' is perhaps a good place to commence with this aspect of Malthus's thought. After quoting and summarizing Ricardo's 'position that capital cannot be redundant' (Malthus, *Principles*, I, 356), and after also referring to James Mill's *Commerce Defended* (1808) and the work of Jean-Baptiste Say, Malthus addresses the limitations of these figures' ideas in the following terms. One of the 'fundamental error[s] into which' these writers 'and their followers appear to have fallen is, the not taking into consideration the influence of so general and important a principle in human nature, as indolence or the love of ease' (Malthus, *Principles*, I, 358). Hence –

> [i]t is taken for granted that luxuries are always preferred to indolence, and that the profits of each party are consumed as revenue. [. . .] The effect of a preference of indolence to luxuries would evidently be to occasion a want of demand for the returns of the increased powers of production supposed, and to throw labourers out of employment. The cultivator, being now enabled to obtain the necessaries and conveniences to which he had been accustomed, with less toil and trouble, and his tastes for ribands, lace and velvet not being fully formed, might be very likely to indulge himself in indolence, and employ less labour on the land; while the manufacturer, finding his velvets rather heavy of sale, would be led to discontinue their manufacture, and to fall almost necessarily into the same indolent system as the farmer. That an efficient taste for luxuries, that is, such a taste as will properly stimulate industry, instead of being ready to appear at the moment it is required, is a plant of slow growth, the history of human society sufficiently shews; and that it is a most important error to take for granted, that mankind will produce and consume all that they have the power to produce and consume, and will never prefer indolence to the rewards of industry, will sufficiently appear from a slight review of some of the nations with which we are acquainted. (Malthus, *Principles*, I, 358–9)

In comparison to what we observed of Ricardo's terminology surrounding idleness, it is worth observing that Malthus here privileges the morally pejorative term 'indolence' even though, in my previous quotation from him, this term seemed synonymous with the more neutral – or even positive – 'love of ease'. At this stage in Malthus's *Principles*, which is quite late on in his treatise but before he has begun to unpack the implications of human idleness directly, inertia is seen through a lens of distrust, or in a manner that favours the commercial advancement of human society. Working slightly against the grain of this bias, however, one should note that again labour itself is cast as hard and troublesome, in a phrase inherited this time from Smith, 'toil and trouble'. Thus the farmer here, in the more advanced stage of economic progress being referred to, can obtain his 'necessaries and conveniences [. . .] with less toil and trouble' than previously. Standing somewhere between these alternatives, the phrase 'to indulge himself in indolence' seems to partake of both moral judgement and a sympathetic comprehension of human desires. It is as if inertia were a commodity of dubious morality that commercial society would nevertheless not wish to obviate.

If this passage is, structurally or generically speaking, a version of Ricardo's 'South Seas' paragraph – albeit that Malthus is commenting on the state of Ricardo's treatise after that passage's deletion[23] – then we must also note that the setting and time-frame of Malthus's scene is considerably more modern and flexible than Ricardo's. The 'manufacturer' of 'velvet' and the 'cultivator' of a farm are contemporary figures, not chronologically or geographically distant ones, and the desire to 'indulge' oneself in 'indolence' is thus firmly placed in the present. Furthermore, amongst all of political economy's versions of this observation of the human tendency to idleness written before Malthus (and there are many of these, almost always based on historically or spatially remote 'savage' life), it is a strikingly new feature to describe the indolence of the worker as a kind of contagion that might work its way up the social strata. The manufacturer here, finding his product slow to sell, would 'fall almost necessarily into the same indolent system as the farmer'. Indolence is consequently somewhere between a dangerous moral infection and a fashionable social more in this formulation. It threatens to undermine the whole system of a specialized economy, and could do so in a matter of weeks or months, as Malthus expresses it. We should thus see in this passage that while Malthus is ultimately making a very similar observation to Ricardo's – that 'an efficient taste for luxuries', one that 'will properly stimulate industry', is needed by any commercial society – he is doing so in a manner that gives much more weight, theoretically and practically, to the human tendency to idleness.

In accordance with this emphasis, similar observations are scattered throughout Malthus's *Principles*, most often in the conventional form of referring to 'savage' life. He notes in passing within a discussion of different levels of activity among the 'labouring classes', for instance, that 'society proceeds from the indolence of the savage to the activity of the civilized state' (Malthus, *Principles*, I, 314). (This again is support for Berg's judgement that observations concerning 'primitive' man are very often deployed as analogies for the contemporary 'poor'.) A discussion of 'New Spain' and its reliance on the easy-to-grow banana includes the notion that 'the luxury

of doing little or nothing', which apparently stems from 'habits of indolence', is more powerful than the 'luxury of possessing conveniences and
comforts' (Malthus, *Principles*, I, 382). And again, at various points in his
treatise, Malthus applies such an emphasis to even his present, non-savage
examples in formulations such as the following, found in his discussion of
rent: 'If an active and industrious family were possessed of a certain portion
of land . . . ' (Malthus, *Principles*, I, 142). Neither human productivity nor
even activity is taken for granted here, for Malthus considers the threat of
idleness in almost all the relevant examples he gives.

    In the later stages of his treatise, Malthus augments these observations
into a series of maxims that relate to modern commercial societies. He
states, for instance, that it is 'by no means uncommon in the most
improved states' for 'the workman' to 'consider indolence as a greater
luxury to those which he' might 'procure by further labour' (Malthus,
Principles, I, 379). He then promotes the role of indolence to that of
a fundamental economic force, in a passage this time taking issue with
Smith:

> Adam Smith has observed 'that the desire of food is limited in every man by
> the narrow capacity of the human stomach; but the desire of the conve-
> niences and ornaments of building, dress, equipage, and household furni-
> ture, seems to have no limit or certain boundary.' That it has no *certain*
> boundary is unquestionably true; that it has no limit must be allowed to be
> too strong an expression, when we consider how it will be practically limited
> by the countervailing luxury of indolence, or by the general desire of
> mankind to better their condition, and make provision for a family[.]
> (Malthus, *Principles*, I, 468)

Note here that it is the compound, morally ambiguous phrase 'the luxury
of indolence' that is selected to represent rule of the tendency to idleness.
Malthus elevates a desire for ease that is somewhere between moral failing
and worthwhile indulgence into a principle of economic analysis.

    It would be fair to observe of statements such as the previous
quotation – and indeed of many of my quotations from Malthus –
that the morally ambivalent language in which human idleness is
couched represents an irresolution, or even a confusion, around the
categories of human repose and inertia. Malthus, one might contend,
identifies an important tension in the logic of political economy, and
indeed gives that tension a significant amount of attention and space in
his treatise, but does not meaningfully resolve such tension into a clear
statement of doctrine or opinion. This contention would be justified,
from what we have seen of Malthus's thought so far. But his *Principles*

in fact progress from ambivalence and partial confusion on such topics to a much clearer and more direct set of observations on human idleness and the role it could have in commercial society. Malthus disentangles the compound vocabulary we have seen him deploy so far, that is, in a closing section of his treatise that also anticipates one of the key innovations of Mill's political economy. The passages I am referring to follow on from the last quotation modifying Smith, and are to be found amongst his account of high-wage economies and their alternatives, where Malthus considers the possible and likely outcomes of various scenarios for both the working classes and society at large. This context, and the cumulative effect of the previous observations surrounding idleness, leads Malthus to stand back from the hypothetical and make a more direct judgement of what he considers desirable:

> I have always thought and felt that many among the labouring classes in this country work too hard for their health, happiness, and intellectual improvement; and, if a greater degree of relaxation from severe toil could be given to them with a tolerably fair prospect of its being employed in innocent amusements and useful instruction, I should consider it as very cheaply purchased, by the sacrifice of a portion of the national wealth and populousness. But I see no probability, or even possibility, of accomplishing this object. To interfere generally with persons who are arrived at years of discretion in the command of the main property which they possess, namely their labour, would be an act of gross injustice; and the attempt to legislate directly in the teeth of one of the most general principles by which the business of society is carried on, namely, the principle of competition, must inevitably and necessarily fail. (Malthus, *Principles*, I, 473–4)

Idleness is figured here in language notably more positive than morally pejorative. The phrase 'relaxation from severe toil' constructs a notion of a just reward from a style of labour that is verging on unfairly harsh, for the adjective 'severe' necessarily indicates more than simply strenuous exertion. It is as if, in this formulation, the life outside of labour is now the decisive element in one's status, even though the pervasive standpoint of political economy usually figures labour as the vast majority of human existence, especially among the lower classes. Malthus's perspective in this passage is thus unusual, in the context of both his treatise and political economy more widely, in that it allows the categories of 'intellectual' wellbeing, 'amusement' and 'instruction' – the last two being passive engagements in comparison to the activity of manual labour – to swing into focus.[24] This statement thus recognizes a whole set of values in what was formally the 'luxury of indolence' and demonstrates the extent to which both individual and social life might be enriched and enhanced by a just consideration of such values.

But of course this passage is also an identification of the impossibility of achieving the phenomenon of human wellbeing that Malthus foregrounds. Commercial society functions by the 'principle of competition' and by the individual's liberty to engage in that competition. Thus, as he goes on to say, 'without a simultaneous resolution on the part of all the labouring classes to work fewer hours in the day, the individual who should venture so to limit his exertions would necessarily reduce himself to comparative want and wretchedness' (Malthus, *Principles*, I, 474).[25] Furthermore, it is more likely that such abstinence from labour and from the field of competition would be instigated, if it occurred at all, by the 'general habits of indolence and ignorance, which so frequently prevail in the less improved stages of society'; 'such leisure', Malthus makes explicit, would be 'of little value' (Malthus, *Principles* I, 474). This is a direct restatement of the manner in which, in the long quotation above, 'innocent amusements and useful instruction' also necessarily invoke their opposite, problematic alternatives. The spectres of moral vice and useless dissipation that were previously housed in the term 'indolence' haunt even this attempted positive account of human idleness, therefore. This disentanglement of the treatise's previously morally mixed language of idleness finds the positive categories of repose precariously close to a kind of unacceptable alienation from the norms of getting on and using time usefully. Idleness stands in this sense as a fundamental challenge to the assumptions and tenets of commercial society. And Malthus's now direct consideration of the logic of idleness allows him to name very directly the ideas and institutions that inactivity threatens and challenges. We have 'competition', utility, economic advancement, and to these we should add 'private property'. For Malthus's ruminations on this problem lead him to conclude that all economic progress in the form of 'increased consumption, whether desirable or not on other grounds, must always have the specific effect of preventing the wealth and population of a country, under a system of private property' (Malthus, *Principles* I, 475). 'Wealth' is used here in a sense that includes the intellectual and spiritual wellbeing of the majority of the community. Within the 'system of private property', consequently, the holistic account of human wellbeing that includes the tendency to idleness can never be realized. Thus Malthus's consideration of idleness ends with an account of the considerable obstacles standing in the way of a system that might privilege repose and 'ease' but, simultaneously, with a very clear sense of the pertinence and desirability of passivity within modern commercial life. Where Ricardo cast the problem of idleness into a geographical elsewhere, and then closed down the implications of human repose through his 1819 alterations, Malthus positions these issues very much in the present – in both 1820 and his second edition of 1836 – and ultimately casts commercial society as straining against the desirability and persistence of idleness. In Malthus's hands, political economy is thus not fully in thrall to the ideologies of commercial society. Instead, it can stand back from such investments with a disinterestedness and a level of insight absent from the work of his predecessors.

We will see, presently, that Malthus's analysis of the ideologies and institutions that idleness challenges is replicated and taken significantly further in John Stuart Mill's political economy. Even though Malthus's following of the logic of idleness ends in the powerful impasse of competition and private property, therefore, the attempt to unpack the implications of human idleness is nevertheless a very important step along the way to a mode of economic thought that can reconcile repose and labour, liberty and competition. This synthesis may take nearly three decades to arrive – for Mill's *Political Economy* is not published until 1848 – but arrive it does. Before we turn to Mill, however, we must note at this point that Keats and Shelley's analyses of idleness with which we began this study have now taken on a very direct significance to political economy itself. Malthus's account of how 'relaxation from severe toil' could oscillate between the realm of useful passivity and morally dubious dissipation is notably undeveloped, in that he gives no sense of what each set of activities might be, or of how the constructive and the destructive might be kept apart. Even this ultimately positive account of the social and individual utility of idleness is lacking any real description, or knowledge, of idleness's workings, in other words. And Malthus's work does not make reference to a body of thought that might do this work for him. Yet such bodies of thought – of quite diverse provenance – do indeed exist at the time Malthus's treatise is written. One such repository would be Jeremy Bentham's educational thought, published as the *Chrestomathia* between 1815 and 1817, which is almost entirely framed around the danger of intellectual instruction tipping over into harmful dissipation, and which thus theorizes the precariousness of repose, idleness and contemplation very directly.[26] The other collection of ideas that do this work, as already implied, and as we have already seen, is the Romantic tradition of inquiry into the metaphysical dangers, and the moral and spiritual benefits, of idle contemplation, of which Keats and Shelley's works are late examples. Because of their different emphases, when taken together, Bentham and the Romantic tradition represent a comprehensive account of idleness's pertinences and pitfalls, in commercial society.

Thus, while it would be grossly unfair to castigate Malthus for not synthesizing his treatise with such diverse ideas, we should note that the development of political economy in the first few decades of the nineteenth century has led to it becoming a complementary mode of inquiry to the consideration of human contemplative agency that is to be found in the thought of Keats and Shelley. Even though Keats's ruminative letters opposed aesthetic contemplation and economic activity, therefore, and even though this opposition was foundational for key writings of Cowper, Wordsworth, Coleridge, Wollstonecraft and others, political economy's working through of the problem of idleness that we have witnessed so far in fact brings these overtly opposed traditions into some kind of adjacency. And if this alignment is visible – or inferable – now that we have looked at Malthus's political economy in some detail, it will become pressing, immediate and impossible to ignore in Mill's economic thought, to which we turn now.

Mill's primary work of political economy which, as already stated, was published in 1848, goes some way to announcing its ambitions in its full title, *Principles of Political Economy, with Some of Their Applications to Social Philosophy*. Mill's purview thus moves beyond the narrowly technical mode of political economy we saw Ricardo develop and invokes the wider concerns of the discipline's Scottish Enlightenment progenitors, Smith and Ferguson. The nascent political economy of these latter figures repeatedly addressed fundamental questions of social organization and the principles underlying civil society because of their indebtedness to the classical republican tradition and its implicit cultural relativism. Mill's correspondence with Auguste Comte in the 1840s 'opened his eyes', according to Schwartz, 'to the merits of Adam Smith'.[27] But such relativist impulses in Mill's *Principles* were also augmented by the influence of the French socialist Saint-Simonians. Again, according to Schwartz, this group 'insisted on the historical relativity of ideas, creeds and institutions' and 'sought to replace the "anarchical" system of free competition by a centralized organization of the economy'.[28] Thus, Mill's political economy, in a marked departure from the British tradition before him, made a new distinction between 'laws of production and laws of distribution'. Schwartz's summary of how 'Mill contrasted' these 'two types of laws in the economic field' is instructive:

> On the one hand, he said, 'the laws and the conditions of the production of wealth partake of the character of physical truths. There is nothing optional

or arbitrary in them.' On the other hand, he affirmed that 'it is not so with the Distribution of Wealth. That is a matter of human institution solely. The things once there, mankind, individually or collectively, can do with them as they like.'[29]

Because of Mill's considerable influence – his *Principles* stand as *the* authority on economic matters until the 1890s[30] and go through seven editions during his lifetime, 'including a cheap edition for working-class readers that sold over 100,000 copies before his death in 1873'[31] – this distinction is extremely important. As we shall see, it puts Mill in a position to stand back from the ideologies of 'competition' and 'private property' that we saw Malthus run up against, and to cast institutions such as these as one set of choices among many. It also leads Mill to stress the human qualities in commercial interactions with a sense of their mutability. Thus, rather than making use of political economy's fiction of *homo oeconomicus* – who follows his or her precise self-interest in every transaction – Mill stresses how 'custom' (Mill, *Principles*, I, 244) and 'carelessness' (Mill, *Principles*, II, 460) shape all kinds of human interactions. Custom's power is so far-reaching, for instance, that its influence must be 'applied whenever relevant, whether expressly mentioned or not, to the conclusions contained' in Mill's whole 'treatise' (Mill, *Principles*, I, 244).[32] In one sense, this is Mill making the same proviso implicit in the Ricardian method, foregrounding the fact that, in Schwartz's terms, 'the political economist's conclusions' are 'only true in the abstract'.[33] But Mill nevertheless gives such considerations a genuine human shape in his political economy.

Beyond the immediate economic contexts for Mill's thought, there are also wider concerns that must be seen to stand behind the considerable engagement with questions of idleness that we will find in his *Political Economy*. These concerns are expressed by Mill, in his posthumously published *Autobiography* of 1873 as stemming from his deep questioning of his own beliefs and upbringing that took place in 1826. In that episode, Mill concluded that the famously intensive mode of education given to him by his father and Bentham was too biased towards the destructive powers of 'analysis' and lacked cultivation of the 'passive susceptibilities' and 'the internal culture of the individual'.[34] His solution, reading the poetry of William Wordsworth in the first instance and then broadening his aesthetic reading to Coleridge, Goethe and 'other German authors',[35] made him 'feel that there was real, permanent happiness in tranquil contemplation', and that he had an 'interest' in 'the common feelings and common destiny of human beings'.[36] We will see many echoes of these ideas in the *Principles*, and we will thus trace, in what follows, the extent to which Mill's political economy bridges the gap between economic and aesthetic activity that we saw enunciated by Keats. For these brief extracts from his *Autobiography* make clear that what Mill takes from his Romantic and aesthetic reading – the importance of 'tranquil contemplation' and the notion of 'passive susceptibilities' – are exactly those ideas we saw probed in detail in Shelley and Keats's thought. Mill is thus a direct follower of both the systems of thought that might have aided Malthus in his account of the various states of idleness. He is intimately acquainted with both Benthamite Utilitarianism and the tradition of contemplative inertia that Shelley and Keats follow. It is therefore no surprise to find Mill's political economy engaging very thoroughly indeed with the logic of idleness.

This is not to say that the treatment of Mill's political economy I am about to offer is a commonplace, however. It is a striking result of the specialization of academic thought that Mill's economic writing has not been read with an eye to this notion of 'tranquil contemplation', and has not been considered in the context of his formative Romantic reading. In his thorough and detailed account of Mill's political economy and its intellectual background, for instance, Schwartz devotes considerable space to Mill's intellectual crisis, but ultimately reads it as an instance of intellectual 'rebellion' from his father, and from Utilitarianism, rather than as important because of the actual content of the ideas he encountered there. The very close coincidence of terminology between the *Autobiography* and my treatment of Shelley and Keats thus offers a new path into Mill's economic writing, just as the present chapter offers a reconsideration of the workings and pre-occupations of nineteenth-century political economy more generally. To consider how Mill partially follows the Romantic tradition is therefore not to see him as simply moving away from key ideas and beliefs of political economy. Mill's version of this discourse in fact draws out and extends exactly the tensions we found in Ricardo and Malthus.

Mill's mode of political economy, then, in accordance with the broad set of influences we have just surveyed, highlights human labour's position amongst a spectrum of non-economic qualities, and very often views the capacity for labour itself as a mixed blessing. In his discussion of 'The Degree of Productiveness of Productive Agents', we thus find the notion that the '[e]nergy of labour' is 'not an unqualified good, nor one which it is desirable to nourish at the expense of other valuable attributes of human nature'. And this idea serves as a summary of a long passage on the pitfalls of the English and American work ethic:

> In ['the thoroughness of their application to work on ordinary occasions'], the English, and perhaps the Anglo-Americans, appear at present to surpass every other people. This efficiency of labour is connected with their whole character; with their defects, as much as with their good qualities. The majority of Englishmen and Americans have no life but in their work; that alone stands between them and ennui. Either from original temperament, climate, or want of development, they are too deficient in senses to enjoy mere existence in repose; and scarcely any pleasure or amusement is pleasure or amusement to them. Except, therefore, those who are alive to some of the nobler interests of humanity (a small minority in all countries), they have little to distract their attention from work, or to divide the dominion over them with the one propensity which is the passion of those who have no other, and the satisfaction of which comprises all that they imagine of success in life – the desire of growing richer, and getting on in the world. (Mill, *Principles*, I, 103–4)

Not only is the 'energy of labour' here opposed to 'the nobler interests of humanity', but 'mere existence in repose' is held up as a kind of pure, unadulterated and fundamental mode of human existence.[37] This state, moreover, is contrasted with one that features heavily in Bentham's writing: 'ennui'. In his *Chrestomathia*, for instance, Bentham also positioned stultifying 'ennui' as the frequent accompaniment to the English culture of labour, and also advocated cultivating the life of the mind as its cure.[38] Mill, as T. W. Heyck observes, 'accepted what Bentham had not – the qualitative superiority of intellectual or spiritual pleasures over physical' ones.[39] But Mill's passage here nevertheless focuses directly on the shared ground between Bentham's utilitarian account of ennui and Romantic passivity, because the phrase 'mere existence in repose' would also usefully summarize the state celebrated by Keats's letters. In this quotation then, knowledge of the virtues of such passivity can be synthesized with the energies of labour to create a more complete portrait of human existence and priorities. We should note too, in this passage, that Mill's language stands at some distance from his predecessors' morally pejorative terms such as 'indolence' or 'indulgence'. 'Repose' might seem a more neutral term; but here it is aligned directly with 'pleasure', 'amusement' and 'nobler interests'. Idleness is thus configured as above labour in the hierarchy of human engagement, and an over-predominance of labour is equated with a lack of sensibility and an ignorance of the higher features of human life.

We should remember that Malthus's expression of the idea that most labourers work 'too hard' did not denigrate the energy of labour in this manner. And we have not seen, up until this point, such a direct statement of the purity of 'repose' as a fundamental feature of human existence – except in Keats's vision of how human existence might become like that of 'the flower', of course. Mill's awareness of the implications – and the still contemporary relevance – of idleness thus continues the movement of nineteenth-century political economy towards a position of compatibility with the Romantic model of repose. Mill's thorough conception of inactivity also allows him to express what was formerly the 'indolence' of 'savage' life in much more even-handed terms than Ricardo or Malthus. From the very beginning of Mill's *Principles* – in even his 'Preliminary Remarks', for instance – early stages in the development of commercial society are attributed positive qualities, and are described without the implicit judgement of his predecessors' moral language. Thus, in 'the nomad state', 'a part of the community, and in some degree even the whole of it, possess leisure'. That is, '[o]nly a portion of time is required for procuring food, and the remainder is not engrossed by anxious thought for the morrow, or necessary repose from muscular activity' (Mill, *Principles*, I, 11–12). That 'leisure', 'necessary repose' and 'anxious thought' are distinguished here demonstrates the precision of Mill's vision of the categories of idleness, in comparison to the other texts considered in this chapter. 'Leisure' here thus invokes a culture of complex and significant modes of being outside of labour. And the status of this description as about 'nomadic' life already implies – at this early stage of Mill's treatise – that contemporary commercial society might reduce man's capacity for certain experiences that he considers positive.

Mill is still writing political economy here, however, and his analysis is thus compatible with many of the concepts and beliefs we have observed in Ricardo and Malthus. These observations on 'nomadic' life thus lead to the familiar idea that '[s]uch a life is highly favourable to the growth of new wants, and opens a possibility of their gratification' (Mill, *Principles*, I, 12). But one must recognize that Mill's more positive conception of repose has important consequences for his depiction of 'the growth of new wants'. In comparison to Ricardo's two versions of his South Seas passage, for instance, economic man is rendered less of a forced construction with undesirable side-effects in Mill's account. Rather than engendering the problematic consequences that were implied in Ricardo's phrase 'all legal means', Mill's 'new wants' and 'gratifications' seem more innate and straightforward, and are more connected to the self-chosen leisure activities of the figures he describes. The development of economic man in this account thus harnesses the apparently natural tendencies of 'leisure', and is not a mode of colonial imposition in accordance with a problematic conception of 'humanity'.[40]

It is not just in the realm of idleness that Mill's *Principles* build on what we observed in earlier political economy, however. Mill's depiction of labour also takes further the awareness of work's considerable arduousness that we observed in Malthus. And we will see that Mill's *Principles* give this conception of labour a very important place their overall system. The very first idea of Mill's first chapter is that 'it is necessary to include in the idea' of labour 'not solely the exertion itself, but all the feelings of a disagreeable kind, all bodily inconvenience and mental annoyance, connected with the employment of one's thoughts, or muscles, or both, in a particular occupation' (Mill, *Principles*, I, 25). This is a notion of labour's arduousness that extends even to intellectual work and to the struggles of contemplative activity, elements of human life that are normally ignored by political economy because of their preoccupation with the productivity of manual labour. We observed how Ricardo's work, for instance, almost unconsciously privileged manual labour as a kind of pure category in no need of elaboration, in his account of the 'fanciful' values of wine and art. Mill's depiction of work, by contrast, is physical, nuanced and precise. This opposite but comparable emphasis to what we have seen of Mill's version of idleness is also matched by a clear awareness of labour's power and value in the world. In his chapter, 'On Peasant Proprietors', as one example, he quotes at length an English traveller's account of Swiss peasant labour as evidence of 'unwearied assiduity, and what may be called an affectionate interest in the land' (Mill, *Principles*, I, 256). The labour that garners this approving summary – as reported by H. D. Inglis in his 1830 *Switzerland, the South of France, and the Pyrenees* – is both attentive and long: 'When I used to open my casement between four and five in the morning to look out upon the lake and the distant Alps, I saw the labourer in the fields; and when I returned from an evening walk, long after sunset, as late, perhaps, as half-past eight, there was the labourer mowing his grass, or tying up his vines' (Mill, *Principles*, I, 256). On this occasion, these observations do not meet with a countervailing sense of how repose is disallowed by such constant activity. In this way, Mill's text could be described as portraying in detail, and almost as celebrating, both labour *and* leisure. Mill's *Principles* are also, therefore – for most of their duration – an extension of the Janus-faced tradition of nineteenth-century political economy. They juxtapose – especially in their early sections – detailed but contradictory portraits and judgements of human powers, and cast human life as poised between the complexities of idleness and the intensities of labour.

This powerfully plural vision in Mill's thought, this clear awareness of the opposing tendencies towards idleness and labour in previous political economy, and of the compound nature of human life, also stands behind his *Principles'* flexibility with larger ideological issues. For Malthus, the institutions of private property and competition were monolithic in that their incompatibility with human leisure marked the end of the road for that author's attempt to think through the implications of idleness. Mill's mode of political economy, by contrast, builds on the different perspectives of the Saint-Simonians, of Smith, and of the Romantic consideration of idleness, in order to take a much longer view of these same institutions. Mill first develops this style of analysis at the point of his work where he departs from the immovable 'laws and conditions of the production of wealth' in order to consider the 'human institution' of the 'Distribution of Wealth' (Mill, *Principles*, I, 199). This is the work's second book, on 'Distribution' as opposed to 'Production'. In the discussion 'Of Property' to be found there, Mill thus contrasts the traditional distribution of resources in commercial society with the recently developed joint-ownership models of the followers of Robert Owen in Britain and of Charles Fourier in France (the reference to 'Communism' at the end of this quotation is thus not a reference to Marxist versions of that term):[41]

> [I]f the institution of private property necessarily carried with it as a consequence, that the produce of labour should be apportioned as we now see it, almost in an inverse ratio to the labour – the largest portions to those who have never worked at all, the next largest to those whose work is almost nominal, and so in a descending scale, the remuneration dwindling as the work grows harder and more disagreeable, until the most fatiguing and exhausting bodily labour cannot count with certainty on being able to earn even the necessaries of life; if this or Communism were the alternative, all the difficulties, great or small, of Communism would be as dust in the balance. (Mill, *Principles*, I, 207)

Private property, as it has been practised hitherto, is fundamentally contradictory in this passage because it fails to reward exertion and unfairly supports inactivity. Thus, both the intense disagreeableness of labour and the complex value of idleness that Mill stresses throughout his work are invoked here in order to expose private property's current absurdities. The pure, unadulterated existence that is repose is given to large numbers of those whose work is simply 'nominal' or who do not work at all. A community's working population, meanwhile, must experience all the constant disagreeableness and toil of labour, even though it is this group that contributes most to the nation's prosperity. Where Malthus found 'relaxation from severe toil' impossible for most people under the system of private property, then, Mill inverts and extends this observation. Private property is faulty here because its current implementation does not align with the rounded and visceral view of human existence that Mill has developed in the early stages of his treatise.

But this is only the first stage of Mill's discussion of private property. As this section of his work develops, he is at pains to demonstrate that this institution is not by definition incompatible with the portrait of human nature that he has constructed. On the contrary, in its ideal form private property could mediate between the poles of labour and leisure, we are told. Mill describes the removal, for instance, of the private property's historical injustices in the following manner:

> The social arrangements of modern Europe commenced from a distribution of property which was the result, not of just partition, or acquisition by industry, but of conquest and violence: and notwithstanding what industry has been doing for many centuries to modify the work of force, the system still retains many and large traces of its origin. [. . .] To judge of the final destination of the institution of property, we must suppose everything rectified, which causes the institution to work in a manner opposed to that equitable principle, of proportion between remuneration and exertion, on which in every vindication of it that will bear the light, it is assumed to be grounded. We must also suppose two conditions realized, without which neither Communism nor any other laws or institutions could make the condition of the mass of mankind other than degraded and miserable. One of these conditions is, universal education; the other, a due limitation of the numbers of the community. (Mill, *Principles*, I, 207–8)

Just 'proportion between remuneration and exertion', together with equally distributed 'education' and population control,[42] would bring about a fair trial of private property here. And the emphasis in this passage is that the inequalities of education and reproduction are more pressing for human society than the difference between remunerating work directly and sharing all in common. The parallel emphases on the toil of labour and on the pleasures of idleness that we observed in Mill's earlier analysis come together here, therefore, in the idea that both should be distributed among society in equal measure. Mill's ultimate rule of private property, in its correct implementation, is that the hardships of labour and the pure experience of repose must both be experienced by each individual, and must be equated in direct 'proportion'. This is private property's 'equitable principle' that will 'vindicate' its existence. In Ricardo and Malthus's works, labour and repose were in tension, or even in contradiction. But Mill here brings these two features of human life into direct and unproblematic proximity. Such a vision of correctly ordered society can only be glimpsed thanks to the considerable attention that Mill pays to the details of both labour and idleness. The toil of labour and the tranquillity of repose are thus now figured as two sides of the same coin of human experience. To experience one and not the other is to partake in an unfair distribution of life's resources. Current society, in its imperfect state, thus 'guarantees' to many of its members 'the fruits of the labour and abstinence of others, transmitted to them without any merit or exertion of their own' (Mill, *Principles*, I, 208). Idleness and repose are figured in this image as the 'fruit' of labour, as its nourishing, rewarding, beautiful product. This image thus also captures the ideal relationship between work and rest in commercial society. Mill is synthesizing, in other words, the complexities of Romantic passivity with an enhanced, visceral conception of the category that is the mainstay of political economy: labour.

There is clearly a vision of a logical and fair society implied in these extracts from Mill's chapter 'Of Property'. But it is notable that Mill does not depict that society directly, at this point in his treatise. Even the complex rhetoric surrounding the phrase 'proportion between remuneration and exertion' makes that society hard to grasp. Mill's *Principles*, however, are unique among eighteenth- and nineteenth-century political economy because they contain an extended and direct account of a possible society of the future. This is a vision that accords directly with the emphases on labour and repose that we have traced so far in Mill's work, and the idea of their close union that we have just seen articulated. In Book IV of his treatise, Mill thus goes well beyond the analytical mode of political economy represented by Ricardo, and moves towards the 'social philosophy' of his work's title. This account of how society might be constituted occurs in a chapter titled 'Of the Stationary State', a reference to the notion to be found in the writing of Ricardo and others that economic growth is ultimately limited by the finite nature of natural resources. For Mill, though, the end of the 'progressive state' is by no means a cause for concern. After summarizing the importance of 'progress' and 'growth' for John McCulloch, Smith and Malthus, and after quoting those figures' concern for a time when that growth would cease,[43] Mill gives the following assessment of these views:

> I am inclined to believe that [the stationary state] would be, on the whole, a very considerable improvement on our present condition. I confess I am not charmed with the ideal of life held out by those who think that the normal state of human beings is that of struggling to get on; that the trampling, crushing, elbowing, and treading on each other's heels, which form the existing type of social life, are the most desirable lot of human kind, or anything but the disagreeable symptoms of one of the phases on industrial progress. [...] Most fitting, indeed, is it, that while riches are power, and to grow as rich as possible the universal object of ambition, the path to its attainment should be open to all, without favour or partiality. But the best state for human nature is that in which, while no one is poor, no one desires to be richer, nor has any reason to fear being thrust back, by the efforts of others to push themselves forward. (Mill, *Principles*, II, 754)

The conventional, economic mode of reading statements such as these is represented by V. W. Bladen, in the authoritative scholarly edition of Mill's *Complete Works*. For Bladen, one should distinguish between Mill the political economist and Mill 'the preacher', in his *Principles*, with a passage like this one being very much in the voice of the latter persona. The point of Bladen's distinction is to delimit what is appropriate to political economy as a practical science of social mechanisms, and what belongs in a more speculative, non-empirical discourse. For Bladen, therefore, in the section of Mill's work we are now considering, '[t]he preacher [...] contemplate[s] the Stationary State', when 'the political economist' should be 'concerned with the practical problems of contemporary society'.[44] This is not a fair judgement of the logic of Mill's writing, or of the nature of political economy by this point in the nineteenth century (it also demonstrates the disregard with which 'contemplation' is held in recent economic thought). For we have traced the manner in which the internal tensions surrounding idleness and passivity in a variety of modes of political economy necessitate – even by 1820 – a direct consideration of the moral ambiguities of those states. Furthermore, this passage's critical distance from the current state of society and its 'struggling to get on' recalls Mill's earlier, positive accounts of leisure in the 'nomad' state, a passage with certain political economic credentials. Mill here casts current commercial society as simply 'one of the phases' of man's development in the same way that 'nomadic' society was figured as a stage of development towards commercial society. In the nomadic state, '[o]nly a portion of time' needed to be devoted to labour, and 'the remainder' was 'not engrossed by anxious thought for the morrow'. Here, in the future society of the stationary state, neither work nor leisure are enervated by the 'fear of being thrust back', and the persistent 'crushing' and 'elbowing' of competition has been left behind. This passage therefore again imagines an equitable division of life into labour and leisure, and directly furthers the analysis to be found in earlier sections of Mill's work. And again, instead of these two modes of life being in tension with one another, as they were in Malthus, or as they were in earlier sections of Mill's treatise, these categories are now imagined as in harmony.

The practical features of Mill's future society that would effect this reconciliation of labour and leisure follow on from his earlier critique of faulty versions of private property. Thus, as well as the 'prudence and frugality of individuals', Mill advocates 'a limitation of the sum which any one person may acquire by gift or inheritance, to the amount sufficient to constitute a moderate independence'. Together with an acceptance of the idea of the 'stationary state', this would apparently lead to

> a well-paid and affluent body of labourers; no enormous fortunes, except what were earned and accumulated during a single lifetime; but a much larger body of persons than at present, not only exempt from the coarser toils, but with sufficient leisure, both physical and mental, from mechanical details, to cultivate freely the graces of life, and afford examples of them to the classes less favourably circumstanced for their growth. (Mill, *Principles*, II, 755)

Structurally, this description again works to recall and carefully modify one of Mill's earlier vignettes. This time it is the portrait of the English and American work ethic that is invoked, with its notion that for the 'majority' of the members of these communities there is 'no life but in their work' and no ambition but 'the desire of growing richer, and getting on in the world'. In the stationary state of the future, by contrast, a removal of the culture of 'getting on', and the consequent high proportion of leisure time, gives space 'to cultivate freely the graces of life' and to develop what were formerly termed the 'nobler attributes' of human nature. Mill is notably realistic in the idea that such interests would not characterize every individual's life. But this is nevertheless a portrait of society that balances labour and leisure very differently to how they are arranged in contemporary Britain, and that imagines these two realms of existence in harmonious alliance for a far greater proportion of a population. The result would be the creation of more rounded and complete citizens than the stunted profit-seeking machines of contemporary English and American society. Mill's text, in its first edition, contained the judgement that, for all its social advantages, in American society 'the life of the whole of one sex is devoted to dollar-hunting, and of the other to breeding dollar-hunters' (Mill, *Principles*, II, 754). This portrait of the stationary state is therefore one that seeks to harness the idea that human leisure time is often filled with an intensity of activity that exceeds that attained in working hours. Mill makes this point, which was also a feature of Ferguson's thought and of the philosophies of Owen and Fourier, in his extended discussion of Fourier's ideas: 'scarcely any labour, however severe, undergone by human beings for the sake of subsistence, exceeds in intensity that which other human beings, whose subsistence is already provided for, are found ready and even eager to undergo for pleasure' (Mill, *Principles*, I, 212–3). With this conception of human energy in place, the emphasis of Mill's stationary society on 'the graces of life' seems justifiable.

It is worth observing that Mill devotes much more space, in this description of future society, to the 'passive susceptibilities' than to its attendant culture of work. The latter is a slightly restricted, but not much altered, version of everything that has been described in the rest of the treatise, and the rest of political economy more broadly. The former is more of a new development, and is especially in need of thorough explanation in the context of political economy's conventional mode of understanding culture, which was largely represented by Ricardo's handling of wine and art.[45] Mill therefore elaborates further the contemplative elements of the model of social and individual wellbeing that would prevail in the stationary state, demonstrating that the 'passive susceptibilities' and 'tranquil contemplation' are both very much at issue. Following a brief consideration of the significance of population control to any stationary state, it is aesthetic meditation of the style we observed in Shelley and Keats's thought that is cast as a key feature of the future state:

> A world from which solitude is extirpated, is a very poor ideal. Solitude, in the sense of being often alone, is essential to any depth of meditation or of character; and solitude in the presence of natural beauty and grandeur, is the cradle of thoughts and aspirations which are not only good for the individual, but which society could ill do without. Nor is there much satisfaction in contemplating the world with nothing left to the spontaneous activity of nature; with every rood of land brought into cultivation, which is capable of growing food for human beings; every flowery waste or natural pasture ploughed up, all quadrupeds or birds which are not domesticated for man's use exterminated as his rivals for food, every hedgerow or superfluous tree rooted out, and scarcely a place left where a wild shrub or flower could grow without being eradicated as a weed in the name of improved agriculture. (Mill, *Principles*, II, 756)

The frame of reference needed to understand this passage is not to be found in political economy itself, but in the kind of meditative thought we looked at in Chapter 1 of this study. Indeed, both Shelley and Keats's models of idle contemplation are covered by Mill's account of aesthetic repose. Shelley's 'Mont Blanc' explored in striking detail 'solitude in the presence of natural beauty and grandeur' and also depicted that mode of being as a 'cradle of thoughts and aspirations'. Recall how that poem staged a dramatic encounter with the mountain's voice and its ability to 'repeal / Large codes of fraud and woe'. Keats's model of idle contemplation, meanwhile, stressed the extent to which the individual's contemplative journey was 'not only good for the individual' but also fundamental to ideal social interaction. In Mill's terms, 'society could ill do without' such intense meditation. And of course, in the case of both Shelley and Keats, as is also very strikingly the case for the whole canon of Romantic writing, it is 'the spontaneous activity of nature' that prompts and enriches such states of contemplative existence. Keats's flowers, bees and forest trees are wild and beyond human control, and Mont Blanc itself is quintessentially uncultivated and uncultivatable. Shelley's poem thus describes an attempt to leave human society and consider a scene of wilderness in its own bafflingly complex terms. Even if its final moment seemed to cast that task as an impossibility, Shelley's poem is still structured by exactly the same logic as Mill's passage here.

The intellectual side of Mill's stationary state is not entirely made up of aesthetic contemplation, of course, although this aspect has a real emphasis in his description. Mill positions such repose as complemented by a broad array of 'human improvement' that contrasts with the 'stationary condition of capital and population':

> There would be as much scope as ever for all kinds of mental culture, and moral and social progress; as much room for improving the Art of Living, and much more likelihood of its being improved, when minds ceased to be engrossed by the arts of getting on. Even the industrial arts might be as earnestly and successfully cultivated, with this sole difference, that instead of serving no purpose but the increase of wealth, industrial improvements would produce their legitimate effect, that of abridging labour. Hitherto it is questionable if all the mechanical inventions yet made have lightened the day's toil of any human being. (Mill, *Principles*, II, 756)

This passage further fleshes out the 'nobler interests of humanity' than 'getting on'. Human life is imagined as expanding here into various and diverse realms of thought, being and knowledge that leave making money looking like a poor and cramped mode of existence. The conceit of this description is that these vast areas of human wellbeing can only be signalled in short-hand from contemporary commercial society. The 'Art of Living', for example, is a term that is vague but provocative enough to imply that human potential has only been glimpsed in commercial society. Again, this term might be said to recall the 'leisure' of nomadic life, as if there are elements of human existence invisible to the narrow consciousness engendered by the system of economic competition. This passage thus contains both an implicit and an explicit critique of the purview of political economy in the nineteenth century. Its implicit critique is that the system of wealth promoted by that discourse is comprehensively stultifying for human mental life, even to the extent of limiting consideration of what society might be. Its explicit critique is that 'industrial improvements' have been denied their 'legitimate effect' of 'abridging labour' by the ideology of growth and expansion.[46] For Mill's stationary state is not a vision of a far-distant future for society. On the contrary, 'this ultimate goal is at all times near enough to be fully in view'; society is apparently 'always on the verge of it' and it could be grasped at any moment (Mill, *Principles*, II, 752). It is for this reason that Mill again evokes the spectre of labour's considerable arduousness, in this account of the potential 'mental culture' of mankind: several centuries of technological improvements have not significantly 'lightened the day's toil of any human being'.

Rejecting growth in wealth and population would thus allow, in Mill's scheme, for growth in the genuine wellbeing of individuals and their communities. This is a vision of the future of human society that unites the central ideas of the early nineteenth century's diverse reactions against economic progress. Berg records that the 'staunchly Tory outlook' in these decades 'spurned industrial society altogether', while '[r]adicals and workers [...] attributed poverty and unemployment to the machine in the hands of capitalist employers', and 'hoped to harness' technology's 'benefits to themselves'.[47] Mill's idea of a society that would cease to exploit labour for the sake of profit, and that would significantly foster non-industrial modes of passivity, might thus be seen as having it both ways.[48] It is also striking that taking seriously the categories of idleness, repose and leisure, as we are doing in this study, allows us to see Mill's comprehensive radicalism very clearly. This is an important revaluation of Mill's economic thought because, for commentators from Raymond Williams to Donald Winch, Mill has been 'awarded', in Winch's terms, 'the status of a flawed or failed romantic, capable of appreciating the private consolations of literature, but lacking those liberating qualities that would have allowed him to uphold (or anticipate) an alternative vision of society'.[49] Mill's *Principles*, as we have understood them here, are deeply at odds with this judgement. Mill certainly 'anticipates' and 'upholds' an 'alternative' society, one liberated from the ideologies of technological progress, from the culture of the individual simply 'getting on', and from the historical deformities of the institution of private property. And Mill should also be understood to thoroughly synthesize a key element of Romantic poetics – the emphasis on contemplative repose – with the quantitative and technical purview of political economy.

We have now seen the full development of political economy in the first half of the nineteenth century, and witnessed its considerable – and, over the course of these decades, growing – preoccupation with the categories of idleness, repose and contemplation. We are thus now in a position to assess this discourse's conception of idleness as a whole and to comment on its relationship to the intensely positive accounts of human contemplation we followed in the writing of Keats and Shelley. One must note, to begin with, that political economy's increasing engagement with questions of repose and inertia moves it closer and closer to the Romantic discourse of idleness, until, by the end of Mill's *Principles*, the two fields effectively meet. Mill's thought thus comprehensively synthesizes an awareness of labour's features and significance with an understanding of idleness and its considerable rewards very close to that of Keats and Shelley. If Mill gives more space, at the end of his treatise, to the delineation of passivity's many states and qualities than he does to the style of labour that might be practised in the stationary state, one might say that this is because that knowledge of idleness is a new and unusual presence in the discourse in which he is working. Alternatively, one might conclude that the nineteenth century's powerfully commercial and industrialized society is in need of the corrective that Romantic idleness can offer. This second interpretation is supported by Mill's 1850 essay 'On the Negro Question' – a reply to Thomas Carlyle's 'Occasional Discourse on the Negro Question' of the previous year – and the manner in which he there 'assert[s]' a 'gospel of leisure' in order to redress Carlyle's apparently inflated conception of labour:

> The worth of work does not surely consist in its leading to other work, and so on to work upon work without end. On the contrary, the multiplication of work, for purposes not worth caring about, is one of the evils of our present condition. [...] In opposition to the 'gospel of work', I would assert the gospel of leisure, and maintain that human beings *cannot* rise to the finer attributes of their nature compatibly with a life filled with labour.[50]

A notion of 'passive susceptibilities' very close to that elaborated on in the *Principles* is here used to counter Carlyle's notion that slave labour is a step on the path to polite society. Again, in other words, Mill stresses one side of his leisure and labour synthesis in order to challenge contemporary patterns of thought.

When one stands back even further from the development of political economy in these decades, and from individual conflicts such as this, that discourse's account of human nature appears to be almost paradoxical. Political economy once focused on – and indeed championed and celebrated – human labour, in all its manual and productive manifestations. By the mid-nineteenth century, by contrast, in a development of which Mill's work is the culmination, but which can certainly be found before his treatise's publication, the discourse is distinctly suspicious of the stunted single-mindedness of economic man, and accordingly of the category of labour itself. In the glimpses of colonial idleness we saw in Ricardo, in Malthus's cumulative awareness of the 'luxury of indolence', and of course in Mill's wholesale account of the passive arts of living, economic productivity is rendered a kind of second nature. It is desirable, in the logic we have picked out of these texts, for a society's members to toil and to produce. But that productivity is a short-lived feature of a stage in social development, or a problematic imposition by the colonial mindset. Far from celebrating labour, and from demonstrating the extent to which man is a fundamentally economic animal – as Smith's *Wealth of Nations* did at length – nineteenth-century political economy in fact constructs a portrait of human nature in which it is often the tendency to idleness that seems primary and permanent. This tendency may be seen through the lenses of various moral and intellectual ideologies, and may thus be cast as morally suspect 'indolence', as proto-civilized 'inertia', or indeed as man's 'noblest' quasi-classical achievement. But a reader of the texts considered in this chapter may very fairly be left with the impression that the human capacity for labour is in need of constant stimulation, and careful care – the impression, in other words, that economic man is an ongoing and problematic construction. The human tendency to idleness, meanwhile, is positioned by these texts as innate, as always present, and as standing behind the true health and success of any community. It is only Mill, in these decades, that resolves the tensions of this Janus-faced discipline, therefore. And it is striking that he does so by bringing the Romantic positive conception of idleness into the same fold as political economy's conventional focus on labour. The category of idleness, in political economic thought, thus develops from being something like a simple category of stasis in the late eighteenth century – a cessation of successful, productive activity – to the state in which man's primary nature can be expressed and developed, in the strand of thought that culminates in Mill's writing. Mill, therefore, strives to synthesize the psychological category of idleness to be found in Romantic poetics with the more external conception of inertia belonging to political economy. By the mid-century, therefore, one might say that Keats's and Shelley's intensely psychological models of idleness are left looking like powerful insights into the complexities of man's primary nature – not derivative or elitist accounts of literary leisure. The distinction that Keats made in his letters between economic and aesthetic activity is thus upheld, but reinterpreted by Mill. Rather than man being the 'flower' instead of the 'bee', Mill's political economy contends that man might be both.

CHAPTER 3

The 'Gospel of Work'

Nineteenth-century political economy's preoccupation with questions of idleness, culminating in John Stuart Mill's celebration of a stationary state that fosters passive and aesthetic susceptibilities, is remarkable in the context of that discourse's history. But Mill's particular synthesis of the aesthetic and the economic is also noteworthy because it stands in stark opposition to one of the primary currents of nineteenth-century thought outside political economy. For the dominant voices of cultural description and critique across the century share an emphasis, not on repose and contemplation, but on labour and activity. From the early 1830s onwards, the nineteenth century witnesses a repeated proclamation of what is termed the 'gospel of work', sometimes even from the same tongues that thoroughly challenge the type of work actually taking place in Britain's advanced industrial economy. This body of thought – as it is formulated between approximately 1830 and 1860 – will form the subject of the present chapter, because it constitutes a powerful and far-reaching counter-narrative to the Millite and Romantic positive conceptions of idleness that we have considered so far. The influence of this ideology of labour is in fact so marked that throughout the rest of the century – and the rest of this study – the category of idleness will almost always be seen through its lens. As we will find in Chapter 4, for instance, even the celebrations of idle contemplation and aesthetic consciousness that are written between 1850 and 1880 transform aesthetic passivity into an arena for diligent and arduous work.

But the 'gospel of work' also has a second, and a rather paradoxical, relevance for the present study. At the same time that this body of thought argues against human repose, it also founds its conception of correct, full and genuinely productive labour on a previous generation's theorizations of the categories of idleness and aesthetic consciousness. What this means, as we shall see at some length, is that the many examinations and celebrations of aesthetic idleness that are contemporary with Keats and Shelley might be said to contain the seeds of their own refutation, and downfall. This unlikely and paradoxical genesis of the 'gospel of work' also creates a situation in which the particular type of work that exemplifies mid-nineteenth-century labour is actually aesthetic creation and concentration itself. This is not to say, however, that contemporary conceptions of ideal labour are simply synonymous with aesthetic activity, or that the considerable influence of the 'gospel of work' effects the direct transmission of earlier positive conceptions of idleness. On the contrary, as we shall see in the analysis that follows, in both contemporary and more recent contexts, the 'gospel of work' is understood simplistically and straightforwardly. Its advocates and theorizers are repeatedly and consistently read as promoting a concentration on arduous and useful labour above all else, and as denigrating idleness and repose in extreme and forthright terms.

In order both to lay out this paradoxical situation and then to clarify its complex effects, the present chapter will be divided into two sections. Firstly, it will examine the 'gospel of work' in its most influential and far-reaching forms by considering Thomas Carlyle's and Karl Marx's depictions of ideal labour. Secondly, it will turn to the effect of this powerful ideology by considering some of the poetic accounts of idle contemplation that stand in the wake of the 'gospel of work'. Poetry, in the earliest years of the nineteenth century, was the bastion of positive conceptions of idle contemplation, as we saw in Chapter 1. In the shadow of Carlyle and Marx, however, as we shall see presently, poetry becomes that category's consistent opponent, repeatedly contrasting aesthetic consciousness with the apparently superior virtues of labour and activity.

The most extreme and forthright manifestation of the 'gospel of work' may be the writing of Samuel Smiles, whose *Self-Help* of 1859 energetically celebrates the diligent pursuit of activity, and repeatedly and loudly proclaims the virtues of the individual who 'spar[es] neither labour, pains, nor self-denial'.[1] But our present purposes require us to take a longer view of the 'gospel of work', and to consider both its intellectual origins and its most complex and complete expressions. For this reason, we must begin this account of the passivity at the heart of the period's ideology of 'work' with the thought of Thomas Carlyle. Carlyle, as we shall see, is the heir to the Romantic philosophical tradition that – in England as in Germany – had espoused idle aesthetic contemplation as the culmination of human activity and intellect. Carlyle's most important early work, moreover, *Sartor Resartus* (1833–4), develops his conception of correct 'work' at the same time as paying complex homage to this inheritance.

Although it is frequently read by intellectual historians and some literary critics as a straightforward autobiography,[2] *Sartor Resartus* is in fact a deeply ambiguous serio-comic 'hoax', to use Anne Mellor's term. Here is Mellor's useful account of the work's context:

> Both in content and in structure, this is a work of 'transcendental buffoonery'. It is, first and foremost, a hoax, a book-length review of a book that does not exist ... Carlyle adapts to his own purposes the familiar wit of *Fraser's Magazine* and *Blackwood's*, the wit of Oliver Yorke and Christopher North, those endearing and irascible editors who also do and do not exist. Carlyle of course expected the more faithful and subtle readers of *Fraser's* to see through his hoax, to penetrate his disguises and recognize *Sartor Resartus* for the jocoserious production that it was ... To help his less knowledgeable readers, Carlyle ... included the American and English reviews of *Sartor*, which revealed it for the hoax it was, in its first book-form publication in England in 1838.[3]

Carlyle's multi-layered text must therefore be recognized as extremely slippery. Not only is its comically conservative, sceptical and fictional editor guiding readers through the thought of a comically obscure, and also fictional, philosopher, Diogenes Teufelsdröckh, but the editor gradually becomes aware of Teufelsdröckh's own 'humouristico-satirical tendenc[ies]', 'underground humours' and 'intricate sardonic rogueries' (*Sartor*, 153). Because these terms apply not simply to Teufelsdröckh and his hopelessly confused autobiographical fragments, but also to Carlyle himself in the case of this text, the entire design of *Sartor* is gradually revealed to be a kind of Laurence Sterne-style meta-fiction in which ideas and judgements are simultaneously proposed, lauded and subtly mocked. For Janice Haney, *Sartor* is thus 'an overdetermined fiction, a text that lays fiction upon fiction'.[4]

Within this scheme, Teufelsdröckh's pervasive 'passivity' holds something of a privileged position, for it is repeated and reaffirmed throughout the text, and seems to be both celebrated as the embodiment of the protagonist's transcendental insight, and satirized as a kind of flimsy affectation. *Sartor*'s editor casts this posture of repose as the linking characteristic throughout Teufelsdröckh's life, but almost always does so at the same time as foregrounding its absurdity. Take the following summary, for instance:

> [I]n much of our Philosopher's history, there is something of an almost Hindoo character: nay, perhaps in that so well-fostered and every-way excellent 'Passivity' of his, which, with no free development of the antagonist Activity, distinguished his childhood, we may detect the rudiments of

much that, in after-days, and still in these present days, astonishes the world. For the shallow-sighted, Teufelsdröckh is oftenest a man without Activity of any kind, a No-man; for the deep-sighted, again, a man with Activity almost superabundant, yet so spiritual, close-hidden, enigmatic, that no mortal can foresee its explosions, or even when it has exploded, so much as ascertain its significance. A dangerous, difficult temper for the modern European; above all, disadvantageous in the hero of a Biography! (*Sartor*, 78)

The comic absurdity of this portrait lies in the particular type of 'Activity' Teufelsdröckh represents. This 'spiritual', 'enigmatic' 'Activity' hidden beneath surface 'Passivity' apparently 'astonishes the world'. And yet, because even the 'deep-sighted' cannot 'ascertain' the 'significance' of such 'explosions' of 'Activity', and because Carlyle's syntax keeps open the possibility that the 'deep-sighted' might not even be able to tell when this 'Activity' 'has exploded', this description is self-defeating. On its surface, therefore, this passage celebrates Teufelsdröckh's vast powers of philosophic contemplation. It also positions them as central to any consideration of the philosopher. But at the same time, this description serves to comically undermine such intense passive contemplation as rendering Teufelsdröckh all but useless to the world – even to its 'deep-sighted' members – and certainly unfit to be the subject of the present partial attempt at 'Biography'. Passive contemplation is thus configured here as both a powerful posture of the philosopher's mindset and an absurd caricature of that profundity and power.

   Of course, the sceptical implications of this humour are offset, in *Sartor*, by the space it devotes to the philosopher's clothes-philosophy itself, and by the considerable extent to which that philosophy resembles Carlyle's own worldview. In general terms, for instance, Teufelsdröckh's focus on clothing and raiment parallels the complex notion of 'machinery' that Carlyle had developed in his earlier *Signs of the Times* (1829). And *Sartor's* editor oscillates dramatically between the comically flawed celebration of the previous quotation, periods of unalloyed scepticism and also frequent periods of whole-hearted awe at the implications of Teufelsdröckh's ideas. It is in the latter mode, for instance, that the following passage from Teufelsdröckh's writing is excerpted. And this passage again casts the philosopher as passive contemplator of the world's complexities:

With men of a speculative turn ... there come seasons, meditative, sweet, yet awful hours, when in wonder and fear you ask yourself that unanswerable question: Who am *I*; the thing that can say 'I' . . .? The world, with its loud trafficking, retires into the distance; and, through the paper-hangings, and stone-walls, and thick-plied tissues of Commerce and Polity, and all the living and lifeless Integuments (of Society and a Body), wherewith your Existence sits surrounded, – the sight reaches forth into the void Deep, and you are alone with the Universe and silently commune with it, as one mysterious Presence with another. (*Sartor*, 42)

To withdraw into, but beyond, oneself, to transcend the trappings of 'Existence' but to reach its essential heart, to 'silently commune' with the 'Universe' in a 'meditative . . . yet awful' manner: this mode of being must be understood to recreate the aesthetic contemplation of the Romantic and idealist traditions. Thus, one might describe this posture of contemplation as highly comparable to the state dramatized by Percy Shelley's 'Mont Blanc'. For that poem described being alone with the powerful 'mysterious Presence' of the mountain and silently communing with its voice and import. Carlyle's description after this quotation indeed goes on to closely parallel Shelley's language in the poem. Teufelsdröckh describes how, in this intense idleness, 'sounds and many-coloured visions flit round our sense; but Him, the Unslumbering, whose work both Dream and Dreamer are, we see not; except in rare half-waking moments, suspect not' (*Sartor*, 43). Much like Shelley's trance-like vision of the spinning 'universe of things' and their God-like central mountain, Carlyle's passage defines studied, practised, 'half-waking' aesthetic contemplation as a kind of fundamentally pure mode of being that can picture the human place in the world with a clarity otherwise unavailable. And if one compares these ideas to Carlyle's own philosophical beliefs, one finds a precise match. According to Mellor, Carlyle viewed the universe at the time of writing *Sartor* as 'a mysterious, anarchic force that is vitally alive, always moving, changing, making and unmaking', a 'divine power' that 'can be apprehended . . . not through mechanistic logic, but only intuitively'.[5]

Sartor Resartus, however, does not simply recreate the kind of worldview to be found in Shelley's 'Mont Blanc', or in Coleridge's *Biographia Literaria* (1817), which also, in part, serio-comically celebrates the philosopher's intense aesthetic contemplation. For Carlyle, such a mode of meditative passivity is only the first step towards fully realized human behaviour. It is for this reason that other moments of Teufelsdröckh's passive contemplation within *Sartor* that are highly comparable to the one quoted above soon have their potential pathos thoroughly punctured. On contemplating a beautiful mountain scene midway through the life-journey that structures the text, for instance, as the beauty of the setting sun causes 'a murmur of Eternity and Immensity, of Death and of Life' to steal through Teufelsdröckh's 'soul', the 'Spell' of such intuitive contemplation is 'broken' by the emergence of the philosopher's former lover and former friend – Blumine and Herr Towgood – now married and travelling on their honeymoon in their 'gay barouche-and-four' (*Sartor*, 117–18). On this occasion the moral to be gleaned from this bathetic episode is provided by the editor, through his own reading of Teufelsdröckh's clothes-philosophy, and through quotation from Aristotle. The pure contemplation of such beauty stood no chance of ultimately satisfying Teufelsdröckh, and therefore some such bathos was inevitable, because '*The end of Man is an Action, and not a Thought*' (*Sartor*, 120). Educated by Teufelsdröckh's ideas themselves, *Sartor*'s editor thus casts idle aesthetic contemplation as not an unqualified good in itself, but a step along the way to correct humanity. But the fact that this clear moral is quoted from no less an authority than Aristotle, rather than from the slippery, partially comic and certainly fictional Teufelsdröckh himself, serves to make this lesson stand out as genuine, almost timeless, philosophical truth in the scheme of *Sartor*'s serio-comic half-satire.

Passive contemplation of the universe's complexities is thus but one step towards correct being, for Teufelsdröckh and his now-converted editor. Accordingly, *Sartor* progresses from revealing the intuitively ascertained universe of its philosopher, and from dramatizing the intense passivity that allowed for that intuition, to describing how one must act and participate in that universe. One such moment is to be found in Teufelsdröckh's marginal notes on his friend Hofrath Heuschrecke's Malthusian tract 'entitled *Institute for the Repression of Population*' (*Sartor*, 172). There, Teufelsdröckh defines the 'two men' alone that he 'honours' in the world:

> First, the toilworn Craftsman that with earth-made Implement laboriously conquers the Earth, and makes her man's. Venerable to me is the hard Hand; crooked, coarse; wherein notwithstanding lies a cunning virtue, indefeasibly royal, as of the Sceptre of this Planet. ... A second man I honour, and still more highly: Him who is seen toiling for the spiritually indispensable; not daily bread, but the Bread of Life. Is not he too in his duty; endeavouring towards inward Harmony[?] (*Sartor*, 172–3)

Action here, in both its physically humble and spiritually pure manifestations, is positioned as the ideal participation in the universe's complexity. For if the universe is 'vitally alive, always moving, changing, making and unmaking', then to move and to create is to participate in it in a direct and harmonious manner. The land-worker's 'hard Hand' should thus be seen as 'the Sceptre of the Planet'. And he who creates in an inward, spiritual sense is participating in the universe's activity in a manner just as pure.

If the two models of action were to be combined into a single figure, moreover, '[s]uch a one will take thee back to Nazareth itself' and 'thou wilt see the splendour of Heaven spring forth from the humblest depths of Earth, like a light shining in great darkness' (*Sartor*, 173). For Teufelsdröckh, in other words, both manual and spiritual work move man towards the condition of divinity, and the significance of Jesus lies in his harmonious synthesis with the intellectual and physical forces and complexities of the universe.

It should be recognized, at this point, that even this evangelical celebration of physical and spiritual labour is not very far removed from the Romantic aesthetics of idleness that we saw Carlyle recreate in the first sections of *Sartor*. Because one of the primary intertexts of this work is Coleridge's *Biographia Literaria*, it is pertinent to recall that the central moment of that text also depicted aesthetic contemplation as approaching the condition of divinity. Coleridge cast the human imagination as no less than a 'repetition' of the 'act of creation' itself, no less than the 'infinite I AM'.[6] He thus positioned the poet, he who uses the imagination in the most sophisticated and organic fashion, as the fullest realization of quasi-divine creativity. Carlyle assumes a comparable position in *Sartor*, when he has Teufelsdröckh describe the 'Work of Art' as 'divine', and when he explains how the 'Artist or Poet' can rise into a 'Prophet' in whom 'all men can recognize a present God' (*Sartor*, 169). Likewise, one must observe that the 'second man' that Teufelsdröckh honours, who works towards 'inward Harmony', is also a figure taken to some extent from Romantic or idealist aesthetics. In the same way that the notion of aesthetic contemplation's divinity is shared by Coleridge and a whole generation of German idealists, so too the idea of 'inward Harmony' is rehandled and reasserted across a similar constituency.[7] Friedrich Schiller is perhaps the fullest analyst of this idea in his 1795 *Über die ästhetische Erziehung des Menschen, in einer Reihe von Briefen* (*On the Aesthetic Education of Man, in a Series of Letters*). Schiller contends for the passive contemplation of 'Fine Art' as the ultimate balancing act for the human mind, because aesthetic objects simultaneously put into play man's physical and spiritual capabilities.[8] A comparable notion of harmonious 'free play' and of the development of the 'whole man' is also explored at length in Coleridge's *Biographia* and in several contemporary English and German texts.[9]

What these connections, or intellectual debts, show us about the ideas to be found in *Sartor*, are that at the very base of Carlyle's celebration of 'work' – be it manual or spiritual – is the aesthetics of passive contemplation developed by the Romantic tradition in England and the idealist tradition in Germany. Carlyle's emphasis is certainly different from that of Coleridge or Schiller, who place more stress on the powers of contemplation itself, and do not cast that state as forcefully as a step along the way to correct activity.[10] Nevertheless, the place of *Sartor* in Carlyle's literary career serves to position the idle aesthetics of his intellectual forebears as the bedrock of his conception of ideal human action. This is the case because Carlyle's later, non-satirical work restates Teufelsdröckh's complex honouring of labour and activity in even more heightened and impassioned terms. *Past and Present*, Carlyle's 1843 work of cultural criticism that, as its central gesture, contrasts nineteenth-century and medieval behaviour and priorities, is the clearest example of this restatement. It is to this work that we will now turn.

Past and Present begins by taking issue, as we saw Mill and Malthus do, with the discrepancy between Britain's national wealth and the state of wellbeing of the majority of its citizens. Christening this unresolved issue the 'condition of England' question (*Past*, 71), Carlyle describes how

> the world has been rushing on with such fiery animation to get work and ever more work done, it has had no time to think of dividing the wages; and has merely left them to be scrambled for by the Law of the Stronger, law of Supply-and-demand, law of Laissez-faire, and other idle Laws and Un-laws, – saying, in its dire haste to get the work done, That is well enough! (*Past*, 87)

This overemphasis on production and 'half-frantic velocity' (*Past*, 84) has led not simply to 'work and ever more work', but also, paradoxically, to 'the deadest-looking stillness and paralysis':

> Workers, Master Workers, Unworkers, all men, come to a pause; stand fixed, and cannot farther. Fatal paralysis spreading inwards, from the extremities, in St. Ives workhouses, in Stockport cellars, through all limbs, as if towards the heart itself. Have we actually got enchanted, then; accursed by some god? (*Past*, 75)

In one sense, this description is simply a restatement of the problem of the manual labourer's stultification that has been a key feature of political economy since Adam Ferguson's *Essay on the History of Civil Society* and Adam Smith's *Wealth of Nations*. An advanced division of labour, for these writers and all their nineteenth-century followers, tends to contract the mental and moral capabilities of its workforce to an alarming and problematic extent.[11] But Carlyle's heightened, visionary formulation of this commonplace, in which the nation's workforce is 'enchanted' or 'accursed by some god', renders the problem of stultification much more immediately one of spiritual and cosmic concern. The pervasive materialism of laissez-faire political economy 'spread[s] inwards', here, as if the 'heart[s]' and souls of the nation's citizens are being turned to stone. Taken as a whole, British society is thus apt to be described using the language of a fairy tale, and is in need of being dramatically delivered from its bondage.

Before turning to *Past and Present*'s version of such deliverance, to what Carlyle's rhetoric has set up as an almost magical solution that will redress this cosmic curse, we should note that this text has already configured passivity and idleness in slightly different terms to *Sartor Resartus*. In the earlier work, Teufelsdröckh's intense 'stillness', 'passivity' and aesthetic contemplation were positioned as the postures of intuition needed to adequately comprehend an anarchic and vitalistic universe. But they were also subtly mocked, or cast as problematically extreme, and it was only by learning from, and passing through, that process that correct and harmonious life-activity could be identified. In *Past and Present*, comparably, one might describe paralysis and 'enchantment' as problematic versions of idleness in need of a corrective conception of labour and life-activity. In this sense both texts might be read as casting total passivity as somehow misguided, or even lopsided. But it seems impossible to ignore the more pejorative implications of Carlyle's cosmic, or fairy-tale language in *Past and Present*, by which to 'stand fixed' or even to 'pause' is now to display the symptom of a widespread disease. In this sense, passivity would seem to be quite straightforwardly villainized here. This reversal, or inversion, of the significance of idleness from *Sartor* to the opening of *Past and Present* might lead one to attribute even more satire to the early stages of *Sartor* than I allowed in my treatment of it. Alternatively, one might conclude that, when removed from the Sternean, Coleridgean, or generally satirical metaphysical contexts of German philosophy, intense passivity cannot carry anything other than negative associations for Carlyle. Either way, one cannot get away from the fact that the opening of *Past and Present* covers over the passive roots of Carlyle's thought, even as Carlyle prepares to deliver the same work-based conclusion that he deployed in *Sartor*.

Turning to the climax of *Past and Present*, to its eleventh chapter, entitled simply 'Labour', one finds a similarly complex situation with regards to passivity and activity. On the one hand, idleness is there again overtly and directly denigrated, as if again it is the great and alien evil besetting humankind. On the other, though, Carlyle's climactic justifications of work again make central use of the language of idleness to be found in Romantic and idealist aesthetics. While this discrepancy might be

explained by the issue of class, which we will consider below, it is nevertheless the case that Carlyle writes of idleness, in this key section of *Past and
Present*, in seemingly contradictory terms. The chapter on 'Labour' thus
commences by celebrating work and aggressively denigrating passivity:
'there is a perennial nobleness, and even sacredness, in Work. Were he
never so benighted, forgetful of his high calling, there is always hope in
a man that actually and earnestly works: in Idleness alone there is perpetual
despair' (*Past*, 223). We would seem here to be in territory far removed
from Teufelsdröckh's fictionally famous 'Passivity' and the penetrative
intuition it fostered. The path to truth no longer lies in brooding, meditative complexity or in 'silently communing' with the universe. Pervasive
inactivity is now synonymous with the 'perpetual despair' of the
'enchanted' and the 'accursed'. And yet, only a few sentences later, as
Carlyle reaches the crux of his celebration of labour, we find an echo of
Teufelsdröckh's language itself, and a direct verbal allusion to the idealist
aesthetics of idleness:

> It has been written, 'an endless significance lies in Work;' a man perfects
> himself by working. Foul jungles are cleared away, fair seedfields rise
> instead, and stately cities; and withal the man himself first ceases to be
> a jungle and foul unwholesome desert thereby. Consider how, even in the
> meanest sorts of Labour, the whole soul of man is composed into a kind of
> real harmony, the instant he sets himself to work! Doubt, Desire, Sorrow,
> Remorse, Indignation, Despair itself, all these like helldogs lie beleaguering
> the soul of the poor dayworker, as of every man: but he bends himself with
> free valour against his task, and all these are stilled, all these shrink murmur-
> ing far off into their caves. (*Past*, 223)

The echo of Teufelsdröckh here, and of the aesthetics of idleness he was
used to ventriloquize, lies in the references to 'harmony' and to 'the whole
soul of man'. We observed how the 'inward Harmony' of *Sartor* could be
traced to Schiller's formulation of 'aesthetic education' in quite general
terms. But in this instance Carlyle's phrasing alludes even more precisely to
Coleridge's *Biographia* and its analysis of the central contemplative power,
the imagination. Drawing on his detailed reading of German idealism, one
of Coleridge's most focused expressions of the activities of the imagination
held that '[t]he poet described in *ideal* perfection, brings the whole soul of
man into activity, with the subordination of its faculties to each other,
according to their relative worth and dignity'.[12] It is useful to note that in
this phrasing, 'the subordination' of the 'faculties to each other' very neatly
sums up the aesthetic sense of Schiller's play drive. Carlyle's contention
that in 'Labour' the 'whole soul of man is composed into a kind of real

harmony' thus recalls Coleridge's intricate portrait of imaginative contemplation and further blends it with the 'harmony' Schiller found in aesthetic meditation. For all three figures, consequently, the activity being described rebalances man's stunted or lopsided sensibilities, and brings about full or ideal humanity, even in the midst of the troubled present.[13] And yet, while Coleridge and Schiller attribute these powerful achievements to various species of passive aesthetic contemplation, for Carlyle, in what we have seen of *Past and Present* so far, they are to be found in work, in 'even' the 'meanest sorts of Labour', and occur immediately, 'the instant' man 'sets himself to work'.[14]

With this array of similarities and intertextualities between Carlyle, Coleridge and Schiller, and with a mode of fond humour for Coleridgean and idealist types so central to *Sartor Resartus*, it would be extremely surprising were *Past and Present* to maintain the villainization of passivity that we traced in its opening moments. Carlyle's conception of 'Labour' thus frequently tips over into passivity and aesthetic contemplation itself. When it comes to applying his proclamation of work to the immediate reader of *Past and Present*, for example, Carlyle makes clear that 'for the present', for each individual, 'almost nothing' is actually 'to be done' (*Past*, 90). Instead, the focus for each man should be

> if possible, to cease to be a hollow sounding-shell of hearsays, egoisms, purblind dilettantisms; and become, were it on the infinitely small scale, a faithful discerning soul. Thou shalt descend into thy inner man, and see if there be any traces of a *soul* there; till then there can be nothing done!
> (*Past*, 90)

Carlyle's conception of work thus in fact accommodates both manual labour and the spiritual, inward labour that one might describe as contemplative, or passive. *Past and Present* therefore oscillates between a language divorced from the aesthetics of passivity – as we saw in the case of the work's central passage considered above – and one so close to that tradition that the implicit workshop for this kind of self-improvement must be art or beauty. For a 'discerning soul' is surely one with a heightened and practised sense of judgement and taste, one that – in the idealist tradition, we have seen Carlyle tied to as much as in the classical tradition – holds beauty as its highest aspiration. It is for this reason that, in the chapter immediately after that on 'Labour', quoted above, as Carlyle unpacks the worth and significance of work, he frequently returns to poetry as his most apt and telling example. The following is just one of several instances of this association of work and poetry: 'He that works, whatsoever be his work, he bodies forth the form of Things Unseen; a small Poet every Worker is' (*Past*, 229). Where Coleridge made poetry the exemplary mode of human achievement, Carlyle, in this formulation, inverts Coleridge's terms but maintains precisely the same implication. Every mode of work, of whatever type, is poetry in miniature. Poetry is thus configured by this formulation as the pinnacle of both physical and spiritual work. One might say that the role held by Jesus in Teufelsdröckh's celebration of inward labour is here taken up by the poet.

On one level, then, Carlyle's argument in *Past and Present* might seem contradictory, or even nonsensical. British society is blindly carrying on its commercial work with too much energy and with too little justice, leading to a kind of cosmic curse on the population. And the answer to this is apparently the 'gospel of work', for each individual to labour with all his soul. Work is the answer to too much work. Absurdity is certainly the conclusion Mill came to on this aspect of Carlyle's thought in his reply to Carlyle's 1849 'Occasional Discourse on the Negro Question', as we saw in Chapter 2. But the more in-depth look we have now taken at Carlyle's model of work allows us to see that Mill's position in his *Principles* is in fact quite close to that of Carlyle's in *Past and Present*. Just as Mill synthesized the discourses of labour and of passive contemplation to envisage a social arrangement promoting both these poles of life, so Carlyle constructs an ideology of labour that includes the intricate passive and aesthetic engagements of the Romantic and idealist traditions. Carlyle's work is thus not simply blind, self-justifying productivity, but a balancing of the inward aesthetics of harmony with the outward nobleness of duty and achievement. And while Frederic Ewen contends that Carlyle's model of work stems primarily from Goethe, we have now seen how it in fact takes its contemplative elements from a broad constituency of English and German authors.[15] While the terms themselves – 'work' and 'labour' – that Carlyle uses to deploy this new model of activity may not differ at all from those of his predecessors or even opponents, his model of labour includes an inward, meditative, spiritual disposition not strictly acknowledged in that term, that will follow the 'radical universal alteration' of society's 'regimen and way of life' (*Past*, 88) predicted by *Past and Present*. The visionary, revolutionary opening of *Past and Present* from which these terms are taken notably positions inner, spiritual life as the prime agent of the new way of being:

> [t]here will be an agonizing divorce between you and your chimeras, luxuries, and falsities, take place; a most toilsome, all-but 'impossible' return

to Nature, and her veracities and her integrities, take place: that so the inner
fountains of life may again begin, like eternal Light-fountains, to irradiate
and purify your bloated, swollen, foul existence[.] (*Past*, 88)

The remarkable rhetoric of this famous passage renders the 'inner fountains of life' the essential pay-off of Carlyle's revolution, by positioning
them after the colon and the revelatory clause, 'that so'. Their effect,
moreover, 'to irradiate and purify' a currently 'foul existence', again
approximates the harmonizing, contemplative effect of fine art as described
by Schiller. Inner, spiritual, meditative life will here counteract the
mechanistic 'chimeras' of contemporary life. Carlyle's 'work' after this
transformation will be 'divorced' from the 'luxuries' and 'falsities' multiplied by laissez-faire consumerism. In this sense, Carlyle's future state
recreates what Michael John Kooy describes as the citizen's new 'attitude
to the object at hand' that will follow Schiller's aesthetic education.[16] That
is to say that while, to outward appearances, work may still appear to be
work, its alignment with the spiritual, the inward, the harmonious, the
aesthetic and the contemplative, will render it a true life-activity rather
than a 'paralysis' of one's humanity.

While Carlyle must be understood to villainize pervasive passivity in the
opening set-piece of *Past and Present*, then, he also builds this work's
conception of ideal 'labour' very directly on what was formerly the aesthetics
of idleness. In this sense, idleness and passivity here fulfil a kind of double
function. Man would seem to be at risk of a dangerous predominance of
passivity, a kind of harmful total inertia, for Carlyle. But, importantly,
passive, aesthetic, spiritual elements are the ultimate guarantees of purity in
the model of work that will exist after society's great transformation. When
phrased in this manner, *Past and Present* does not seem to stand that far from
Sartor Resartus. In that work too, Teufelsdröckh's total passivity was the
subject of repeated humour and bathos, as if in that mode the philosopher
was an absurd caricature of an idealist or a Coleridgean. When combined
with an Aristotelian ethos of action, by contrast, the aesthetics of idleness were
deployed to much more serious effect. They provided, for instance,
a profound insight into the significance of New Testament thought. If 'in
Idleness alone there is perpetual despair', then one might say that, for Carlyle,
in idleness properly deployed lies the human path to divinity.

As is well known, Carlyle exerts a profound influence on the thought of
his immediate contemporaries. For Jonathan Mendilow, for instance,
Carlyle inspired 'two generations of disciples', and led 'clergymen' to fear

'that Carlyleanism might "supersede the soul saving gospel of Christ"'.[17] One of the key elements of this influence is what Mendilow terms Carlyle's 'theory of man as *homo faber*'[18] rather than *homo oeconomicus* which, from what we have seen in this chapter so far, should now be understood to include an implicit aesthetics of passivity. It is a model in which outward, physical work is combined with a previous generation's theorizations of idleness to produce total, harmonious humanity. And because among those powerfully influenced by Carlyle are John Ruskin and William Morris, we will have several occasions over the course of this and the next chapter to trace the effects and development of this hybrid cluster of ideas. For the present, however, we must observe that even among those nineteenth-century cultural critics that do not stand in Carlyle's immediate sphere of influence, the pattern of thought that we have identified in Carlyle's 'gospel of work' is to a large extent replicated. That is to say that for Karl Marx, for instance, work in commercial society is also to be classified as not fully work but as a type of disease or curse. And again, Marx positions a more spiritual, inward or harmonious model of work as the answer to commercial society's ills. What this means is that Carlyle's handling of work and idleness is not simply the idiosyncratic result of his particular reading or temperament. Rather, what we are witnessing in the first half of this chapter represents the widespread legacy that theorizations of idleness from the end of the eighteenth century exert over considerations of commercial society well into the nineteenth century.[19] Considering Marx in this context may thus necessitate stepping slightly outside of the chronology of British thought this study is tracing – Marx's *Captial*, his most important work, was not translated into English until 1890 as we shall see, although *The Communist Manifesto* was published in England in 1850 – but it allows us to consider the long-standing and transnational relevance of the complex Victorian relationship between idleness and labour.

Turning to Marx's writing, then, one finds a relationship between aesthetic consciousness and productivity that stands extremely close to Carlyle's thought. For Marx also uses the work of artistic creation as the ultimate example of unforced, unrestricted human labour, and casts the communist project of human emancipation as one that will return man to a state something like Carlyle's post-transformation society, or Schiller's 'Aesthetic State'. But yet this aspect of Marx is notably elusive in his oeuvre, as if picturing post-revolutionary society too clearly will itself limit – and problematically harden – human potential. Marx's focus is instead on the logical and technical injustices of the present, which, to be seen clearly, necessitate the formulation of a whole new mode of political economy divorced from what he sees as the class-interests that infect the discipline's analysis. It is striking, however, that in almost every brief glimpse of the communist future Marx offers, there is reference to a language of contemplative aesthetics very similar to the one we identified in Carlyle. Take the case of the *Grundrisse*, Marx's draft workings towards his wholesale critique of political economy composed 1857–8, which is slightly more effusive than that critique itself, *Das Kapital* (1867–94), when it comes to questions of human drives and potential. In 'Notebook VI' of the *Grundrisse*, Marx takes issue with Adam Smith's notion that human happiness lies in 'tranquillity' and freedom from work, and does so by a now-familiar reference to human creativity:

> Daß das Individuum „in seinem normalen Zustand von Gesundheit, Kraft, Thätigkeit, Geschicklichkeit, Gewandtheit" auch das Bedürfniß einer normalen Portion von Arbeit hat, und von Aufhebung der Ruhe, scheint A. Smith ganz fern zu liegen. Allerdings erscheint das Maaß der Arbeit selbst äusserlich gegeben, durch den zu erreichenden Zweck und die Hindernisse, die zu seiner Erreichung durch die Arbeit zu überwinden. Daß aber diese Ueberwindung von Hindernissen an sich Bethätigung der Freiheit – und daß ferner die äusseren Zwecke den Schein bloß äusserer Naturnothwendigkeit abgestreift erhalten und als Zwecke, die das Individuum selbst erst setzt, gesetzt werden – also als Selbstverwirklichung, Vergegenständlichung des Subjekts, daher reale Freiheit, deren Aktion eben die Arbeit ahnt A. Smith ebenso wenig. [...] Wirklich freie Arbeiten, z. B. Componiren ist grade zugleich verdammtester Ernst, intensivste Anstrengung.[20]

> It seems quite far from Smith's mind that the individual, 'in his normal state of health, strength, activity, skill, facility', also needs a normal portion of work, and of the suspension of tranquillity. Certainly, labour obtains its measure from the outside, through the aim to be attained and the obstacles to be overcome in attaining it. But Smith has no inkling whatever that this overcoming of obstacles is in itself a liberating activity – and that, further, the external aims become stripped of the semblance of merely external natural urgencies, and become posited as aims which the individual himself posits – hence as self-realization, objectification of the subject, hence real freedom, whose action is, precisely, labour. [...] Real free working, e.g. composing, is at the same time precisely the most damned seriousness, the most intense exertion.[21]

For Coleridge, Wordsworth, Shelley, Schiller and many others, aesthetic contemplation may look like sheer passivity, but it is in fact arduous and serious labour. Schiller, as we have seen, casts aesthetic activity as the harmonious work of the whole man. Shelley, likewise, depicts poetry as the fullest human engagement in his *Defence*. Coleridge makes versions of this claim many times in the *Biographia*. These ideas, moreover, in Schiller's work as in that of his English counterparts, were deployed as a means of undermining the apparently restrictive notion of productive labour as it appeared in political economy. Marx, therefore, in this extract from the *Grundrisse*, should be understood to be harnessing exactly this tradition – indeed, much to the same effect – but, like Carlyle, as changing its emphasis from passivity to activity. In a comparable manner to the opening of *Past and Present*, this passage thus both villainizes pure inertia – here Smith's 'Ruhe' or 'tranquillity' – and classes a species of aesthetic passivity – 'Componiren', 'composing' – as the pinnacle of human engagement.[22] Intense aesthetic contemplation is thus the model for liberated, genuinely voluntary labour here, and communist society could be classified as the full embodiment of the Romantic and idealist aesthetics of idleness. For Marx in the *Grundrisse*, Man thirsts for the 'Selbstverwirklichung' of 'intensivste Anstrengung' – the 'self-realization' of the 'most intense exertion' – that recreates, or approximates, aesthetic contemplation.

Many more examples of this pattern of thought are to be found in Marx's oeuvre. For he time and again rejects Smithian 'tranquillity' and other forms of pure inertia to cast labour as the eternal condition of human life. But whenever he gives any level of detail of the features of labour after the revolution, he does so in a manner that recalls the Coleridgean, Schillerian or Carlylean notion of aesthetic wholeness. Examples of the former include the repeated idea, in *Capital*, that labour is 'ewige Naturnotwendigkeit, um den Stoffwechsel zwischen Mensch und Natur',[23] 'an eternal natural necessity which mediates the metabolism between man and nature'.[24] Or the suggestion, also in *Capital*, that the 'abolition of the capitalist form of production'[25] ('[d]ie Beseitigung der kapitalistischen Produktionsform'[26]) would not lead to a drastic reduction in the length of the working day, because of the self-directed energy of labour in its then-liberated citizens. An important example of the latter is to be found back in the *Grundrisse*, where Marx's observations on the classical obsession with virtue (as opposed to the modern obsession with financial gain) lead him to define wealth outside of the terms given by either culture. Here again, it is the notion of aesthetic creativity that immediately surfaces:

> [W]enn die bornirte bürgerliche Form abgestreift wird, was ist der Reichtum anders, als die im universellen Austausch erzeugte Universalität der Bedürfnisse, Fähigkeiten, Genüsse, Produktivkräfte etc der Individuen?

Die volle Entwicklung der menschlichen Herrschaft über die Naturkräfte, die der s. g. Natur sowohl, wie seiner eignen Natur? Das absolute Herausarbeiten seiner schöpferischen Anlagen [...]? [W]o er sich nicht reproducirt in einer Bestimmtheit, sondern seine Totalität producirt? Nicht irgend etwas Gewordnes zu bleiben sucht, sondern in der absoluten Bewegung des Werdens ist? In der bürgerlichen Oekonomie – und der Produktionsepoche der sie entspricht – erscheint diese völlige Herausarbeitung des menschlichen Innern als völlige Entleerung; diese universelle Vergegenständlichung als totale Entfremdung, und die Niederreissung aller bestimmten einseitigen Zwecke als Aufopferung des Selbstzwecks unter einen ganz äusseren Zweck.[27]

[W]hen the limited bourgeois form is stripped away, what is wealth other than the universality of human needs, capacities, pleasures, productive forces etc., created through universal exchange? The full development of human mastery over the forces of nature, those of so-called nature as well as of humanity's own nature? The absolute working-out of his creative potentialities [...]? Where he does not reproduce himself in one specificity, but produces his totality? Strives not to remain something he has become, but is in the absolute movement of becoming? In bourgeois economics – and in the epoch of production to which it corresponds – this complete working-out of the human content appears as a complete emptying out, this universal objectification as total alienation, and the tearing-down of all limited, one-sided aims as sacrifice of the human end-in-itself to an entirely external end.[28]

Man's 'creative potentialities' ('schöpferischen Anlagen'), his 'totality' ('Totalität') and his 'absolute movement of becoming' ('absoluten Bewegung des Werdens') here all configure non-commercial 'Reichtum', 'wealth' as a matter of Schillerian wholeness and Coleridgean innate creativity. These terms delineate a full image of unfettered humanity, one which recalls the whole aesthetic tradition from the turn of the nineteenth century, and in so doing cast commercial society as a set of intense limitations and constraints. In contemporary life, such many-sided, aesthetic, contemplative and spiritual human development is not only denied but utterly inverted. Instead of developing in a harmonious and whole manner, man undergoes a 'völlige Entleerung', a total depletion or evacuation of his identity and capabilities, and experiences a 'totale Entfremdung', a 'total alienation' from his surroundings and engagements. And of course, even if one does not read this kind of terminology as a series of allusions to idealist and Romantic patterns of thought, it should be noted that Marx's language is still thoroughly entwined with notions of passivity and aesthetic consciousness. To 'work out' one's 'creative potentialities' is to know oneself through a sustained process of aesthetic and contemplative consideration. To 'produce' one's 'totality' is to supplement the mechanical, non-intellectual and non-spiritual components of current life with ruminative, inward, passive accomplishments. What this important passage sets out, in other words, is a version of humanity based in contemplative and aesthetic passivity. And again, as was the case with Carlyle, Marx's vision is one in which these primary elements of human wholeness are fostered in and through non-alienated, unforced, labour.

While it is possible to detach Marx from idealist and Romantic thought like this, it is nevertheless common to view Marx's project in the light of Schiller's aesthetic education. Terry Eagleton, for example, also records how Marx 'inherits Schiller's "disinterested" concern with the all-round realization of human powers as an end in itself', but ironically renders the 'process by which this might historically come about [...] as far from classical disinterestedness as one could imagine'.[29] For Eagleton, Marx's 'scandalous originality' thus lies in harnessing 'this noble Schillerian vision of a symmetrical, many-sided humanity to highly partial, particular, one-sided political forces'; in valuing a 'traditionally conceived *Humanität*' but in suggesting that it 'will be brought to birth by those whose humanity is most crippled and depleted'.[30] From what we have seen in this chapter so far, one should consider a comparable irony to lie in the relationship between Schillerian passive aesthetic contemplation and Marx's emphasis on work. Not only will the segment of the populous most deficient in aesthetic culture engender the fullest possible Aesthetic State, in Marx's thought, but the human engagement most opposed to Schillerian passivity – labour, that is – will become the embodiment of an aesthetic and spiritual consciousness that was first conceived as the antidote to commercial society's over-emphasis on labour. Marx's project thus performs a complex and paradoxical inversion of the terms of idealist aesthetics, but maintains idealism's conception of aesthetic consciousness, and inner, spiritual contemplation as the key to full humanity. Marx's central category of 'labour', much like Carlyle's 'gospel of work', becomes a complex species of passivity, creativity and contemplative wholeness. And Marx's thought – like Carlyle's – villainizes pure inertia, or animal 'tranquillity', at the same time as being preoccupied with the moral and spiritual complexities of aesthetic passivity.[31]

We have now reconstructed the significance of the nineteenth-century 'gospel of work' in a manner that includes its contribution to the ongoing debates surrounding idleness and aesthetic consciousness. And while we will have occasion to consider Ruskin and others' further contributions to this cluster of ideas in Chapter 4, it is nevertheless an apt time to note that this portrait of the 'gospel of work' departs significantly from those that have appeared in recent criticism of Victorian thought. Gregory Dart's consideration of Ford Madox Brown's 1865 painting, *Work*, for example, summarizes Carlyle's conception of that category as follows: 'While professing to sympathize with the political and economic grievances of the working man, Carlyle continually suggested that only if a man devoted himself to his labor would he be able to receive it back in its sacramental form, as *work*, that which was its own reward.'[32] Note here that labour is simply labour; the 'working man' must continue to work, as if the activity Carlyle is theorizing were identical with that currently practised by the nation's labouring classes. Rob Breton makes a very similar set of assertions in his account of Morris's handling of Carlyle's thought. The 'Victorian Gospel of Work' is apparently 'the idea that work is a good in itself; that it ennobles; that it fosters a sense of stable identity or community; or that through it one accrues intrinsic development and satisfaction'.[33] Again, here, Carlyle's positive outcomes of work are associated with an unspecified form of labour, as if every style of labour were equally worthwhile and as if Carlyle were a celebrator of specialized labour *tout court*. Even Rancière, as we saw at the commencement of this study, configures nineteenth-century work as straightforward labour with added moral significance: 'The nineteenth century [saw] the assertion of [work's] positive value as the very form of the shared effectivity of thought and community.' What we have seen in the present analysis, by contrast, allows us to see clearly the role that the passive susceptibilities – and that aesthetic consciousness as the pinnacle of these susceptibilities – play in Carlyle's thought. And since this central paradigm to Carlyle's oeuvre is echoed and replicated in Marx, as we have seen, it is not an exaggeration to say that its significance for Victorian cultural politics is considerable. These texts might thus be said to represent a continued process of consolidation between the categories of labour and idleness that parallels that process as we traced it in the period's political economy. Or, alternatively, one might describe the dual role of idleness in these texts as a manifestation of the decreasing political acceptability of idleness across the nineteenth century (more of which below). Either way, to describe the 'gospel of work' without its implicit aesthetics of passivity is to significantly misrepresent its complexity and significance.

It is time to turn away from these highly influential theorizations – and proclamations – of labour, and from their closely connected degradations of pure, unmixed repose. Because to continue the process of understanding the significance of idleness and aesthetic consciousness in the middle years of the nineteenth century, we must now turn our attention to the period's literary representations of passivity that stand in the shadow of this 'gospel of work'. We must turn, that is, to the writing of Alfred Tennyson, Matthew Arnold and Gerard Manley Hopkins. The work of these figures that considers the issue of idleness is aligned with the outward form of the 'gospel of work' in the sense that it is either straightforwardly negative about poetic repose, or that it frames contemplative passivity in such a way as to lament its present impossibility. What the texts we are about to examine demonstrate, therefore, is that Carlyle's proclamation of the 'gospel of work' is made in a society that is already turning against the complex passivities of Romantic thought and that is therefore specially prepared to receive the headline news of that proclamation and to ignore or discount its more paradoxical details (much as we have just seen recent criticism of this field do). Poetry in this period should thus be seen to claim, time and again, that the Romantic model of passivity is unsustainable, unworldly and self-indulgent.

It is with Tennyson that we should begin this section of analysis, and with his most direct account of idleness, 'The Lotos-Eaters' of 1832. This poem is an interesting text for this study for more than one reason. In one sense 'The Lotos-Eaters' demonstrates very clearly how idleness as a subject of discourse can be ignored or occluded in scholarship of Victorian thought. For recent approaches to the poem include Francis O'Gorman's attempt to read it as inflected by contemporary parliamentary failures to act on the subject of electoral reform,[34] and Isobel Armstrong's analysis of Carlylean or Marxist 'alienated labour' in the poem.[35] Both these approaches, however, serve to turn critics and readers away from the all-encompassing inertia that the poem explores in considerable detail in order to focus on matters distinct from the text's actual terms. Armstrong, for example, sees the poem as 'both the *expression* of the addictive desire in which drug requires further drugging, and an *analysis* of the conditions under which the unhappy consciousness and the unhappy body come into being'. Because these 'conditions' are, for Armstrong, 'the horrors of' contemporary 'labour' practices, her reading of the poem must constantly go beyond the text's idleness itself in order to recreate 'the world of mechanised labour'.[36] It is by no means my contention, with these comments, that the poem is unrelated to labour practices, to the analyses of Carlyle and Marx, or indeed to contemporary reform debates. Rather, simply, that the poem also has a large amount to tell us about contemporary conceptions of idleness itself, and is indeed a very direct contribution to the period's complex debates about idleness and aesthetic consciousness. A second significance of this poem for the present analysis lies in its relationship with other work by Tennyson that does not consider idleness as directly, but that includes oblique and often puzzling references to states of repose or of intense, unworldly, aesthetic contemplation. There are a large number of Tennyson's works that fall into this category, but the most important is perhaps *The Princess* (1847), which contains repeated reference to a kind of involuntary trance-like state experienced by its male protagonist. Eve Sedgwick, like many others, is unable to unravel the mystery of what she calls these 'fugue state[s]' in her comprehensive and otherwise extremely impressive analysis of the poem.[37] 'The Lotos-Eaters', however, and the analysis of its handling of idleness that I am about to develop, offers a way of dealing with this issue. Such states would seem to represent the kind of involuntary accesses of aesthetic contemplation that were celebrated by the Romantics but that, for Tennyson and his contemporaries, represent problematic instances of otherworldliness, effeminate passivity and a valuing of the realms of fantasy above those that correspond more straightforwardly with the 'gospel of work' and its martial, masculine ethos. 'The Lotos-Eaters' is in this sense a kind of touchstone for later Tennyson and for mainstream Victorian values, and a very direct indication of the extent to which those values are animated by an interaction with questions of idleness, repose and aesthetic contemplation.

Tennyson's 'The Lotos-Eaters', then, tellingly stands at a considerable distance from the literary depictions of idleness that have already been considered in this study. Where Shelley's 'Mont Blanc', Keats's depiction of a society built on aesthetic contemplation and even parts of *Sartor Resartus* all cast intense passivity as powerfully productive in terms of the states of consciousness or social and moral conditions it could engender, Tennyson's poem renders idleness in dramatically negative terms. We saw, for instance, how Shelley's 'Mont Blanc' dramatized a reception of knowledge that was unavailable elsewhere, seized from the mountain's dangerous and troubling physicality. In 'The Lotos-Eaters', by contrast, intense passivity becomes, not a truthful and powerful engagement with the world's sensuousness, but a giving in to sensuality and also – perhaps more importantly considering the development of conceptions of idleness in the second half of the century – a giving in to one's inner anxieties and moral weaknesses. Take the following example of the poem's particular justification of idleness, one of many extended passages in the poem that function in this manner:

> Why are we weigh'd upon with heaviness,
> And utterly consumed with sharp distress,
> While all things else have rest from weariness?
> All things have rest: why should we toil alone,
> We only toil, who are the first of things,
> And make perpetual moan,
> Still from one sorrow to another thrown;   ('LE', 57–63)

It is not only in looking at this poem in the context of the contemporary 'gospel of work' that statements such as these seem deeply problematic. Because the poem is a dramatic monologue, it is inflected with a pervasive irony that invites a thorough reconsideration of all of its judgements. Alan Sinfield sums up this general effect of nineteenth-century dramatic mono- logue neatly: '[w]hat we experience in dramatic monologue [. . .] is a divided consciousness. We are impressed, with the full strength of first-person pre- sentation, by the speaker and feel drawn into his point of view, but at the same time are aware that he is a dramatic creation and there are other possible, even preferable perspectives'.[38] The complaint of these lines, that 'rest' is granted to 'all things' except man, is thus partially seductive but is more pressingly objectionable or challengeable, in this context. The spectre of a more con- ventional model of manly virtue is raised by these lines, in other words; one in which hardship, 'sharp distress' and 'toil' are embraced as generative schools of character and life. One should note that Romantic accounts of idle contem- plation such as Shelley's 'Mont Blanc', or Coleridge's 'Frost at Midnight', did not invoke or imply any consideration of active virtue in this manner. Rather, this is a direct effect of the form and dramatic construction of Tennyson's poem, and it is an effect which can be registered in almost every line. In this quotation, for instance, the mariners' song is characterized by the facile repetition of such phrases as 'All things have rest' and 'We only toil', both of which weakly restate, rather than advance, the singers' argument. These restatements serve to dilute the mariners' case for inertia and, in Sinfield's terms, to play against the force of the poem's 'first-person presentation'. In this context, furthermore, the notion that human life is one of 'perpetual moan[ing]' is especially ironic, for it invokes the idea that this is only the case for these particularly benighted and wrong-headed figures and for this parti- cular expression of the human lot.

Now, as well as the obvious allusion to the *Odyssey*, from which the plot of Tennyson's poems is taken, it is also frequently observed that 'The Lotos-Eaters' alludes extensively to, and quotes almost verbatim from, James Thomson's *The Castle of Indolence* of 1748. Thomson's poem is a highly suitable intertext for Tennyson because it also explores the seductions of idleness at considerable length, but ultimately rejects this realm in favour of an active philosophy of virtue, even if it keeps open the possibility that its poet-protagonist is still yearning for the world of languid and aesthetic indolence located in the poem's eponymous castle.[39] It has not been observed, however, that 'The Lotos-Eaters' also closely parallels – and synthesizes – several examples of the Romantic poetics of idleness. Coleridge's 'Eolian Harp' is invoked throughout the fifth and seventh sections of the mariners' song,[40] for instance, which cast their posture of passivity as one '[w]ith half-shut eyes' ('LE', 100) or '[w]ith half-dropt eyelid' ('LE', 135), seeing, but not fully paying attention to, 'the far-off sparkling brine' ('LE', 143). Such a posture was the central, powerfully contemplative state of Coleridge's poem, which describes the poet as 'behold[ing]', 'thro' [...] half-clos'd eyelids', the 'sunbeams dance, like diamonds, on the main'.[41] By recreating the terms of this posture within the pervasive irony of nineteenth-century dramatic monologue, and by divorcing these lines from their powerful philosophical pay-off ('And what if all of animated nature [...]'), Tennyson renders Coleridge's posture of passivity one of irresponsible selfishness and indulgence. 'The Lotos-Eaters' also invokes Coleridge's more obviously problematic depictions of calm and intertia in 'The Rime of the Ancient Mariner' (1798), in its introductory description of the lotos-eaters' island. The phrase, '[t]he charmed sunset linger'd low adown / In the red West' ('LE', 19–20), as one example, recalls Coleridge's portrayal of his vessel being becalmed while '[t]he charmed water burnt alway / A still and awful red'.[42] This time the allusion serves to recreate the same moral failings to be found in the original poem, as these lines invoke Coleridge's mariner's thoughtless and ill-omened actions.

Even more immediately for the present study, however, 'The Lotos-Eaters' can also be read against Keats's contemplative society of social idleness that we found in his correspondence. Back in the 'Choric Song' of Tennyson's poem, the mariners record how 'sweet' it is to shut them-selves off from any other form of society and

> To dream and dream, like yonder amber light,
> Which will not leave the myrrh-bush on the height;
> To hear each other's whisper'd speech;
> Eating the Lotos day by day,
> To watch the crisping ripples on the beach,
> And tender curving lines of creamy spray;
> To lend our hearts and spirits wholly
> To the influence of mild-minded melancholy;
> To muse and brood and live again in memory[.]   ('LE', 102–10)

These lines dramatize embracing a world made up entirely of aesthetic contemplation in which the shoreline's 'ripples' and 'spray' can occupy one's full attention, and revelling in the restricted society of other passive contemplators, 'hear[ing]' only 'each other's whisper'd speech'. In this sense these lines stand very close to Keats's description of immersing oneself in the ruminations that stem from a 'page full of poesy' and then 'whisper[ing]' the 'results' of one's passive 'journey' to one's 'neighbour', building thereby a 'grand democracy' of aesthetic passivity. But again, it is crucial to the design of Tennyson's version of this idea that 'The Lotos-Eaters' renders these lines a problematic over-statement, a kind of doubled discourse that says one thing and most urgently implies the opposite. In this instance, this effect is even underlined by the ending of the stanza that glosses 'mus[ing] and brood[ing] and liv[ing] again in memory' as becoming '[h]eap'd over with a mound of grass', and ending up as '[t]wo handfuls of white dust, shut in an urn of brass' ('LE', 112–13). In other words, Keats's intensely positive and radical vision of an alternative society of idleness has become, in Tennyson's poem, synonymous with the insensibility of death. To be at one with the natural world in this manner, to commune only with one's close compatriots and shared contemplators, is to become effectively inanimate here. It is to be swallowed up by the earth and to return to 'dust' as in cremation, or burial. One should also note here that this quasi-Keatsian state is brought about, and sustained, not by the reading of poetry or by the innate aesthetic energy of each individual. Instead, the mariners' apparently indulgent and irresponsible repose is engendered by their constant '[e]ating' of the Lotos. Whether one sees this fruit as a version of contemporary Britain's reliance on various forms of opium or whether one reads it in any other manner, in comparison to Keats's, Mill's and others' arguments for the innate-ness of aesthetic or passive susceptibilities, Tennyson's poem should be understood to cast this form of pervasive passive contemplation as fundamentally artificial. The mariners' contentment with this Keatsian existence is only sustained by their particular location and by their particular pattern of consumption. Thus, in this fundamental sense, 'The Lotos-Eaters' serves to cast aesthetic contemplation – especially in this extreme and total form – as an artificial attribute of human nature, and a deeply undesirable one at that.

Tennyson's 'The Lotos-Eaters' has several close parallels within early and mid-Victorian literature, because its conception of idleness's relevance for contemporary Britain is entirely in accord with that of many contemporary figures. Matthew Arnold is perhaps the most notable of these contemporaries, for his early poetry repeatedly dramatizes idle aesthetic contemplation in accordance with various Romantic models, but always does so in order to stress its inapplicability to – or impossibility in – the present. 'The Strayed Reveller', the title poem of Arnold's first volume of poetry published in 1849, is a case in point. This poem casts the intuitive immersion in the universe's complexities that we observed in Shelley's 'Mont Blanc' and in *Sartor Resartus* as a form of artificial intoxication akin to that of the lotos-eaters' prolonged inertia. It is when drunk on the goddess Circe's wine that the poem's eponymous protagonist experiences the world as a 'wild, thronging train' and a 'bright procession / Of eddying forms' that '[s]weep through' his 'soul' ('SR', 294–7). This formulation recalls the opening paralysis of Shelley's poem, or the notion, in Coleridge's 'Eolian Harp', that the mind receives – and is nearly swept away by – the world's 'intellectual breeze'. But Arnold's circular poem does not build to an insightful moral pay-off that justifies such intuitive immersion (as Coleridge's and Shelley's poems do). And its setting, like 'The Lotos-Eaters', in a mythic, Odyssean past, renders this posture of aesthetic contemplation comprehensively outmoded. The youthful protagonist of 'The Strayed Reveller' and his aesthetic vision are thus doubly – or triply – distanced from the poem's reader: the youth is lost, benighted and out of his depth in Circe's 'palace'; his passivity is thoroughly contrasted with Ulysses's own heroic and active masculinity; and he is of course thoroughly insulated from contemporary Britain and its commercial modernity that framed Shelley's and Coleridge's poems.

Arnold's poem 'The Scholar-Gipsy', published four years after 'The Strayed Reveller' in 1853, passes a more detailed and direct, but ultimately very similar judgement on idle aesthetic contemplation to the earlier poem. Its central personage is again used to represent a mode of intense aesthetic contemplation that aligns with Romantic conceptions of that act (it is for this reason that the poem has been described by William Ulmer as a 'Romantic critique of Victorian alienation'[43]). And again this figure – the scholar-gipsy himself – is from the distant past: he is taken from Joseph Glanvill's 'extended apology for skeptical philosophy',[44] *The Vanity of Dogmatizing* of 1661. But this time, the poem repeatedly underlines the manner in which modern life differs from that surrounding its aesthetic exemplar, making it an overt contention of the poem's speaker that idle aesthetic contemplation has little to offer the present. 'The Scholar-Gipsy' is thus an extended elegy for a lost world of meaningful and powerful idle contemplation. The contrast comes most

dramatically towards the end of the poem, where modern intellectual
power is defined against the intense and focused poetic imagination of
the title figure (to whom the 'thou' of the first line of this quotation refers):

> Thou waitest for the spark from heaven! and we,
>   Light half-believers of our casual creeds,
>   Who never deeply felt, nor clearly will'd,
>   Whose insight never has borne fruit in deeds,
>   Whose vague resolves never have been fulfill'd;
>   For whom each year we see
>   Breeds new beginnings, disappointments new;
>   Who hesitate and falter life away,
>   And lose to-morrow the ground won to-day—
>   Ah! do not we, wanderer! await it too?
>
> Yes, we await it!—but it still delays,
>   And then we suffer! and amongst us one,
>   Who most has suffer'd, takes dejectedly
>   His seat upon the intellectual throne;
>   And all his store of sad experience he
>   Lays bare of wretched days;
>   Tells us his misery's birth and growth and signs,
>   And how the dying spark of hope was fed,
>   And how the breast was soothed, and how the head,
>   And all his hourly varied anodynes.   ('SG', 171–90)

The context for this contrast is that the poem's eponymous scholar has – albeit
in the distant past – committed himself to the world of poetic imagination by
following a 'gipsy-crew' who can 'rule' the workings of men's brains and 'can
bind them to what thoughts they will' ('SG', 44–7). He has dedicated his life
to the 'spark from heaven' that can make this imaginative feat occur and awaits
it with a singular purpose. (The poem's rendering of the scholar's story in the
present tense is a part of its sense that this figure is a persistent image of what
we in the present are not, and its half-serious claim that the scholar's extreme
focus on imaginative contemplation confers on him immortality because he is
not prey to the tendency of the fragmented modern world to eat away – by
endlessly dividing – intellectual power.) In these two stanzas, therefore,
modern intellectual fragmentation is depicted by a syntax that is almost
endlessly divided into further qualifications, rather than direct statements.
The 'we' of the first line of this quotation is qualified by nine separate clauses in
that stanza alone before the energy of the speaker's definition is dissipated by
a rhetorical question rather than a definite statement: 'do not we, wanderer!
await it too?' In the second of these stanzas, connectedly, modern artistic

expression is classed as an ever-more detailed expression of suffering, rather than of positive, active experience or moral certainty. Thus the modern equivalent of a figure like the scholar-gipsy is he who 'most has suffer'd' and whose poetic expression is simply made up of 'all his store of sad experience' and a detailed record of the life of 'his misery'. Modern art is thus a constantly repeated and minutely varied description of medicating the disease of life in this portrait: the best poet is he who can dramatize 'all his hourly varied anodynes' most intricately.

This is, of course, a disturbing and far-reaching portrait of cultural degeneracy, and its notion of an aesthetics of failure and loss is one that we will see echoed several times in the rest of this study. It is striking, that is, that modern aesthetic concentration can only look inward, in this depiction, and can only unravel almost endless worlds of misery and pain. For our present purposes, however, we should note that Arnold has rendered idle aesthetic contemplation on the Romantic model a historical fact in 'The Scholar-Gipsy', but one that emphatically cannot be revived in the present. The poem's extended descriptions of the scholar's wanderings, and of various fleeting glimpses of him, serve to dramatize the longing for this historical model of poetic concentration. But these descriptions are simply fantasies, and thus again render aesthetic passivity a kind of myth that haunts the present, rather than a current, relevant and worthwhile human engagement. It is also pertinent to the present analysis to observe that Arnold's depiction of contemporary aesthetic activity – in the two fragmented stanzas from the poem that we looked at – cast it as the arena for almost endless, arduous intellectual work. In contrast to the scholar's instantaneous access to aesthetic activity, and therefore his easy spontaneity, the poem's speaker and his contemporaries must constantly work and fail: 'each year' of their lives apparently '[b]reeds' new 'beginnings' and an equal number of new 'disappointments'.

These three poetic accounts of idleness thus complement the contemporary valorization of the 'gospel of work' by overtly denigrating contemplative and aesthetic idleness, and by contrasting it with virtuous activity – in the case of 'The Lotos-Eaters' and 'The Strayed Reveller' – or with arduous and constant, even if ultimately sombre, work – in the case of 'The Scholar-Gipsy'. But there is also a strand of contemporary poetry that denigrates contemplative and aesthetic idleness without contrasting that state with the more active virtues of labour. Instead, such poems cast the capacity for aesthetic and spiritual consciousness as innate, but as quickly lost after early childhood. They thus serve to mourn the loss of aesthetic and transcendent capability, and depict contemplative idleness as non-

existent in, or sadly inapplicable to, the mature Victorian world of rationality. In contrast to the abundant Romantic and idealist depictions of
aesthetic consciousness's pertinence for – and constant existence in – the
present, and in contrast to Mill's advocacy of a society that materially
fosters such contemplative idleness, these poems thus subtly but powerfully
distance aesthetic consciousness from contemporary Britain.

    The first such poem we will consider is another by Arnold that was published
in his first volume of poetry in 1849, 'To a Gipsy Child by the Sea-Shore'. This
text describes at length the transcendent and spiritual consciousness that seems
to be indicated by the eponymous child's strikingly 'meditative guise' ('GC', 3).
For Arnold's speaker, the depth of this contemplative idleness is so remarkable
that it seems to invoke worlds and experiences far beyond the child's possible
knowledge or history:

> Glooms that go deep as thine I have not known:
> Moods of fantastic sadness, nothing worth.
> Thy sorrow and thy calmness are thine own:
> Glooms that enhance and glorify this earth.
>
> What mood wears like complexion to thy woe?
> His, who in mountain glens, at noon of day,
> Sits rapt, and hears the battle break below?
> Ah! thine was not the shelter, but the fray.
>
> What exile's, changing bitter thoughts with glad?
> What seraph's, in some alien planet born?
> No exile's dream was ever half so sad,
> Nor any angel's sorrow so forlorn.
>
> Is the calm thine of stoic souls, who weigh
> Life well, and find it wanting, nor deplore:
> But in disdainful silence turn away,
> Stand mute, self-centred, stern, and dream no more? ('GC', 17–32)

It is aesthetic passivity that is invoked in descriptions such as these, and in the
poem's numerous other stanzas in this vein, because the child's extreme
'calmness' and resignation seem to denote the powerful and solid possession
of otherworldly knowledge and experience. This association of childhood with
contemplative profundity is of course a Wordsworthian commonplace by the
mid-nineteenth century, but one that also works to invoke the models of
aesthetic contemplation we have already considered in this study. Like
Shelley's cataloguing of the countless worlds, experiences and processes that
seemed to be reflected in Mont Blanc's vast complexity – Shelley's poem
dramatized his quest to seize that knowledge through contemplative

intensity – Arnold's child's powerfully 'meditative guise' seems to imply that he is already the possessor of such experiences and knowledge. The child's acquaintance with what Keats describes as 'mysteries' and 'doubts' thus seems to exceed that of 'any angel' on 'some alien planet born', or of any 'grey-hair'd king [. . .] [w]hose mind hath known all arts of governing' ('GC', 33–5), as Arnold has it just after this quotation.

The point of Arnold's detailed elaboration of this child's transcendent knowledge, however, is that it is both innate and will be quickly lost in the currents and preoccupations of adult life. Arnold's poem thus concludes by predicting how the child's knowledge of the world's 'tale / Of grief' will be 'eas'd' by 'a thousand sleeps' ('GC', 51–2), how the 'blank sunshine' or life will 'blind' the child and thus erase his past knowledge ('GC', 61), and how 'Wisdom', the personification of the child's current transcendent awareness, will henceforth be 'too proud / To halve a lodging that was all her own' ('GC', 63–4). Yet a small glimmer of something like hope occurs in the poem's final stanza, where Arnold suggests that such knowledge will return, 'once', before the child's death:

> Once, ere the day decline, thou shalt discern,
> Oh once, ere night, in thy success, thy chain.
> Ere the long evening close, thou shalt return,
> And wear this majesty of grief again.   ('GC', 65–8)

This, above all, is a melancholy conception of aesthetic consciousness. Arnold's child will 'wear' his 'majesty of grief again', but only in his final – presumably deathly – knowledge of life's limitations, of the 'chain' that binds all human life. What this means is that the innate, transcendent, aesthetic capability that is the primary subject of Arnold's poem is cast emphatically as a forerunner of death, and not in any way as an active means of contributing to contemporary life, or to its adult commitments. This poem is thus intensely sombre, and ultimately tragic, in mood. It records the power and possibilities of aesthetic consciousness in majestic terms, but only does so in order to comprehensively lament that state's rare occurrence in human life, and its considerable brevity even in the lives of those few who are blessed with its appearance. In this sense 'To a Gipsy Child' stands at a considerable distance from the writing of Keats, Shelley, Schiller or Mill, and conforms to the ideology of labour that this chapter is following by systematically reducing the significance of aesthetic idleness to contemporary society.

In order to demonstrate that this lament for aesthetic consciousness's impermanence becomes something of a sub-genre of poetry in its own right, let us move now to a slightly later but ultimately very similar poem, Gerard Manley Hopkins's 'Spring and Fall', which was composed in 1880.[45] Again, like Arnold's 'Gipsy Child', this poem depicts intense, spiritual and otherworldly aesthetic consciousness, but only to predict that capacity's decay as its child-protagonist matures. In Hopkins's hands, and in this poem's spare symbolic scheme, such intense aesthetic capability is denoted by the child's grief at autumn's extensive fall of leaves, at 'Goldengrove unleaving' ('SF', 2). Such grief again recalls the intimate physical connection that Shelley's 'Mont Blanc' dramatizes, or that is also explored at length in Tennyson's 'Lotos-Eaters '. It is also very closely related to the emotion explored in Tennyson's 'Tears, idle tears, I know not what they mean' of 1847. In Hopkins's hands, however, this emotional and spiritual reaction is interesting, primarily for its impermanence:

> Ah! as the heart grows older
> It will come to such sights colder
> By & by, nor spare a sigh
> Though worlds of wanwood leafmeal lie;
> And yet you will weep & know why.   ('SF', 5–9)

The coldness Hopkins stresses directly restates the 'eas'd' and sun-blinded state Arnold predicts for his child's adult life. The intensity of childhood's untutored aesthetic consciousness, here, is thus rendered a stark contrast to cold and solipsistic adulthood. In the latter state, for Hopkins's speaker, huge quantities of misery and sorrow – 'worlds of wanwood leafmeal' – will not raise a 'sigh', let alone a tear. In other words, whereas the child's aesthetic and spiritual consciousness is so acute and active that a scene of natural beauty and decay has the effect of a powerful tragedy, the adult's spiritual life will be characterized only by overt, known and immediately apparent griefs: 'you will weep & know why'.

Again like Arnold's 'Gipsy Child', Hopkins's 'Spring and Fall' also positions its child's innate aesthetic consciousness as a premonition of the unique spiritual insight provided by death. Hopkins makes this point, subtly and beautifully, in his poem's final lines:

> Now no matter, child, the name:
> Sorrow's springs are the same.
> Nor mouth had, no nor mind, expressed
> What heart heard of, ghost guessed:
> It is the blight man was born for,
> It is Margaret you mourn for.   ('SF', 10–15)

The aesthetic consciousness that enables the child to mourn for Goldengrove's 'unleaving' is here classified as an instance of her spirit, or 'ghost', grasping at, and 'guess[ing]', the profound sorrows that she will eventually suffer. This is the primary manner in which Hopkins renders the child's grief a matter of transcendent, otherworldly knowledge. But it is also a means of disconnecting aesthetic consciousness from quotidian, adult life. As in Arnold's similar poem, the effect of Hopkins's adult speaker's commentary is to categorize aesthetic, spiritual consciousness as the stuff of childhood, and of final, deathly consciousness, but therefore not of rational, normal life. This subject can only form the matter of a poem, in other words, because such aesthetic knowledge is conceived of as marginal, hidden and effectively irrelevant, to any adult auditor or reader of the poem. We should also note here, finally, that the conception of aesthetic consciousness embodied in this poem – as indeed in 'To a Gipsy Child' – is one so intensely negative that that state has become synonymous with a kind of morbid introspection that any successful adult will studiously ignore. For to grasp at spiritual knowledge in the manner of Hopkins's child is to 'guess' at, and intuitively seize, one's fundamentally diseased and lost state. This, in Hopkins's starkly powerful terms, is 'the blight that man was born for'. The child's spiritual awareness is identical with her 'mourning' her own metaphysically fallen state.

I want to conclude this chapter by noting that the melancholy flavour of this poetry of idle contemplation that we have now considered is a feature not just of the present impossibility of aesthetic consciousness, to the mid-century mind influenced by the 'gospel of work'. These texts surely also function as laments for a world in which adult consciousness could be conceived as innately spiritual, as laments, therefore, for the very model of intellectual capability that the Romantics exemplified and that Mill strove to cast into his future 'stationary state'. In this sense, this melancholy poetry of aesthetic idleness's brief appearance in human life – or of its relevance only in some other, historical or fictional location – is also, in part, utopian. These poems sustain the knowledge and appreciation of aesthetic, spiritual consciousness – or the desire to maintain one's innate childlike sensibility – even among a world of commercial rationality and technological progress that negates the relevance and utility of such states. The following is another way of saying this. Even if a poem like Tennyson's 'Lotos-Eaters' does not itself actively mourn the loss of aesthetic consciousness – so overt and powerful is its case against contemplative idleness – it nevertheless encapsulates the idea of a land where aesthetic consciousness predominates, and allows that encapsulation to be the starting point for a different type of imaginative portrayal. What we have seen in the second half of this chapter might thus be described as the transformation of idle contemplation into something like a 'myth', with all the desperate longing and distilled human aspiration that term evokes. Such a status is by no means hypothetical, or potential, in the nineteenth century, moreover. Tennyson's mythic land is indeed the starting point, and the touchstone, for subsequent imaginative, and actively political, accounts of human capability. The most important and high-profile of these is certainly William Morris's *News from Nowhere* of 1890, which builds on many of the texts considered in this chapter, including Marx's *Capital*, which Morris read in its French translation in the 1880s, and which was translated into English in the same year that Morris's novella was published. *News from Nowhere*'s time-travelling Victorian protagonist thus considers the anarcho-communist utopia of 'Nowhere' to recall 'the Lotos-Eaters' land [. . .] where it was always afternoon', a reference that both grounds Morris's novella in the kind of earlier literary laments for aesthetic idleness that we have traced here, but that also foregrounds Nowhere's absolute unreality.[46] It is therefore no surprise that Morris's narrative – with its intensely positive account of an aesthetically led society – ultimately takes the form of a dream vision, of a fantastic glimpse beyond the bounds of current possibility. What this indicates is that the century's literary portrayers of aesthetic consciousness are never in a position to return the positive conception of idle contemplation to the present. The texts considered in the second half of this chapter are in this sense representative of the double-edged relevance of idle contemplation for a significant strand of Victorian literature. Aesthetic consciousness is both mourned as a now-vanished presence in contemporary life, and transformed into a myth. These texts thus embody a kind of desperate hope that a future human society might be able to reconcile the apparent incompatibility of contemplative repose and virtuous, diligent labour.

Let us finish this chapter by tying this knowledge together with what we learned from our analysis of Carlyle and Marx. The mid-Victorian ideology of work can now be seen to represent a powerful and a widespread counter-narrative to earlier, positive conceptions of idleness, even though it is itself constructed on that category's earlier theorizations. The second half of this chapter has begun the task of charting the influence of this body of thought across the century, but this influence is so considerable that this task will in part characterize the rest of this study. In the immediate wake of

Carlyle and Marx, however, it is now clear that meditative poetry, which was the bastion and constant celebrant of aesthetic consciousness at the beginning of the century, has become that category's opponent and sometimes its mourner. The knowledge to be gleaned by any contemporary reader of the texts considered in this chapter is thus that Victorian adult, virtuous life is the arena for diligent and arduous work, and that contemplative idleness represents either a species of childlike spontaneity, soon to be lost, or the stuff of fictional, alternative, mythic realities. What this means for the development of the categories of idleness and aesthetic consciousness this study is charting is that such states are consistently configured – in these examples of mid-Victorian thought – as the antitheses of correct, mature, civilized life. Idle contemplation thus becomes a species of amoral self-indulgence here. But at the same time, in Carlyle, in Marx and in the poetry written in their wake, idleness and aesthetic consciousness retain the trace of their earlier positive and even revolutionary associations. The gospel of work may confidently announce itself by villainizing inertia and passivity, in other words, but the complexities, subtleties and manifold possibilities we traced in Mill's 'gospel of leisure' and in Romantic poetics do not seem to be so easily negated.

CHAPTER 4

Cultural Theory and Aesthetic Failure

We saw, in Chapter 3, how idle contemplation is repeatedly villainized in mid-century theorizations of ideal labour, as well as in the meditative poetry of aesthetic consciousness that stands in that ideology's shadow. The field we are to turn to now – the cultural theory of the 1850s, 1860s and 1870s – represents, by contrast, a discourse that accommodates aesthetic consciousness in strikingly positive terms even as contemporary poetry turns against that category. The thought of John Ruskin, the later thought of Matthew Arnold and the work of Walter Pater form our focus here. Each of these figures contends explicitly for the powers and pertinence of idle aesthetic contemplation. But each does so at the same time as modifying, and destabilizing, the aesthetic moment as it was conceived at the beginning of the nineteenth century. Because these modifications elongate and professionalize the aesthetic encounter, as we shall see, we are still dealing in one sense in this chapter with the considerable influence of Carlyle and others' 'gospel of work'. Idle aesthetic consciousness becomes, in these decades, a conscious and willed life-process, rather than a spontaneous or even involuntary access of intuition. Connectedly and importantly, the objects that bring about these newly diligent aesthetic experiences are repeatedly understood, by these figures, not as natural occurrences, like Shelley's Mont Blanc, but as studied, man-made, art-objects. The cultural theory of the second half of the nineteenth century thus returns the act of idle contemplation to the present – in comparison with texts like Tennyson's 'Lotos-Eaters' and Arnold's 'Scholar-Gipsy' – but does so while significantly distancing this category from untutored, quotidian activity.

We shall begin with the oldest of these three cultural theorists, John Ruskin, and with his hugely influential architectural analysis, *The Stones of Venice*, published between 1851 and 1853. *The Stones of Venice* is a three-volume work of staggering breadth and detail. It offers a comprehensive account of the architectural history of Venice in which as much attention is paid to the vast ideological transformations that stand behind the city's different epochs as to the stylistic minutiae of the city's buildings and monuments. And on top of this vast coverage – all illustrated with Ruskin's own drawings and diagrams – *The Stones of Venice* also exerts a profound influence over wider socio-cultural thought in the period, through the strikingly original analysis of its central chapter, 'The Nature of Gothic'. It is the intellectual hallmark of this chapter that can be felt throughout Morris's *News from Nowhere* (every time its narrator refers to any architecture and design), and that indeed to a large extent configured the entirety of Morris's career.[1] 'The Nature of Gothic' also contributed directly to the architectural practices of Victorian Britain and led to Ruskin's own development of a direct and far-reaching critique of contemporary political economy in his 1862 work *'Unto This Last'*. It is this central chapter of *The Stones of Venice* that also holds the most pertinence for the present analysis, because in it Ruskin addresses the notions of aesthetic capability and the practicalities of aesthetic consciousness in ways that reflect the period's changing conceptions of those categories.

'The Nature of Gothic', published in 1853 in the second volume of *The Stones of Venice*, develops a way of considering architecture – and by extension any cultural object – as 'an index [. . .] of religious principle' (*Stones*, II, 156). The term 'religious', in this phrase, is one we might want to gloss as 'social' or indeed 'cultural', because what Ruskin means here is that architectural artefacts are apt to be read for the ideas about society and human capability that have informed their production. His primary examples all serve to make a distinction between those systems of religion, and thus society, that enslave the individual workman and forbid his creative impulses, and those that liberate the workman and that sanction his involvement in architectural and other forms of cultural creation. Of the former, the principal schools are the 'Greek, Ninevite, and Egyptian', although the 'servility' of each society and therefore of each architectural style is 'of different kinds' (*Stones*, II, 156). Of the latter, it is in 'medieval' and 'especially Christian' building – and therefore culture – that 'this slavery is done away with altogether', 'Christianity having recognized, in small things as well as great, the individual value of every soul' (*Stones*, II, 157). The terms of this distinction obviously contain an implicit reference to contemporary Britain. Not only does Ruskin observe that, in terms of its problematic admiration for 'servility' and 'perfection', the 'modern English mind has [. . .] much in common with that of the [ancient] Greek' (*Stones*, II, 158), but he also goes on to expand on the 'individual value of every soul' by depicting the process of mental stultification frequently commented upon (and sometimes lamented) by contemporary political economists.[2] Ruskin's manner of describing this process – his use of imperatives, for instance – maintains a productive ambiguity between its historical and more recent occurrences:

> [O]bserve, you are put to stern choice in this matter. You must either make a tool of the creature, or a man of him. You cannot make both. Men were not intended to work with the accuracy of tools, to be precise and perfect in all their actions. If you will have that precision out of them, and make their fingers measure degrees like cog-wheels, and their arms strike curves like compasses, you must unhumanize them. All the energy of their spirits must be given to make cogs and compasses of themselves. [. . .] The eye of the soul must be bent upon the finger-point, and the soul's force must fill all the invisible nerves that guide it, ten hours a day, that it may not err from its steely precision, and so soul and sight be worn away, and the whole human being be lost at last – (*Stones*, II, 159)

In terms of its imagery and politics, this analysis obviously follows that of figures like Schiller and Carlyle on the same subject – and indeed the analysis of Marx and Friedrich Engels in *The Communist Manifesto*, as this was published in English just a year before *The Stones of Venice*. This passage's sense of the human worker being 'lost' as he turns himself into a set of 'cogs and compasses' recalls, for example, Schiller's notion of man becoming simply the 'imprint of his occupation or of his specialized knowledge'[3] and Marx and Engels's notion of the worker's complex alienation. Ruskin's location of this problematic process at once in the present and in the distant historical past, however, sets up a situation in which the grand and abundant gothic buildings of Britain stand as concrete evidence against the inhumanities of advanced specialization. Because, for Ruskin, medieval and Christian gothic architecture is a physical manifestation of the opposite of this widespread process of stultification. This is 'perhaps, the principal admirableness of the Gothic schools of architecture', in his analysis: rather than requiring the perfection of execution from the worker who has been shaped into a 'tool', 'out of fragments full of imperfection, and betraying that imperfection in every touch', they 'indulgently raise up a stately and unaccusable whole' (*Stones*, II, 157–8).

This is the central idea of Ruskin's 'The Nature of Gothic', and one that connects this text to a highly influential strand among conceptions of aesthetic consciousness across the nineteenth century, as we shall see presently. 'Imperfection' is not only natural, but laudatory. And Ruskin goes on to explore this idea in a number of closely connected ways.

Following his portrait of historical and contemporary stultification, for example, we are offered an account of the slow and problematic processes of creativity that stem from liberating the worker rather than enslaving him in the name of 'precision':

> On the other hand, if you will make a man of the working creature, you cannot make a tool. Let him but begin to imagine, to think, to try to do anything worth doing; and the engine-turned precision is lost at once. Out come all his roughness, all his dulness, all his incapability; shame upon shame, failure upon failure, pause after pause: but out comes the whole majesty of him also; and we know the height of it only when we see the clouds settling upon him. And whether the clouds be bright or dark, there will be transfiguration behind and within them. (*Stones*, II, 160)

Carlyle, in *Past and Present*, described the process of work as revelatory and transformative in its instantaneous positivity: 'Even in the meanest sorts of Labour, the whole soul of man is composed into a kind of real harmony, the instant he sets himself to work!' Any negativity was immediately 'stilled' for Carlyle's worker: 'Doubt, Desire, Sorrow, Remorse, Indignation, Despair itself, all these like helldogs lie beleaguering the soul of the poor dayworker, as of every man: but he bends himself with free valour against his task, and [. . .] all these shrink murmuring far off into their caves.' Schiller and the English Romantics – in a comparable vein, albeit for the benefit of passivity rather than activity – consistently portray aesthetic consciousness as a species of spontaneous and innate access to the realms of beauty and perfection and to its direct analogy, moral awareness. Keats's poetic contemplators and Schiller's overworked labourers thus need no training or practice to construct their aesthetic democracies. Keats and Schiller's visions of aesthetic contemplation are, rather, direct and instantaneous. This central passage of Ruskin's 'The Nature of Gothic', by contrast, completely reimagines aesthetic consciousness. In Ruskin's hands artistic contemplation is attended straight away – but also for an extended period of time – with failure, with doubt, with sorrow and with incapacity. '[S]hame upon shame, failure upon failure, pause after pause': Ruskin's language is extreme almost to the point of being damning, but above all represents both the personal, moral failings and the artistic and technical deficiencies of the freed worker as considerable in both duration and scope. Just before this passage Ruskin had phrased this issue as one of technical competency exclusively: he told us that 'if you ask' the worker to 'think' about his work, 'to consider if he cannot find [. . .] better [forms to create] in his own head', then 'he stops; his execution becomes hesitating; he thinks, and ten to one he thinks wrong; ten to one he makes a mistake in the first touch he gives to his work as a thinking being' (*Stones*, II, 159). In the 'shame upon shame' passage, by contrast, these technical issues have been amplified into wholesale moral and character flaws. The attempt to experience aesthetic consciousness falters not just on technical inexperience, but on wider personal and mental issues that seem to inhibit adoption of the correct aesthetic attitude: 'roughness', 'dulness' and 'shame'. Ruskin's passage does – obviously – depict these considerable problems as ultimately surmountable. Out of this process of repeated failure there also comes 'the whole majesty' of the worker. One should note again, though, that even in this celebration of the worker's contemplative and aesthetic potential, there is a dark overtone to Ruskin's formulation. We are to 'know the height' of the worker's 'majesty' only after considerable time, when we see 'the clouds settling upon him'. But even then, because these clouds may 'be bright or dark', the possibility seems to be left open that the worker's aesthetic consciousness may be negative or somehow foreboding in its intent and its ambition.

This remarkable passage thus celebrates aesthetic consciousness as the primary and most important terrain of human life, but also, simultaneously, cuts against the grain of all previous statements of that sort by associating with passive contemplation a series of large-scale moral problems. In this sense, Ruskin's version of aesthetic experience is a kind of meeting point between early nineteenth-century comprehensively positive conceptions of that field and more recent, pejorative accounts of idle contemplation like Tennyson's 'Lotos-Eaters'. Recall how that poem cast pervasive repose as utter moral laxity because of its ideological lack of interest in active, martial and personal virtues. To be benighted in Tennyson's contemplative society was to forsake one's responsibilities to one's home and to oneself in an artificially sustained delirium.[4] Ruskin's account of attempted aesthetic consciousness resulting in moral and technical failure thus demonstrates the powerful influence of the 'gospel of work' – and its attendant distrust of idle contemplation – even over positive considerations of artistic culture. We might thus class Tennyson's poem as representative of a powerfully negative strand of thinking about aesthetic consciousness that can be felt even in an ultimately celebratory account of man's creative and contemplative potential published two decades after the poem. Ruskin's *Stones of Venice*, after all, is positive enough on this subject to be classed by Linda Dowling within the field of contemporary writing on 'aesthetic democracy'.[5]

Ruskin's analysis of gothic 'imperfection', and his delineation of an aesthetic encounter with failure, leads him on, in 'The Nature of

Gothic', to the quite thorough development of a critique of political economy. In contrast to the stark originality of that consideration of imperfection, however, Ruskin's account of political economy at this stage in his career largely follows the patterns of thought of his intellectual forebears in this territory, many of whom we have already considered in this study. Ruskin thus passionately observes the widespread misconception, in contemporary Britain, as to 'what kinds of labour are good for men', and the continuance, instead, of a system founded on the 'degradation of the workman'. The 'great cry' that can be heard 'from all our manufacturing cities' is consequently 'that we manufacture everything there except men', that 'we blanch cotton, and strengthen steel, and refine sugar [. . .]; but to brighten, to strengthen, to refine, or to form a single living spirit, never enters into our estimate of advantages' (*Stones*, II, 163). This phrasing, and this overall idea, is again reminiscent of Schiller, Coleridge or Carlyle's take on commercial society, although this time Ruskin uses commercial processes as emblems of the care and attention men themselves forego. A few pages further on, connectedly, Ruskin's mode of analysis echoes the final position taken on the relationship between human activity and passivity by Mill in his *Principles of Political Economy*, which was published just five years before this second volume of *Stones of Venice*. Just as Mill depicted the ideal human life of his stationary state as divided into – and synthesizing – labour and contemplative repose, so Ruskin critiques the separation between worker and gentleman in contemporary society:

> We are always in these days endeavouring to separate [manual and intellectual labour]; we want one man to be always thinking, and another to be always working, and we call one a gentleman, and the other an operative; whereas the workman ought often to be thinking, and the thinker often to be working, and both should be gentlemen, in the best sense. As it is, we make both ungentle, the one envying, the other despising, his brother; and the mass of society is made up of morbid thinkers, and miserable workers. Now it is only by labour that thought can be made healthy, and only by thought that labour can be made happy, and the two cannot be separated with impunity. (*Stones*, II, 167)

While not phrased explicitly as a vision of the future like Mill's similar statements, this passage nevertheless advocates the synthesis of contemplative passivity with the energy of labour to create ideal human 'health' and 'happ[iness]'. And since we have already touched on Morris's *News from Nowhere*, it is striking the extent to which a passage like this provides the blueprint for labour there, and for Morris's notion that even manual labour requires considerable thought.[6]

One might thus characterize Ruskin's position in a passage like this as conventional, by 1853. It follows the central patterns of thought of figures like Carlyle and Mill in its vision of reordered society, one that is less commercially narrow-minded than contemporary Britain, but that is still intensely productive and is, importantly, also creative in a contemplative and aesthetic sense.[7] Ruskin's 'Nature of Gothic', however, cannot as a whole be characterized as a conventional text. Because after drawing out the social and the political economic consequences of its religious critique of architectural modes in this manner, Ruskin returns to his notion of 'imperfection' and the aesthetic and moral failures that attend on it. In this sense, the ordered and harmonious image of the worker thinking and the thinker working, and of both being gentlemen 'in the best sense', is undercut by the darker portraits of aesthetic complexity that bookend 'The Nature of Gothic'. Returning to gothic architecture, then, Ruskin addresses the two primary human qualities that inform its creation, 'the great truths commonly belonging to the whole race, and necessary to be understood or felt by them in all their work that they do under the sun' (*Stones*, II, 178). (The 'race' in question here is the people of northern Europe taken as a whole, and thus Ruskin is essentially speaking of the architecture that is innate to the British climate and temperament.) These primary qualities are 'the confession of Imperfection, and the confession of Desire of Change' (*Stones*, II, 178). Ruskin explains them as follows:

> The building of the bird and the bee needs not express anything like [these qualities]. It is perfect and unchanging. But just because we are something better than birds or bees, our building must confess that we have not reached either the perfection we can imagine, and cannot rest in the condition we have attained. If we pretend to have reached either perfection or satisfaction, we have degraded ourselves and our work. (*Stones*, II, 178)

Again, this idea might be characterized as a synthesis of previous, intensely positive conceptions of aesthetic action with the nagging negativity that informs Tennyson's 'Lotos-Eaters', or the three poems of Arnold's we considered.[8] Seeing human artistic creation as the expression of the 'great truths' that inform all man's existence would seem to configure aesthetic objects as pure and direct expressions of the best and most profound elements of life. This is a position that would sit harmoniously alongside Schiller's radical idealism, for instance, in which the free and harmonious play of man's highest faculties spontaneously generated aesthetic experience. But yet, because Ruskin renders these 'great truths' troubling and melancholy in nature – 'the confession of Imperfection, and the confession of Desire of Change' – he also at once renders aesthetic creation a kind of confrontation of, and an intense encounter with, man's moral and spiritual limitations. The very phrasing of these 'truths' casts them in a maudlin and apologetic light: they are 'confessions' of doubts and desires that undermine, and sully, everyday experience. '[O]ur building must confess' that we have failure at the very heart of our experience, and that 'we cannot rest' in our present 'condition', it is so unsatisfactory to us. We are almost in the world of the Byronic hero, here, and of his sublime melancholy that reaches beyond but is nevertheless cruelly bound by human life. For Byron's Manfred, for instance, man is '[h]alf dust, half deity, alike unfit / To sink or soar', and is constantly in the grip of a 'mixed', 'conflict[ing]' 'essence' that 'breathe[s] / The breath of degradation and of pride'.[9] Ruskin's notion of being 'something better than birds or bees' has the same effect as Byron's tragic, degraded yet proud posture, because this higher condition is marked by the discrepancy between our lofty 'imaginations' and our limited, worldly means.

Despite this intense maudlin consciousness at the heart of Ruskin's exposition of gothic architecture, even these passages of 'The Nature of Gothic' are by no means tragic in mood. In Ruskin's exposition such spiritual complexity is a matter for celebration because of the aesthetic and human interest it imbues into northern building. In comparison to the bold and severe 'servility' and 'perfection' of Greek architecture, for instance, the gothic is 'full of wolfish life[,] fierce as the winds that beat, and changeful as the clouds that shade them' (*Stones*, II, 155). These phrases are taken from the opening set-piece of 'The Nature of Gothic', where Ruskin summarizes northern geography and its attendant temperament. But he makes very similar statements immediately after the Byronic account of imperfection we have just been considering. There again, dark complexity is celebrated, rather than mourned:

> It is that strange *disquietude* of the Gothic spirit that is its greatness; that restless dreaming mind, that wanders hither and thither among the niches, and flickers feverishly around the pinnacles, and frets and fades in labyrinthine knots and shadows along wall and roof, and yet is not satisfied, nor shall be satisfied. The Greek could stay in his triglyph furrow, and be at peace; but the work of Gothic art is fretwork still, and it can neither rest in, nor from, its labour, but must pass on, sleeplessly, until its love of change shall be pacified for ever in the change that must come alike on them that wake and them that sleep. (*Stones*, II, 178–9)

Gothic building is the ultimate expression of a dark, troubled but full contemplative life in this portrait. It is thus the manifestation of an aesthetic complexity partially inhibited by commercial society but nevertheless innate, in Ruskin's view, to the northern temperament that underlies that society. It is also obviously the case that this passage's depiction of 'strange' and noble '*disquietude*' invokes Shelley's 'Mont Blanc' with which we began this study. To 'wander [...] hither and thither among [...] niches', to 'fret [...] and fade [...] in labyrinthine knots and shadows', are exactly the same kind of troubled, contemplative movements that filled Shelley's poem. But such acts in Shelley's poem were a kind of series of trials in order to reach the central presence of the mountain and to understand its epistemological message. In 'The Nature of Gothic', by contrast, it is the feeling of 'disquietude' itself that Gothic building must reflect. What this means is that, for Ruskin, aesthetic experience has become something other than a positive grasping of moral knowledge in the manner of Shelley or Schiller, and therefore something other than a path to a different kind of world and a different kind of society. It is, instead, a direct encounter with one's own limitations and yearnings, an intense reflection of one's troubled self-consciousness that stands behind all the 'work' one does 'under the sun'. In this passage, this negativity is almost total because, in a motif that recalls Arnold's 'Gipsy-Child by the Sea-Shore' and anticipates Hopkins's 'Spring and Fall', Ruskin even casts the aesthetic experience engendered by gothic building as a kind of premonition of death. It is a distilled experience of 'change' that anticipates, and gives forewarning of, the great 'change that must come alike on' all. Aesthetic consciousness is thus a kind of access of moral and indeed total failure, in this portrait, and for all Ruskin's celebration and ennobling of this 'strange *disquietude*', there is nevertheless a sense in which 'The Nature of Gothic' represents something of a nadir in fortunes for aesthetic consciousness and the experience of idle contemplation. Ruskin is, still, a celebrator of aesthetic consciousness and contemplative life. But his formulation of those fields is introspective to the point of morbidity. Ruskin would, in this sense, thus make uneasy company for his intellectual forebears, the early nineteenth-century champions of aesthetic consciousness like Keats and Shelley, as well as for their later followers with their utopian leanings, like Mill and Morris.

Before moving on to Matthew Arnold's differently tempered account of aesthetic consciousness, we should note that this thorough morbidity and Byronic 'disquietude' in 'The Nature of Gothic' barely features in recent criticism of Ruskin's thought. Dowling, for example, in her detailed and far-reaching account of Ruskin's position in contemporary theorizations of aesthetic democracy, offers a distinctly sunny impression of *The Stones of Venice*'s central chapter. 'Ruskin's Gothic cathedral', she tells us, 'came to represent in the eyes of his Victorian readers the promise of a sociality lived completely free from the competitive individualism and degrading power of markets, just as the Gothic workers themselves lived before the capitalist order enforced its maiming divisions of labor on men and women'.[10] There is no mention here at all, or elsewhere in Dowling's impressive study, of Ruskin's 'disquietude'. For Elizabeth Helsinger, perhaps even more confusingly, Ruskin '"democratizes" visual perception by shifting the model of aesthetic experience from the solitary and heroic partaker of the sublime to the more sociable tourists of the picturesque'.[11] In other words, Helsinger reads *The Stones of Venice* as a manual for the polite and earnest tourist, but overlooks the profound complexity at the very centre of the text, the manner in which Ruskin makes the gothic mode represent something much more problematic than picturesque experience. Kenneth Daley, comparably, does observes the Romantic reference implicit in 'The Nature of Gothic', but describes the chapter as 'Ruskin's idealization of the romantic spirit as a remedy for the ills of nineteenth-century England's laissez-faire economic system and its degradation of the industrial labourer'.[12] Again, therefore, Ruskin's original and striking model of aesthetic failure, shame and dullness is ignored in favour of the notion of individual, imaginative liberty associated with the turn of the nineteenth century. Contrary to these accounts of Ruskin's project in 'The Nature of Gothic', and building on Francis O'Gorman's biographical analysis of Ruskin's preoccupation with failure,[13] the present study allows for a detailed historicization of conceptions of aesthetic consciousness and contemplative experience across the nineteenth century, and it is from this perspective that Ruskin's striking originality can be properly appreciated. Ruskin should therefore be understood to stand broadly within the current of thought initiated by the 'gospel of work' that is suspicious of idle contemplation and its claims for aesthetic consciousness. But Ruskin takes this trend in a singular and extreme direction by rendering aesthetic consciousness at once an encounter with practical, moral and metaphysical failure. 'The Nature of Gothic' should thus be placed alongside Tennyson's 'Lotos-Eaters', and Arnold's exactly contemporary 'Scholar-Gipsy', in terms of the association it makes between aesthetic contemplation and troubled, problematic consciousness. But Ruskin's central chapter to *The Stones of Venice* nevertheless mixes this association with an actual celebration of human contemplative life reminiscent of a very different tradition of thought from that of Tennyson and the young Arnold. We will see, when we reach the very end of this study, that Ruskin's profoundly troubled model of aesthetic contemplation is in fact an early anticipation of Sigmund Freud's conception of aesthetic consciousness. Freud, though, casts the aesthetic act in such negative terms in order to severely limit its standing in human life. Ruskin, by contrast, must still be considered as a direct promoter of contemplative, aesthetic experience and thus an advocate of aesthetic democracy, as Dowling maintains. It will be possible to take a much longer view of Ruskinian thought, as well as that of his contemporaries, when we reach the end of this study. For now, let us turn to a work of comparable influence to Ruskin's 'Nature of Gothic', Arnold's *Culture and Anarchy* of 1869.

Culture and Anarchy was published as a one-volume work in 1869, but its six constituent, originally separate essays are the fruit of the slightly earlier 1860s. For Arnold's text began life as his reaction to the Hyde Park riots that took place in July 1866, and the spilling over of reformist discontent into Chester Square, where Arnold lived, and where the angry protestors 'stoned the windows' of Arnold's neighbour, 'the commissioner of police'.[14] *Culture and Anarchy* thus might look, from an overview, much like a Carlylean essay or treatise. It combines fervent and rather derogatory attention to contemporary unrest with the perspectives on social cohesion and political economy provided by German Idealism and by its British Romantic equivalents (Arnold is as steeped in these traditions as Carlyle, as we shall see). Arnold does indeed take one of his central motifs – that of 'machinery' – from Carlyle. But for our purposes *Culture and Anarchy* also stands at some distance from a text like *Past and Present*, because its deconstruction of the notion of 'doing as one likes' takes Arnold into a territory deliberately shunned by Carlyle. This is the field of the moral and therefore social power of beauty and perfection, where aesthetic repose and passive contemplation are allotted the transformative and insightful roles we saw Carlyle satirize in *Sartor Resartus*, and allot to fully realized labour in *Past and Present*.

At the heart of Arnold's argument, and at the heart of *Culture and Anarchy's* judgement of the Hyde Park rioters, are the notions of man's 'best' and 'ordinary' selves (*Culture*, 145–6). The distinction between these poles is founded upon the Romantic reaction against political economy's reliance on 'self-interest' as the primary motive of human action. The Romantic individual, in contradistinction to simplistic *homo oeconomicus*, holds his most interesting and important resources in his contemplative, spiritual, imaginative and social lives. A text like Wordsworth's

Prelude, therefore – which, because it was published posthumously, appeared just before Ruskin's *Stones of Venice* in 1850 – explicitly frames its intensely contemplative self-portrait as a contention with political economy and its apparently '[v]ague and unsound' notions of human life. Wordsworth describes himself in this text as having 'discerned how dire a thing / Is worshipped in that idol proudly named / 'The Wealth of Nations', and describes his long poem as elaborating, by contrast, 'A more judicious knowledge of the worth / And dignity of individual man'.[15] In parallel to this Wordsworthian project, *Culture and Anarchy* locates the individual's 'best self' in the 'fresh and free' play of thought 'upon our stock notions and habits' that 'culture' facilitates (*Culture*, 233). And it classifies the rioter, by contrast, as acting entirely in accord with his 'natural taste for the bathos' (*Culture*, 147) which, without the contemplative and aesthetic guidance provided by culture, is all contemporary society encourages man to follow. The rioter, for Arnold, thus behaves in accordance with his 'ordinary', 'untransformed self', 'taking pleasure only in doing what [he] likes or is used to do' (*Culture*, 135).

It is not difficult to see from this contrast how Arnold's project can be described as treating the struggle for democracy in a rather heavy-handed manner.[16] The essays that make up *Culture and Anarchy* never allow for the possibility that the Hyde Park rioters, and the working classes more generally, have rationally and thoroughly considered the social and political issues affecting them, and have therefore decided that their current activity is the best course of action. Instead, the imaginative, contemplative and rational work of culture is consistently depicted as a point of contrast to current energies. Take the following, entirely characteristic expression of the cultural project, from Arnold's first essay, 'Sweetness and Light':

> the idea which culture sets before us of perfection, – an increased spiritual activity, having for its characters increased sweetness, increased light, increased life, increased sympathy, – is an idea which the new democracy needs far more than the idea of the blessedness of the franchise, or the wonderfulness of its own industrial performances. (*Culture*, 109)

Here, the ideas of 'the blessedness of the franchise' and of Britain's 'industrial' success are rendered simplistic, monolithic, uncritical pieces of dogma in comparison to the airy, nebulous, but suggestive realms of contemplative culture. But 'increased spiritual activity', 'increased life' and 'increased sympathy' are not necessarily at odds with extension of the franchise. In Schiller's *Aesthetic Letters* (which Dowling positions as a direct forerunner of *Culture and Anarchy*[17]), for example, contemplative, aesthetic consciousness was treated as entirely in accord with democratic progress, because the kind of culture that text advocated was one that would enable all classes to capitalize on a social transformation like the French Revolution. Increased 'spiritual activity', for Schiller, was of a piece with – and indeed was to be valued predominantly for – increased moral and therefore political awareness. What we are beginning to see, then, is that Arnold's particular formulation of the case for aesthetic consciousness, in *Culture and Anarchy*, is one that introduces practical and ideological problems that did not pertain to that category in its earlier manifestations. Keats's contemplative society, for instance, was explicitly for high and low alike, and did not stipulate the kind of content that would count as aesthetic consciousness. Mill's imagined future was also thoroughly inclusive in comparison to this aspect of *Culture and Anarchy*, because his *Principles* contain long sections on the rise of working-class consciousness that he saw as having already taken place.[18] Even Ruskin's in many ways deeply negative version of aesthetic consciousness stresses the extent to which it is for all men; this is the glory of Christian gothic architecture.

The problematic nature of *Culture and Anarchy*'s version of aesthetic consciousness is not limited to its handling of class, furthermore. If one considers how one might practice the Arnoldian model of culture, one finds another important hardening of the previously more flexible category of idle contemplation. Thinking back to Keats again, it was a 'page full of poesy' that could invoke aesthetic consciousness and lead one on the path to his 'grand' aesthetic 'democracy'. The brevity and accessibility of this single object was essential to that vision's inclusivity. For Mill, comparably, the stationary state ought simply to include the space for contemplative experience and contact with natural wildness. In Arnold's writing, by contrast, the set of objects that brings about the free play of culture and the aesthetic attitude are not only multiplied, but considerably specialized. That is to say that they take the form of a vastly extensive catalogue of printed, scholarly material. The second essay of *Culture and Anarchy* is one of the places where this aspect of Arnold's culture project is made explicit. There he remarks that 'the culture' of which he has been writing works entirely 'by means of reading, observing, and thinking' (*Culture*, 129). Elsewhere, such as in the first essay of the book where the supposedly admirable 'breadth' of culture is defined, the subject matter of this 'reading, observing, and thinking' becomes apparent:

> religion comes to a conclusion identical with that which culture, – culture seeking the determination of this question through *all* the voices of human

experience which have been heard upon it, of art, science, poetry, philosophy, history, as well as of religion, in order to give greater fulness and certainty to its solution, – likewise reaches. (*Culture*, 93–4)

The strained grammar of this quotation is a function of this problem of 'breadth' in Arnoldian culture. If culture requires 'getting to know' everything that can count as 'the best which has been thought and said in the world' (*Culture*, 233), as Arnold has it in the work's preface, then the man of culture must surely be professionalized, or at the very least provided with some kind of maintenance. For he is to read, observe and think about every 'voice' from 'art, science, poetry, philosophy, history' and 'religion'. And then on top of this, as the preface reminds us, he must, 'through this knowledge, turn [. . .] a stream of fresh and free thought upon our stock notions and habits, which we now follow staunchly but mechanically' (*Culture*, 233–4). Arnold's version of Schiller's and Keats's instantaneous psychological harmony has become, in other words, a matter of a lifetime of study, combined with a programme of applying the ideas of that study to contemporary culture's problems and concerns. It is no surprise, in this context, that Arnold's language might express concern about the task facing the man of culture. Thus, in this awkward quotation concerning '*all* the voices of human experience', this expansion is hurried over – as if the problem of breadth might somehow be concealed – by the squashing of this daunting list of disciplines into a necessarily brief syntactical position. In another forerunner of *Culture and Anarchy*, Coleridge's *On the Constitution of Church and State* of 1829, a whole class of 'clerisy' were to be devoted to the guardianship of the population's spiritual and intellectual development. The idea of professionalizing the man of culture is thus by no means new, in 1869. But Arnold does not advocate this, and Coleridge's system was one in which immediate aesthetic and spiritual experience was to be provided to all by these guides. Instead, Arnold's work seems to demand a lifetime of intellectual and personal commitment from all who care to be involved in any way in political and social matters.

If we briefly stand back from Arnold now, and consider his intellectual positions not as personal choices and political idiosyncrasies but as reflections of the wider currents of thought of the nineteenth century, we will see that there is an important parallel between Arnold and Ruskin in what we have seen so far of their thought. Before the midpoint of the century, aesthetic contemplation – or the Carlylean model of complete, spiritual work that covered over that category but that used its parameters – was consistently depicted as a matter of instantaneous effect. As in the

Romantic and German Idealist traditions, the harmonious, rounded or simply altered consciousness that was to be brought about by the new state of being needed no training, or practice, and did not require repeated, regular performance. Thus, even Tennyson's ultimately negative depiction of aesthetic contemplation in 'The Lotos-Eaters' rendered the effect of that people's narcosis direct, straightforward and instant. Carlyle's phrase, likewise, encapsulates this conception of aesthetic consciousness and its invocation: 'the whole soul of man is composed into a kind of real harmony, *the instant* he sets himself to work'. What we have now seen of the more formal cultural theory of the 1850s and 1860s allows us to pinpoint a sea change that has taken place in this model. And it is a change that, retrospectively, we might also locate in the examples of Arnold's early poetry we considered previously, published in 1849 and 1853. That is, far from being a matter of instantaneously altered consciousness, aesthetic contemplation becomes, around this time, a state requiring careful and regular attention, practice and work. This long process of engendering aesthetic consciousness, furthermore, is now very often cast as one attended by failure, disappointment and melancholy. Arnold's portrait of the contemporary 'intellectual throne' – in 'The Scholar-Gipsy' – being held by he who can tell best 'his misery's birth and growth and signs' is an early instance of this transformation. That poem's portrait of the poetic act is marked both by this intense, personal, psychic failure and by the long quest – the plot of which fills the text – to find and approximate a more fruitful, positive and instantaneous version of aesthetic consciousness. Aesthetic contemplation requires long-studied, esoteric knowledge, in other words, even though it was once simply a matter of heaven-sent inspiration. In *Culture and Anarchy*, comparably, correct, transformative aesthetic contemplation is only able to be performed by a chosen few 'apostles' of culture, as Arnold calls them (*Culture*, 113). Meanwhile, the vast majority of the nation's population rage and riot in a mêlée of failed action while they grope around for correct aesthetic consciousness and the 'right reason' (*Culture*, 235) that it apparently supplies. Ruskin's *Stones of Venice* fits comfortably with these models, because again aesthetic consciousness is depicted as the consummation of a lifetime's failure and near-drudgery. '[S]hame upon shame, failure upon failure, pause after pause' are the fruits of the worker who attempts aesthetic consciousness. For this worker to become an artist, then, and to access anything other than his psychic shortcomings in his approximations of the aesthetic mindset, he must devote many years to his craft. Aesthetic consciousness is thus professionalized and elongated in the 1850s and 1860s. Where once idle contemplation was conceived of as promising instant access to moral consciousness, it has become, for Arnold and Ruskin, a life's work that might never end. This is a highly significant hardening of the category of idle contemplation. Not only does it severely restrict the social and moral power that can be claimed for aesthetic consciousness, but it also inaugurates a situation in which society requires professional men of culture – or critics of aesthetic objects, as will be the case with Pater in the 1870s – in order to guide and temper its actions.

We can also note, at this point, that one might describe this hardening of conceptions of aesthetic consciousness as running counter to the contemporary, society-wide movement towards universal suffrage. At the end of the eighteenth century – as at the beginning of the nineteenth – the moral and political consciousness engendered by idle aesthetic contemplation was frequently invoked as the property of all citizens. This argument is explicit in Schiller and close to explicit in a text like Wordsworth and Coleridge's *Lyrical Ballads* (1798), with its numerous peasant- and statesmen-contemplators. As the actual political influence of the population slowly increases across the nineteenth century, by contrast, these universalizing gestures in the realm of aesthetic consciousness are replaced by more authoritarian accounts of the select few who possess the necessary knowledge and sensibility to perform aesthetic contemplation, and by more cautionary accounts of the psychic moral and practical failures that attend untutored attempts at aesthetic activity. Ruskin and Arnold's works contain elements of both these intellectual positions, even though Ruskin is often considered democratic in his aesthetics.[19] The elements of Ruskin we focused on above were those that might be described as cautionary. Arnold, meanwhile, concentrates in *Culture and Anarchy* on the more authoritarian strain of this argument.

But we might go even further than this generalization concerning democratic reform and delineate the actual historical and logical moment that transforms the dominant conception of aesthetic consciousness. It is no coincidence that the years around mid-century are those that witness this sea change in understandings of – or tactical deployments of – aesthetic contemplation. Charles Kingsley's novels *Yeast* and *Alton Locke*, which I have considered in connected terms elsewhere[20] and which were published in 1848 and 1850 respectively, also respond directly to the Chartist unrest for political reform of the 1840s. *Alton Locke* is set around and dramatizes the bathetic crisis to the Chartist movement, the attempted march on parliament of 1848, for instance; *Yeast* follows the intellectual turmoil of its protagonist as he attempts to come to terms with the educational and financial difficulties of the nation that are the backdrop for this widespread unrest. Kingsley's reactionary strategy for countering contemporary claims for democracy holds elements in common with Ruskin's caution and with Arnold's authority, in that he depicts aesthetic contemplation in both novels as a hollow seduction, and Christianity as providing the only authority that should govern individual or social action. The appearance of these novels after the Chartist failure of 1848 thus demonstrates that the stakes of depictions of aesthetic consciousness are considerably raised – and inflected – by the country's political unrest around mid-century. Kingsley's writing overtly attacks any positive conceptions of aesthetic contemplation: the category itself is a problem for him, and his 'muscular Christianity' sits more easily with the thought of the 'gospel of work'. But what he shows us in this context is that for attempted deconstructions of aesthetic contemplation and for celebrations of that state alike, the country's political unrest is highly significant. Even ultimately laudatory accounts of idleness and aesthetic consciousness – those like Ruskin and Arnold's that stand broadly in the same tradition as Schiller and Wordsworth – are rocked by the same wake of reform that moves Kingsley. What we are witnessing in the present chapter is thus that the most fundamental features of aesthetic consciousness are transformed in accordance with the fraught reformist context of the 1840s, 1850s and 1860s. Indeed, we are tracing how hardened conceptions of aesthetic contemplation flare up – in the early 1850s after Chartism's climax and the European revolutions of 1848–9, and in the late 1860s after the Reform League agitation that led to the Second Reform Act – in direct response to moments of civic unrest around the questions of reform. The accessibility and instantaneousness of idle aesthetic contemplation thus give way, in these fraught moments, to a more studied, a more professionalized, and therefore a more elitist model of cultural education and training. And aesthetic consciousness is no longer conceived as offering instantaneous moral consciousness, and as therefore promising political stability, because the physical and material wants that stand behind contemporary unrest are now understood as more pressing than – and as too concrete to be touched by – issues of psychic attitude or an aesthetic state of mind.

Returning to Arnold's text itself, then, there are a few more elements of *Culture and Anarchy*'s argument that we must attend to in order to give a full account of this work's cultural programme, and of its handling of the category of idle contemplation. We have now seen how aesthetic consciousness has been transformed, in response to contemporary political unrest, into a state tied up with attempts to actively assert cultural and therefore political authority. At the same time, however, *Culture and*

Anarchy also pays constant lip-service to the earlier nineteenth-century model in which aesthetic thought was a species of complete inertia that engendered critical distance from one's society or quotidian concerns. These two conceptions of culture are in constant tension in *Culture and Anarchy*, meaning that many of Arnold's formulations are hybrids of active and passive elements and traditions of thought. It is for this reason that Stefan Collini notes how seemingly passive 'culture' is rendered an 'active force' in Arnold's text: 'culture "*endeavours* to see and learn, and to *make* what it sees and learns prevail", culture "*conceives* of perfection ... as a harmonious expansion of all the powers which make the beauty and worth of human nature", "culture has a rough *task to achieve* in this country", and so on'.[21] Because Arnold is steeped in the aesthetic thought of his intellectual forebears – his poetry alone pays repeated homage to Wordsworth and Keats – these elements of Arnold's expression face two ways at once. They adhere, in one sense, to the celebration of complex aesthetic passivity to be found in the Romantics or in Schiller. But in another they also restlessly demonstrate the pressing and continual engagement that aesthetic consciousness has now become. Arnoldian culture is therefore a synthesis of Schiller, Wordsworth and Mill's passive contemplation with something like the 'gospel of work', even though Arnold distances his cultural project from this latter idea.[22] The 'man of culture', consequently, must dedicate himself to his work and must feel it as a social, active vocation. But that work is above all 'inward' (*Culture*, 234), concerned with cultivating – and with encouraging others to cultivate – the aesthetic attitude and what it has been understood to bring with it for seventy years or more by the time *Culture and Anarchy* is published, the individual's 'best', most rational and rounded self.

This recurrence of synthesized contradictions, or tensions, in *Culture and Anarchy* extends well beyond the poles of activity and passivity. We saw above, for example, what I termed the heavy-handedness with which Arnold might be said to treat working-class, and especially reformist, sentiment. But in accordance with *Culture and Anarchy*'s social vision, its insistence that aesthetic consciousness must be made to 'prevail' (*Culture*, 113), Arnold's work also envisages the eventual negation of all class distinctions, and therefore expresses itself as offering the hand of comfort and kindness to the lower classes. This gesture is made in the work's first essay, 'Sweetness and Light':

> [Culture] does not try to teach down to the level of inferior classes; it does not try to win them for this or that sect of its own, with ready-made

judgments and watchwords. It seeks to do away with classes; to make the best that has been thought and said in the world current everywhere; to make all men live in an atmosphere of sweetness and light, where they may use ideas, as it uses them itself, freely, – nourished, and not bound by them. (*Culture*, 113)

At the same time that it effectively rejects contemporary working-class rationality, then, *Culture and Anarchy* also imagines a scenario in which men of all classes will 'live in an atmosphere of sweetness and light',[23] and in which aesthetic consciousness will 'nourish' and 'free' the individual otherwise 'bound' by the ideologies that belong to his or her particular class. This sentiment is indicative of how Arnold's model of culture conceives of itself as against almost all other means of binding people together by background or belief. *Culture and Anarchy* makes this explicit early in the treatise, amongst a consideration of the contemporary utopian socialists (who Arnold casts as simply the latest pedlars of 'Jacobinism'): 'Culture is always assigning to system-makers and systems a smaller share in the bent of human destiny than their friends like' (*Culture*, 109). This statement, much like that on the extinction of classes just quoted, must give its reader pause. Because Arnoldian culture is surely also a system of thought and behaviour; and even if one has eliminated classes, then Arnold's work itself lays down very clear parameters for separating people into those that 'have' culture and those that have not. This logical problem is considerable in Arnold's thought. By rendering aesthetic culture a platform for arguing against a series of other ideologies and systems, Arnold reinforces the extent to which his own model of culture has become an ideology in its own right. Like his accounts of class consciousness, or of particular sects of Christianity, Arnoldian culture is inseparable, in *Culture and Anarchy*, from a thorough system of education and indoctrination, and a characteristic set of practices and intellectual positions. Again, therefore, we are observing a hardening of thought around aesthetic consciousness and idle contemplation that had not occurred until this particular historical moment. For neither Schiller's relatively simple and light-touch model of the experience of 'Fine Art' bringing about enhanced imaginative and moral consciousness, nor Coleridge's safeguarding of the spiritual and inward cultivation of the individual through the institution of a clerisy necessitated the construction of an ideological programme like that to be found in Arnold's thought. And out of the numerous arguments for aesthetic consciousness written in the years before *Culture and Anarchy*, these texts are the closest to an institutionalized model of aesthetic education.

The final thing we must note about *Culture and Anarchy* is one that will lead nicely into our consideration of Walter Pater's thought of the 1870s. This is the absence of natural occurrences of beauty in Arnold's model. Again, until the midpoint of the century, the predominant conception of aesthetic consciousness was that it was brought about, most naturally and easily, by the beauty of a landscape or by a naturally occurring scene. This was Mill's conception of aesthetic consciousness for his stationary state, as late as 1848. But it was also shared by Kingsley, by Tennyson, by the early Carlyle, by Shelley, by Keats[24] and by many others. In Ruskin's emphasis on architecture and in Arnold's exhaustive lists of 'the best that has been thought and said', by contrast, aesthetic contemplation has come to be associated – totally exclusively in their accounts – with man-made objects. This change fits the contours of the transformation taking place at this cultural moment that have been sketched out above, in that again it represents a hardening, a narrowing and a gentrification of aesthetic consciousness. The bar to admission into the realms of culture has thus been raised from any experience of the natural world, however brief or restricted (think, for instance, of Coleridge's suggestion that his youthful, urban experience of the 'sky and stars' was a spark to his later immersion in natural beauty[25]), to comprehensive access to a well-stocked library, to the time, education and intellectual means to explore it, and to the leisure and financial means to visit the great architecture of continental Europe. This considerable alteration in the conception of aesthetic consciousness is also something of a challenge to the apparent innateness and the profusion of idle aesthetic contemplation. For when natural beauty was the primary instigator of aesthetic consciousness, that state could be described as so abundant that its centrality to human life could barely be questioned. This was one of the primary contentions of the *Lyrical Ballads*, for example. In the world as described by Arnold and Ruskin, by contrast, the individual will only experience the full power of aesthetic freedom, and of the contemplative attitude that could transform society, when he or she becomes acquainted with the best that has been thought, said or built. Until a seminal event of this sort takes place, the aesthetic potential of the individual will apparently lie dormant. Thus, rather than configuring aesthetic consciousness as innate and almost ever-present in natural human life, these cultural systems depict it as in need of artificial, man-made stimulation.

The thought of Walter Pater overlaps, both chronologically and argumentatively, with that of Arnold the prose writer. For while Pater's major work, *Studies in the History of the Renaissance*, was published in book form in 1873, its constituent parts – including his extensive essay on Johann Winckelmann and his 'Conclusion', which will be our focal points here – were written and first published in the late 1860s. In this sense these essays are also part of the same fraught reformist moment as Arnold's cultural theory. When taken together, furthermore, these essays are also readable, like Arnold's, as 'a political tract' designed to bring about what Dowling calls a 'social transformation of Victorian life through an enlarged and emboldened sensuousness'.[26] The Renaissance[27] also shares a central subject matter with Culture and Anarchy, because it is in large part an analysis of the qualities and significance of Hellenism, which is also a key element of Arnold's thought, although one we did not touch on above. Pater's unique novel of 1885, Marius the Epicurean, will be the subject of a brief coda to the present chapter, because it is an extended exploration of the controversial ideas of the 'Conclusion' to The Renaissance, and because both these texts theorize aesthetic consciousness and its position in human life in ways that go beyond the parameters of Arnold's thought. Concluding the chapter with Marius the Epicurean will thus allow us to assess very clearly the standing of idle aesthetic contemplation in the wake of Pater's highly influential and thematically tightly focused writing.

More overtly and clearly than any other figure considered in this study, then, Pater repeatedly emphasizes the centrality of contemplation – and the contemplation invoked by aesthetic experience – to human life. In his 1874 essay on 'Wordsworth', to take one of countless examples, he sums up that poet's timeless relevance with the point that through his poetry 'he conveys' one 'lesson', 'more clearly than all'. This is 'the supreme importance of contemplation in the conduct of life'.[28] Slightly later in the same essay, Pater expands on this point as follows: 'That the end of life is not action but contemplation – being as distinct from doing – a certain disposition of mind: is, in some shape or other, the principle of all the higher morality. In poetry, in art, if you enter into their true spirit at all; you touch this principle, in a measure.'[29] In the later stages of Culture and Anarchy Arnold associated these active and contemplative poles of human life with the terms 'Hebraism' and 'Hellenism' respectively. He also cast the primary work of culture at the time he was writing as more concerned with Hellenism and the breadth of contemplative experience and 'spontaneity of consciousness' it promoted, than Hebraism and its characteristic 'strictness of conscience' (Culture, 165). The rationale for this selection was that, between them, Hellenism and Hebraism encapsulate the intellectual forces that have swayed the human world for its entire history, and that British society had, for the past several centuries, been concentrated too exclusively on Hebraism and its emphasis on energetic and worthy 'doing' (see *Culture*, 190–1). These quotations from Pater's essay on Wordsworth are characteristic of the former's thought then, in that they position Hellenic contemplation, and an enhanced 'disposition of mind', as the primary objects of all human experience while simultaneously shunning the notions of moral or social duty. Elsewhere, as we are about to see, Pater's concentration on Hellenism above all else also restlessly identifies the Greek spirit of passivity and wholeness in any high form of aesthetic culture. Even more forcefully than Arnold, therefore, Pater's writing contends for the development, and the full understanding, of idleness and aesthetic contemplation. We can also see already from these brief quotations, the primary role allotted to art-objects, in Pater's thought. '[I]f you enter into' the 'true spirit' of 'poetry' or 'art', then you encounter 'the higher morality' and its characteristic 'disposition of mind'. Not only is aesthetic experience equated with moral consciousness here, as it was in the idealist and Romantic traditions; but artworks are also associated so strongly with the highest contemplative and moral experiences of life that the figure of the aesthete – of he or she who lives above all for the experience of art – is conjured up as a necessary and logical maximization of human potential. That neither Ruskin nor Arnold's thought invoked this idea, that their emphases on art-objects and their significance did not negate other quotidian and practical aspects of life, demonstrates in one sense what a high-water mark of aesthetic thinking Pater's work represents. But as we will have occasion to consider below, Pater's thought also has a considerable dark, and problematic, side to it. His writing is frequently 'condemn[ed]' and 'caricature[d]' by his contemporaries, as Matthew Potolsky records, although such criticisms are often 'coded attack[s] upon his reputed homosexuality'.[30] He is also frequently charged with 'mislead[ing]' and problematically seducing his readers away from Christian orthodoxy and right living.[31]

Let us turn to Pater's *Renaissance* itself now, and to its longest essay, that on 'Winckelmann', which Pater wrote in 1867. Repose, idleness and aesthetic contemplation feature so heavily in Pater's thought that this essay, like almost all of his writing, contains several different formulations of the contemplative passivity that inheres in art-objects and that is engendered by our experience of them. Of the former, for example, Pater tells us that Hellenic sculpture 'allows passion to play lightly over the surface of the individual form, losing thereby nothing of its central impassivity, its depth and repose' (*Renaissance*, 173). Winckelmann himself, who embodied and made available to his contemporaries the Hellenic spirit which we will see defined presently, apparently 'compares' Greek sculpture 'to a quiet sea, which, although we understand it to be in motion, we nevertheless regard as an image of repose' (*Renaissance*, 174). Of the experience of passivity engendered by art works, Pater observes how Greek tragedy pits the reposing, contemplative individual against noisy, passionate, rival claims to human attention, meaning that this genre 'shows how such a conflict may be treated with serenity, how the evolution of it may be a spectacle of the dignity, not of the impotence, of the human spirit' (*Renaissance*, 178). Statements such as these incrementally accumulate the same idea that we saw Pater express directly in his later essay on Wordsworth, that the highest dignity of human experience lies in contemplative passivity, and that the aesthetic attitude represents a raising of the individual above quotidian concerns into a 'higher morality'. It is for this reason that, in the 'Winckelmann' essay, he defines the spirit of Hellenism, the quality that Winckelmann embodies so fully and so earnestly, in terms that synthesize Arnoldian breadth and a kind of Keatsian[32] concentration on passivity:

> *Heiterkeit* – blitheness or repose, and *Allgemeinheit* – generality or breadth, are, then, the supreme characteristics of the Hellenic ideal. But that generality or breadth has nothing in common with the lax observation, the unlearned thought, the flaccid execution, which have sometimes claimed superiority in art, on the plea of being 'broad' or 'general'. Hellenic breadth and generality come of a culture minute, severe, constantly renewed, rectifying and concentrating its impressions into certain pregnant types. (*Renaissance*, 170)

Pater's use of Winckelmann's German terms to transmit the Greek ideal into English culture encapsulates the trans-historical and trans-European tradition of aesthetic passivity that stands behind this study. For the theorizations of idle contemplation that took place in German idealism and in British Romanticism were both tied to contemporary classical learning and its idealization of Greek intellectual culture. Pater is in this sense more transparent with the heritage to his thought than Arnold, for instance. But the 'Hellenic ideal', in this description, is nevertheless also of its mid- to late nineteenth-century moment. Pater's 'generality' restates Carlyle's 'whole soul of man' that stood in opposition to the problematically narrow specialization promoted by commercial society, while 'breadth' is the same term Arnold uses at this moment in order to invoke the rounded and harmonious individual who could steer society away from its mechanistic obsessions. Pater's use of the term 'blitheness', however, represents another significant development in nineteenth-century conceptions of aesthetic consciousness. This is because this term, when paired with 'repose' in this manner, extends the physical posture of passivity to be found in Arnold and Mill very thoroughly into the fundamental cast of the individual's mind. The 'blithe' individual is one whose cheerfulness and contentment stems from his calm completeness, one whose intellectual and spiritual resources are so thorough that he is impervious to emotional and physical trials alike. Pater's emphasis on passivity is thus even more innate, immanent and total than it has been for any previous theorist of this state. Recall, for instance, the manner in which Shelley's 'Mont Blanc' dramatized the poet ceasing to consciously control his mind. That poem began, for instance, by summarizing the poet's complete mental surrender to '[t]he everlasting universe of things' that '[f]low[ed] through [his] mind'. And in this poem, as in the earlier Romantic tradition before Shelley, this posture of total inertia was attended with a series of significant psychic and physical dangers. In Pater's formulation, by contrast, to be blithe in spirit is to proceed with a serene and pervasive equanimity that stems from internal wholeness. It is to be so complete and calm that one is mentally impervious, but at the same time to remain attentive to, and engaged with, one's surroundings. Pater's blitheness is thus fundamentally distinct from the intense sensibility that characterized Romantic passivity, and that was echoed in Mill or in Carlyle's *Sartor Resartus*.

Despite this very thorough formulation of psychic completeness, it is nevertheless implied in Pater's definition of the Hellenic spirit that such a state is prey to a kind of dissipation or dilution. Pater stipulates, for example, that repose and breadth must be 'constantly renewed' in a 'severe' and exacting manner so as not to sink into a kind of dilettante culture. In the 'Winckelmann' essay Pater gives both historical and present reasons for this qualification. Historically, Pater sets out how the 'Hellenic ideal' serves as a counterforce to the 'universal pagan sentiment' that existed prior to Greek culture and that 'has lingered far onward into the Christian world, ineradicable, like some persistent vegetable growth'. This 'sentiment' is a fundamentally negative view of the world in which the 'human mind' is 'beset by notions of irresistible natural powers, for the most part ranged against man' (*Renaissance*, 160). The intellectual and psychic resources of Hellenism, in other words, insulate the individual from this universal pagan sadness by fostering a sense of man's totality and impenetrability. Pater's conception of the more modern context for the repose of aesthetic contemplation tends in a similar direction. In a portrait highly reminiscent of Arnold's account of modernity in 'The Scholar-Gipsy',

Pater explains that contemporary life is characterized by its 'conflicting claims' and 'its entangled interests', meaning that 'the problem of unity with ourselves, in blitheness and repose, is far harder than it was for the Greek within the simple terms of antique life' (*Renaissance*, 182). This problem of modernity, further, is not susceptible to the exact same treatment as the classical world for Pater. It can 'no longer be solved', we are told, 'by perfection of bodily form', by 'joyful union with the external world', or 'by the direct exercise of any single talent'. '[A]mid the manifold claims of our modern intellectual life', such Greek solutions would apparently only 'end' in 'a thin, one-sided growth' of our humanity (*Renaissance*, 182). Instead, the attitude of aesthetic repose is only to be attained, or constructed, by an exercise of 'breadth' on a scale not known to the Greeks:

> The demand of the intellect is to feel itself alive. It must see into the laws, the operation, the intellectual reward of every divided form of culture; but only that it may measure the relation between itself and them. It struggles with those forms till its secret is won from each, and then lets each fall back into its place; in the supreme, artistic view of life. (*Renaissance*, 183)

Despite the difference in register, this account of modern intellectual priorities is shaped to a large extent like Arnold's conception of culture. For Arnold, man should engage with 'the best that has been thought and said' so that human wholeness can be comprehended, and so that any issue or idea can be framed within a complete and rounded view of human life. Pater, similarly, expresses the intellectual project as examining 'every divided form of culture' in order to construct 'the supreme, artistic view of life'. Both critics thus depict the modern world as necessitating a concentration, and a multiplication, of human intellectual and contemplative activity. And both imagine a powerful interpretative framework to be the result.

Pater's priorities and suggested intellectual activities are, however, quickly distinguished from Arnold's. Because in further explaining the modern Hellenic mode, Pater immediately narrows and focuses his model of aesthetic consciousness well beyond that to be found in *Culture and Anarchy*. First, Pater specifies that 'music and poetry' are actually the only suitable cultural objects for the modern world (*Renaissance*, 184). Then, he refines this judgement even further by letting 'music' fall by the wayside, and defining the contemporary worth of poetry – or 'literary production' – at length:

> What [literary production] has to do in the service of culture is so to rearrange the details of modern life, so to reflect it, that it may satisfy the

spirit. And what does the spirit need in the face of modern life? The sense of freedom. [...] For us, necessity is not, as of old, a sort of mythological personage without us, with whom we can do warfare. It is rather a magic web woven through and through us, like that magnetic system of which modern science speaks, penetrating us with a network, subtler than our subtlest nerves, yet bearing in it the central forces of the world. Can art represent men and women in these bewildering toils so as to give the spirit at least an equivalent for the sense of freedom? Certainly, in Goethe's romances, and even more in the romances of Victor Hugo, we have high examples of modern art dealing thus with modern life, regarding that life as the modern mind must regard it, yet reflecting upon it in blitheness and repose. (*Renaissance*, 184–5)

In this account, 'modern life', as Pater goes on to clarify, 'becomes the tragic situation' (*Renaissance*, 185), to be dealt with in serene 'blitheness' and totality. The 'necessity' that is 'woven through and through us' by scientific and sociological conceptions of human life thus still requires the calm equanimity of aesthetic contemplation. But the complexity that must surround this state in its artistic and intellectual representation is of a different order to the rival passions of Greek tragedy, or the singular excitement of Greek sculpture. In comparison to Pater's initial portrait of self-culture's breadth, then, it is striking that the 'Winckelmann' essay ends with the strong implication that the modern individual in search of self-culture might concentrate, quite appropriately, on just 'literary production'. It would not even be a distortion of Pater's exposition to imagine that individual focusing his or her energies entirely on the 'romances' of Hugo and Goethe. What we are witnessing here, in other words, is a severe narrowing of the discourse of aesthetic contemplation. In Pater's thought, the figure who most embodies the human quest for aesthetic consciousness has become a specialized aesthete of extremely focused predilections. It may still be the case that such specialization is pursued in the interests of psychic 'breadth' and wholeness. But in comparison to the vast catalogue of human thought that Arnold considers necessary for self-culture, or when compared to suggestively broad categories like Schiller's 'Fine Art', or even Ruskin's gothic architecture, Pater's aesthetic objects must be seen to reduce the remit and the social relevance of his man of culture.

This is an apt moment to turn to the famous – or perhaps notorious – 'Conclusion' to *The Renaissance*, because the exact problems found at the end of the 'Winckelmann' essay are considerably amplified in that short concluding piece. The 'Conclusion', composed in 1868 as a part of Pater's account of William Morris's poetry, was omitted from *The Renaissance*'s second edition of 1877, and restored for the work's third and fourth editions in 1888 and 1893. The primary reason for Pater's omission, as summarized by Laurel Brake, was the notice the essay received 'in the pulpits of the university where [its] hedonism [...] was rejected and its danger for students proclaimed by W. W. Capes and others'.[33] Pater also received private objections, such as the letter from his Brasenose colleague John Wordsworth, which took issue with the essay's atheistic inferences and 'the dangers into which [it was] likely to lead minds weaker than' Pater's.[34] These difficulties were referred to by Pater in a note to the 1888 restoration of the 'Conclusion', where he acknowledged that the essay 'might possibly mislead some of those young men into whose hands it might fall' (*Renaissance*, 186). Yet the reinstatement of the 'Conclusion' was apparently now justified by the minor changes he had made to it,[35] and by the fact that *Marius the Epicurean* had been published in 1885. This work, Pater explains in the same note, 'deal[s] more fully [...] with the thoughts suggested by' the 'Conclusion' (*Renaissance*, 186) and therefore reduces the danger of that essay being misconceived.

The key features of Pater's thought that we have picked out so far – his far-reaching emphasis on the blithe repose of aesthetic consciousness, his interest in the individual's 'tragic' encounter with both the 'pagan' and the modern worlds – are both echoed and carried to their logical conclusions in the account of human priorities espoused by the 'Conclusion'. Pater's short concluding essay is almost entirely concerned with the individual's tragic encounter with the world, for instance. It thoroughly casts human experience as that of decay, loss and flux, and makes this judgement in a register that encompasses all past and present life. Take the following account of how 'analysis' complements our experience of the 'physical' and intellectual worlds (*Renaissance*, 186–7):

> Analysis goes a step further still, and assures us that those impressions of the individual mind to which, for each one of us, experience dwindles down, are in perpetual flight; that each of them is limited by time, and that as time is infinitely divisible, each of them is infinitely divisible also; all that is actual in it being a single moment, gone while we try to apprehend it, of which it may ever more be truly said that it has ceased to be than that it is. To such a tremulous wisp constantly re-forming itself on the stream, to a single sharp impression, with a sense in it, a relic more or less fleeting, of such moments gone by, what is real in our life fines itself down. It is with this movement, with the passage and dissolution of impressions, images, sensations, that analysis leaves off – that continual vanishing away, that strange, perpetual, weaving and unweaving of ourselves. (*Renaissance*, 188)

The pessimistic terminology of this account is extreme.[36] The 'pagan sentiment' that motivated the Hellenic spirit was built on suppositions and guesses at the melancholy position of man on earth and within eternity. Here, by contrast, in this inclusive account that supersedes that pagan guesswork, we are 'assure[d]' of a whole set of scientific facts, which all characterize our existence much more significantly by loss than by possession or permanence. Human existence is thus, empirically, a 'continual vanishing away', an experience of flux and decay rather than of being and existence. Even identity is to be understood – analytically, scientifically – as a mirage, or as a cyclic process that might better be described as non-identity: it is a 'strange, perpetual, weaving and unweaving of ourselves'.[37]

As with the 'pagan sentiment' and its counterforce, the 'Hellenic spirit', then, and as with the modern search for 'freedom' and its focus on 'music and poetry', in the 'Conclusion' Pater lays out this intensely pessimistic vision of human existence only in order to frame, to justify and indeed to celebrate its antidote. And yet again, as any reader of the 'Winckelmann' essay will expect, that antidote is the mental repose, and the blithe equanimity, of aesthetic consciousness. Also familiar from the 'Winckelmann' essay will be the rhetorical strategy that Pater employs in the 'Conclusion' of introducing aesthetic repose in generalized terms, but then quickly refining such terms down into the narrow life of the aesthete. Here is the initial, general expression of the aesthetic solution to life's constant flux:

> Every moment some form grows perfect in hand or face; some tone on the hills or the sea is choicer than the rest; some mood of passion or insight or intellectual excitement is irresistibly real and attractive to us, – for that moment only. Not the fruit of experience, but experience itself, is the end. [...] Not to discriminate every moment some passionate attitude in those about us, and in the very brilliancy of their gifts some tragic dividing of forces on their ways, is, one this short day of frost and sun, to sleep before evening. (*Renaissance*, 188–9)

The negativity framing Pater's aesthetic consciousness is here reflected in the winter imagery of the 'short day of frost and sun'. Life is essentially melancholy, in other words, unless one grasps the aesthetic brilliance of the 'moment' and seizes the short but glorious day. It is for this reason that Wolfgang Iser describes Pater as giving his definition of the aesthetic 'in negative terms'; 'time and death are its frame of reference'.[38] It is highly significant too for the development of aesthetic consciousness in the last decades of the century that Pater here rejects the knowledge – and the scope for social application – that Arnold's man of culture gleans from 'the best which has been thought and said'. In Pater's influential formulation, 'experience itself' is its own reward, a reward that is intense but certainly not lasting.

Pater moves immediately on from these intense natural and real-world experiences – the 'tone on the hills' and the 'passionate attitude in those about us' – to recast aesthetic experience as the stuff, once again, of art-objects. Jean-Jacques Rousseau is at first the exemplar of this concentration, because he resolved, in his *Confessions*, to fill the rest of his life with the 'intellectual excitement' to be found 'in the clear, fresh writings of Voltaire' (*Renaissance*, 190). It is with a sense, surely, of the almost absurd narrowness of this resolution that Pater's own support for this decision brings with it a programme of engagement at least slightly more broad, when he states that 'the wisest [. . .] among "the children of this world"' are those who focus upon 'art and song' (*Renaissance*, 190). Much like the final stages of the 'Winckelmann' essay, however, 'song' falls immediately away as Pater makes his final provisos regarding fully realized aesthetic attention:

> Only be sure it is passion – that it does yield you this fruit of a quickened, multiplied consciousness. Of such wisdom, the poetic passion, the desire of beauty, the love of art for its own sake, has most. For art comes to you proposing frankly to give nothing but the highest quality to your moments as they pass, and simply for those moments' sake. (*Renaissance*, 190)

The aesthetic programme here has become one made up entirely of literature and painting. But this is not the only narrowing that has taken place. The phrase 'simply for those moments' sake' in fact represents a wholesale degradation of aesthetic consciousness as it was formerly conceived.[39] Keats's 'page full of poesy' led to a contemplative life that could contain any sort of thinking and that would bring together diverse members of society in a 'grand democracy'. Mill's stationary state was one in which more equal distribution of goods was to be matched by an amicable distribution of aesthetic opportunity, again bringing individuals together in order to circumvent the atomization of laissez-faire capitalism. Arnold's thought also stressed human community above all and imagined the elimination of classes in favour of an aesthetic state that promoted the individual's most public-spirited self. In this famous consummation of Pater's vision, by contrast, the expression of which is taken as a manifesto for more than two decades of cultural priorities, the aesthete is to value his finely honed aesthetic experiences for each moment's sake alone. Art, likewise, is to be loved not for the community it can build and the moral awareness it can foster, but 'for its own sake'. In the context of every instance of aesthetic thought we have considered in this study, therefore, Pater stands out above all else for what he has omitted from aesthetic consciousness. In this category stands the whole tradition of moral thinking that shows any concern for the public good, for the formation of community and for the individual's responsibility to anything other than himself. These fields of thought and action were, up until Pater's thought itself, always structuring and formative components in theorizations of aesthetic consciousness. Pater's so-called higher morality, by contrast, would now appear to be a species of solipsism, a focusing on the glories and complexities of individual consciousness as an end in itself. Of course, Pater could also be seen to represent a partial high point of aesthetic development. He carries one half of the logic of idleness and aesthetic consciousness to its necessary conclusion, emphasizing and amplifying the qualities of the individual's encounter with beauty and repose so that the 'blithe', complete and impenetrable individual is in no need of society's psychic and moral support. But considering Pater's thought in the context of the whole tradition of nineteenth-century aesthetic consciousness, it is hard to resist the conclusion that *The Renaissance* is more pressingly a refinement, and a straining, of aesthetic consciousness to an absurd pitch. Aesthetic repose has become, here, a mode of isolation to divorce the individual from any other human engagement or issue. Blithe passivity has thus become a sealing off of the individual in a kind of glorious sarcophagus of intense experience. We are back, in this sense, in the territory of Tennyson's 'Lotos-Eaters', where aesthetic contemplation possesses a glorious and deeply alluring self-sufficiency, but one that has been bought at the expense of just about everything one would characterize as human.

Dowling's summary of this deeply negative aspect to Pater's thought stresses Pater's considerable influence: by the early 1880s, 'such terms as *Aestheticism, art for art's sake*, and *Culture* had become synonyms, [. . .] to all Britain [. . .], for the apparent betrayal of art and beauty into the hands of a self-nominated and supercilious elite'.[40] The French lineage of 'art for art's sake' of course only made its excesses more unpalatable in Britain. Dowling's term 'supercilious' conforms exactly to the moral and social aloofness shared by Pater's 'Conclusion' and Tennyson's 'Lotos-Eaters'. But the inclusion of the term 'Culture' in her summary also points towards the logical problems we traced in Arnold's thought, and the extent to which the three aesthetic theorists we have considered in this chapter are closely connected in the public consciousness by the last two decades of the century. One might say, consequently, that there is a pressing paradox within all the thought we have considered in this chapter. Ruskin, Arnold and Pater all put forward directly positive accounts of idle contemplation and aesthetic consciousness. In this sense they are all clear heirs to the Romantic and idealist celebration of these categories from the end of the eighteenth and the beginning of the nineteenth centuries. But Ruskin's emphasis on the failure encountered in the aesthetic moment, Arnold's problematic extension of the spontaneous aesthetic attitude to a lifetime's studious work and Pater's extreme narrowing of the remit and purpose of aesthetic consciousness all align as comparably tarnished and troubled attempts at making the case for idle aesthetic contemplation. In one sense, then, the period between the 1850s and the 1880s marks a resurgence in fortunes for the category of idle aesthetic contemplation, in comparison to that state's reputation in the 1830s and 1840s. These first decades of the second half of the century are marked by the celebration and examination of aesthetic consciousness with a depth comparable to – but perhaps more culturally mainstream than – the Romantic focus on that category. And yet these examinations and celebrations are also something like the death throes of positive conceptions of aesthetic consciousness because of the severe problems they introduce, or find, in that state, and because of the lasting damage they do to the reputation of idle contemplation as a socially and morally significant category, as Dowling records and as we shall see in the rest of this study.

Dowling's analysis of the thought that makes up the tradition of nineteenth-century aesthetic democracy ultimately concludes that there is 'an ideal of aristocratic sensibility unrecognized as such' at the heart of all such convictions and expressions.[41] This renders aesthetic democracy, in her account, something like the 'insubstantial dream' of the 'nobleman' who has never fully encountered the material problems of the real world.[42] The perspective on such thought that we have taken up in this chapter allows us to diagnose this period's attempted celebration of aesthetic consciousness slightly differently. We should note, firstly, that the extension of the aesthetic moment is to be found in the thought of all three figures we have considered in this chapter, as it is in Morris's Ruskinian vision in *News from Nowhere* as well. Ruskin, Arnold, Pater and Morris thus all stress the extent to which aesthetic consciousness should fill the entirety of the individual's life, and the extent to which the individual concerned must constantly and persistently work at his or her aesthetic abilities so that he or she is not prey to the ideological or practical dissipation that characterizes the life of those who have not found this calling.[43] The idle repose of aesthetic contemplation has thus become diligent, lifelong work, in this body of thought. This striking similarity across all these aesthetic theorists exists because what we have witnessed in this chapter can be described as the continued influence of the contemporary 'gospel of work' – as that term was theorized by Carlyle and others – on the category of idle contemplation. Idle aesthetic consciousness is recast as diligent, elongated, professionalized activity, in the cultural theory between 1850 and 1880, in accordance with the dominant and widespread conception of work as the most socially purposive and psychically rewarding of human engagements.

The identification of this decisive context puts us in a position to observe another far-reaching transformation in the reputation of aesthetic contemplation that results from this thorough synthesis of work and idleness. We noted above, firstly, that aesthetic consciousness loses its instantaneously transformative potential, and becomes, instead, an occupation like any other. The man of culture must train himself and diligently study, because the aesthetic attitude is not thought of as easily acquired, let alone as innate, spontaneous or accidental, as it was frequently at the turn of the nineteenth century. Secondly, however, we should note that the transformative potential of aesthetic consciousness had been consistently thought of as communicable, through poems like Shelley's 'Mont Blanc', or Coleridge's 'conversation poems'. This fact explains the numerous Romantic texts that strive to encapsulate, and allow for the re-experiencing of, aesthetic experience; it also justifies Keats's high-pitched celebration of 'a page full of poesy'. By the 1860s and 1870s, by contrast, in the thought of Arnold and Pater, aesthetic consciousness – now of more rare occurrence – is only be encountered first-hand, in the direct experience of beauty itself rather than in the artful retelling of that experience. Thus, the cultural theory of this period, and of the figures we have considered in this chapter, must stipulate the set of cultural objects that will begin the slow process of generating the aesthetic attitude. It is for this reason that Pater's *Renaissance* and, to an extent, Arnold's *Culture and Anarchy*, read as critical manuals of what their readers should focus their energies on. The 'man of culture', from the 1860s onwards, is thus no longer he who can – like the Romantic poet – distil aesthetic experience into words. He is, instead, the guide and advisor who can judge which art-objects are most relevant to contemporary society, given society's many ills. The guardian of aesthetic consciousness is thus now the critic rather than the poet. And both figures – think of Arnold the poet and Arnold the critic – have become commentators on the morbidity of quotidian human experience, more pressingly than they are celebrators, or dramatists, of aesthetic consciousness and its moral and social potential. Idle contemplation and aesthetic consciousness are thus configured here again, as they were in Romantic thought, as the key to successful and fully realized life. But these categories are not now psychological states innate to, and therefore ready to be experienced by, any individual. Such states of being function, rather, in the thought of Ruskin, Arnold and Pater, as the end-points of a distant aspiration each individual should harbour. They encapsulate the full potential of each citizen, but thereby indicate how far contemporary society places its citizens from such aesthetic realization.

The final, brief word in this chapter must go to *Marius the Epicurean*, Pater's 1885 novel that, as already stated, was conceived of as a fuller treatment of the ideas of *The Renaissance*'s 'Conclusion'. This novel makes a fitting coda to our account of the cultural theory of Ruskin, Arnold and Pater, because it exemplifies the numerous problems surrounding that category – and that category's fragility – by the final decades of the nineteenth century. This is because what Pater dwells on for the entirety of *Marius* is not the serene and blithe wholeness that aesthetic consciousness casts over the individual. Instead, Pater's focus is on how that state lacks access to – and fails to provide an intellectual position in relation to – the wider moral systems and attitudes that characterize social life and its institutions. It is for this reason that Iser, by far the most insightful critic of Pater's novel, finds its eponymous protagonist, despite the novel's title, to be 'continually drawing away from all such systems as Epicureanism, Stoicism and Christianity' and to ultimately denote only 'the empty space which ideas might fill'. Marius is thus, for Iser, 'an intermediate being, and his indeterminacy demonstrates nothing but a sort of melancholy helplessness'.[44] This fate is clearly the polar opposite of *The Renaissance*'s repeated emphasis on blithe completeness, and exemplifies the problematic superciliousness of contemporary aesthetic consciousness. Pater's novel, again in Iser's terms, thus 'spotlights the spiritual problems arising from' the programme of life announced in *The Renaissance* 'by revealing' the aesthetically enhanced experience of a moment in time to be in fact 'the genesis of longing and anxiety'. The novel, in other words, ultimately expresses 'the failure built into the aesthetic attitude'[45] and casts the defence against the transience of experience that Pater had laid out in the 'Conclusion' as illusory, or misconceived.[46]

We should note, finally, that it is highly significant for the status of aesthetic contemplation towards the end of the nineteenth century that the deeply negative judgement passed on aesthetic consciousness by *Marius the Epicurean* is by no means limited to the ideas featured in *The Renaissance* itself. Pater's novel in fact reads as a catalogue of claims for idle contemplation taken from the Romantics onwards, as well as from a whole range of classical philosophies. What this means for our purposes is that *Marius* casts a very melancholy shadow over the whole tradition of idle contemplation that stands behind Pater's thought (and behind this study), and that the novel actively groups these traditions together as all essentially alike. Pater thus refers explicitly to Coleridge's 'Eolian Harp' when he has Marius intuit 'a far-reaching system of material forces' embodied in 'a thousand combining currents from earth and sky' that animate his seemingly 'active powers', making his consciousness 'a leaf on the wind'.[47] Elsewhere, Pater expresses the culture project in terms that map directly on to *Culture and Anarchy*.[48] And on countless occasions he fuses the aesthetic vocabularies from across the nineteenth century in order to render Marius a representative of aesthetic culture *tout court*.[49] Iser's observations above allow us to see, then, that the fate of these positive expressions of aesthetic consciousness and capability is to be cast as ultimately insubstantial, or as only partial conceptions of human priorities masquerading as systems of totality and wholeness. In this sense *Marius* comprehensively positions the flux and decay of experience, which was expressed so compellingly in the 'Conclusion', as an even more powerful force than Pater acknowledged in that essay. But *Marius* goes further even than this. Pater configures the aesthetic attitude in the novel as precluding Marius from committing himself to any of the more rounded social philosophies he encounters. In the scheme of the novel, and in terms of its relevance for contemporary Britain, early Christianity is the most significant of these philosophical systems. Marius encounters this religion at the very end of the novel, and finds it characterized by socially rich ceremonies which offer a comprehensive justification – and sublimation – of the human experience of decay and flux. Pater's narrator even makes explicit the extent to which Christianity represents a fuller and more rounded system of human capability, echoing Arnoldian or idealist terms by describing it as promoting the 'harmonious development of all the parts of human nature'.[50] But Pater's novel is not consummated by its protagonist's conversion to Christianity, or even by a significant change of intellectual tack on his part. As Iser summarizes, 'in the "great crisis"' Marius 'is finally exposed to the reality of the choice, and the task proves impossible. He does not make the decision. He dies in the awareness of a vague hope'.[51] The novel, in this way, renders its protagonist something like a Wandering Jew figure, or perhaps (anticipating the material we will turn to in the Chapter 5) a kind of Byronic revenant, always tied to – but forever excluded from – human society. The aesthetic attitude is thus rendered something like a curse, in *Marius the Epicurean*, or a secular substitute for the ecstasy of religious contemplation that also precludes the individual from engaging with religion itself. The attempt to live one's life as a maximization of aesthetic consciousness casts the individual above and beyond human sociality, therefore, but in such a way that that distance is felt as an unbridgeable chasm. What Pater consistently expressed, in the 1860s and 1870s, as a 'higher morality', is rendered, in the mid-1880s, a problematic dislocation from conventional moralities and institutions.

CHAPTER 5

The Gothicization of Idleness

The final focus of this study necessitates a departure from the high cultural register of Ruskin, Arnold and Pater, and a consideration instead of the middle- and lowbrow literature of the late nineteenth century. This is because the categories of idleness, aesthetic contemplation and pervasive repose are all central subject matters in Victorian vampire fiction, even though the abundant recent criticism of this field has not had occasion to observe this connection. Novelistic treatments of the vampire figure also form a fitting end-point to the present study because they repeatedly associate idle aesthetic contemplation with the vampire figure him or herself, and thus complete the fall from grace of contemplative repose that began with the early Victorian 'gospel of work'. Idleness here is thus not a component of a desirable new social order, as it was for Carlyle, for Mill or for Arnold, for example. Rather, the texts we will consider in this chapter are all concerned with purging the world of their vampiric antagonists, as well as of the contemplative inertia and spiritual knowledge that those antagonists engender in their victims and embody in themselves. Vampire literature in this period thus energetically performs the cultural work of marginalizing, criminalizing and demonizing the categories of human experience that have been the subject of the present study. And it does so, as we shall see, at the same time as positioning a model of upright, virtuous and work-based masculinity in their stead.

I want to begin this chapter with a text that makes only fleeting reference to the idea of the vampire, however; a text indeed which is most often read in terms quite distinct from the vampiric. This is Emily Brontë's *Wuthering Heights* of 1847. What this novel will enable us to see in some detail is the logical connection, in nineteenth-century gothic and partially gothic writing, between states of contemplative idleness and the vampire's dangerous otherworldliness. Brontë's novel has been repeatedly understood as interacting with the key tenets and figures of Romantic thought in quite general terms. Anne Williams,

Anne Mellor and Michael Macovski's accounts of the text are particularly successful examples of this approach.[1] The ground covered by the present study allows for a new and even more precise consideration of this connection, however. The approach we took to Keats's models of poetic activity and 'negative capability' will enable us to follow Brontë through almost identical territory in *Wuthering Heights*. But whereas the experiential details of aesthetic contemplation were celebrated by Keats, Brontë embodies such aesthetic contemplation in the Byronic, troubled and troubling form of Heathcliff. In this sense, *Wuthering Heights* introduces several layers of ambiguity – at the level of narrative as well as character – to its depiction of aesthetic repose. These ambiguities, as we shall see, coalesce and culminate in the notion that Heathcliff is not just vampiric, but is in fact a vampire.

Brontë's novel alludes directly, though subtly, to negative capability from its very start. Lockwood, the novel's framing narrator, describes the interior of Wuthering Heights itself as its 'penetralium', at the very moment that he encounters Heathcliff for the first time on the house's threshold (*WH*, 4). This term is used a number of times in travel writing in the 1830s and 1840s, but always serves to allude to its first coinage, that of Keats in 1817, in his negative capability letter that we considered at the start of this study.[2] This letter states that 'Coleridge, for instance, would let go by a fine isolated verisimilitude caught from the Penetralium of mystery, from being incapable of remaining content with half knowledge'. The negatively capable poet, by contrast, he or she who can give their full self to the experience of idle aesthetic contemplation, can 'remain content' with 'half knowledge' and thereby immerse themself in mystery's 'Penetralium', its inner heart. Even though Lockwood is repeatedly read as an intensely rational, fundamentally disbelieving auditor of the novel's central narrative, then, this allusion to the contemplative aesthetics of Keats's correspondence serves to imply that what is being accessed in the story of Heathcliff and his household will bear close relationship to the aesthetic grasping at 'half knowledge', 'mysteries' and 'doubts' that Keats celebrates.[3]

If we turn to what is in many respects the central passage of *Wuthering Heights*, the elder Catherine's attempted explanation of her bond with Heathcliff, we will find that this Keatsian promise in the novel's opening is indeed justified. Not only does Catherine there express her dreamy half-knowledge in terms that anticipate Lockwood's dream as well as the novel's remarkable dénouement – stating that were she to find herself 'in heaven' she would break her 'heart with weeping to come back to earth' (*WH*, 81) – but she also makes use of a model of identity that stands very close to Keats's account of the poetic self:

> I cannot express it; but surely you and every body have a notion that there is, or should be, an existence of yours beyond you. What were the use of my creation if I were entirely contained here? My great miseries in this world have been Heathcliff's miseries, and I watched and felt each from the beginning; my great thought in living is himself. If all else perished, and *he* remained, I should still continue to be; and, if all else remained, and he were annihilated, the Universe would turn to a mighty stranger. [. . .] Nelly, I *am* Heathcliff – he's always, always in my mind – not as a pleasure, any more than I am always a pleasure to myself – but, as my own being[.] (*WH*, 82)

We saw Keats define the essence of poetic thought as the ability to 'annihilate' and transcend the self in order to enter into the minds and bodies of those around one. In strikingly similar terms – with an echo of Keats's term 'annihilated', for instance – Catherine here positions the permeability of the self as a fundamental feature of her experience. The assertion that there is 'an existence of yours beyond you' thus directly paraphrases Keats, while giving it even more centrality in human life than Keats's own formulation. In Brontë's passage, the permeability of the self is expressed as characterizing Catherine's whole existence: 'I watched and felt each from the beginning; my great thought in living is himself.' For Keats it was an apt description of the poetic 'fit' alone, of his patterns of aesthetic thought when he was 'free from speculating on creations of [his] own brain'. Brontë's passage might therefore be said to take Keats's thought even further than Keats's own 'poetic self' letter.

Brontë's pattern of reference to Keatsian poetic consciousness is also matched, in *Wuthering Heights*, by a series of references to the inertia or complete repose that, for Keats as for many others, brings about that state. Lockwood's dream might be read as the first example of the novel's emphasis on pervasive idleness, for it is in a state of fitful sleep that Catherine's spiritual prophecy is first shown to come true. But because Brontë renders both Catherine and Heathcliff conscious believers in the powers of aesthetic contemplation, *Wuthering Heights* also contains numerous dramatizations of more overt and willed aesthetic repose. Perhaps the clearest example of this is the sustained embrace between Catherine and Heathcliff that follows their confrontation during Catherine's illness. In this act the spiritual, Keatsian connection between the two protagonists is given physical form. It is for this reason that their embrace is both opaque and other-worldly to Nelly, its observer and narrator:

> His eyes wide, and wet, at last, flashed fiercely on her; his breast heaved convulsively. An instant they held asunder; and then how they met I hardly saw, but Catherine made a spring, and he caught her, and they were locked in an embrace from which I thought my mistress would never be released alive. In fact, to my eyes, she seemed directly insensible. He flung himself into the nearest seat, and on my approaching hurriedly to ascertain if she had fainted, he gnashed at me, and foamed like a mad dog, and gathered her to him with a greedy jealousy. I did not feel as if I were in the company of a creature of my own species; it appeared that he would not understand, though I spoke to him; so I stood off, and held my tongue, in great perplexity. (*WH*, 162)

This embrace, in which Catherine is subsequently shown to be not 'insensible' but an active and equal participant, lasts an unspecified, but clearly inordinate, length of time. After not moving from this position for what might be hours, Nelly is eventually able to separate the two only with the information that Mr Linton will imminently return from church. The embrace is thus a species of intense and sustained passivity that embodies what Catherine sees as the shared identity between her and Heathcliff. In the context of Catherine's Keatsian conception of her identity and the novel's suggestive deployment of the term 'penetralium', this episode thus recalls Keats's own repeated descriptions of pervasive repose as the mechanism for both personal aesthetic consciousness and radical interpersonal connection. We should note here too that Nelly's comparison of Heathcliff to 'a mad dog', and her suggestion that he is, in this instance at least, not a 'creature' of her 'own species', serve to cast the aesthetic passivity of the protagonists' embrace as a bestial, primitive capacity. It is implied, in other words, here and on the many other occasions that Heathcliff is described as some kind of animal, that the capacity for intense aesthetic contemplation is innate and subrational, that it is most often covered over and obscured by civilized life and its attendant education. Lockwood and Nelly, who are almost entirely sceptical of the story they hear and narrate respectively, thus represent civilized, conventional, non-Keatsian thought in the novel.

Following Catherine's death, it is Heathcliff that Brontë uses to sustain the novel's examination of aesthetic consciousness and its attendant posture of repose. And highly significantly for our present purposes, it is in the closing sections of the novel, which focus on Heathcliff in this manner, that Brontë associates intense aesthetic contemplation with the figure of the vampire. The context for this connection is Heathcliff's withdrawal from the physical world of property, power and action into a contemplative and solipsistic realm that he describes as his 'heaven' (*WH*, 328). Finding Heathcliff completely idle and inert for extended periods of time, but also uncharacteristically happy, Nelly intrudes upon his solitude in order to investigate. The scene she encounters is one that directly alludes to Cowper and Coleridge's famous moments of fireside contemplation in *The Task* and 'Frost at Midnight':

> He was leaning against the edge of an open lattice, but not looking out; his face was turned to the interior gloom. The fire had smouldered to ashes; the room was filled with the damp, mild air of the cloudy evening, and so still, that not only the murmur of the beck down Gimmerton was distinguishable, but its ripples and its gurgling over the pebbles, or through the large stones which it could not cover. (*WH*, 329)

We had occasion briefly to consider Cowper and Coleridge's versions of this scene in the first chapter of this study. Here therefore it will be necessary simply to recap that a dying fire, a posture of contemplative repose and a kind of half-attention to the sensual details of one's surroundings – the beck's ripples and gurgles in this case – serve as the most repeated shorthand for the intensities of idle aesthetic contemplation, in Romantic writing and in the early nineteenth century more generally. Brontë's invocation of this trope at this moment has the effect of portraying Heathcliff as concentrating exclusively on aesthetic consciousness and the spiritual realm to which it gives access. In Cowper and in Coleridge, as in Keats, such a state was most often cast as a powerful but temporary focusing of the individual's contemplative potential. Here, in *Wuthering Heights*, it is used to denote Heathcliff's single-minded devotion to the world of aesthetic contemplation – albeit a grimmer and harsher mode of that state than Coleridge's luxurious radicalism – for his 'heaven' comes about from the sustained practising of this mode of being for days at a time.

As with the vast majority of Heathcliff's actions in Brontë's novel, the reader's perception of their import is mediated through the sceptical narration of Nelly. In this instance, therefore, the novel offers us both this portrait of intense contemplative inertia – what Heathcliff describes as his 'Soul's bliss' that 'kills' his 'body' but that 'does not satisfy itself' (*WH*, 333) – and of the opacity of that state to the novel's narrator. Nelly records her response to the fireside scene as follows: 'The light flashed on his features, as I spoke. Oh, Mr. Lockwood, I cannot express what a terrible start I got, by the momentary view! Those deep black eyes! That smile, and ghastly paleness! It appeared to me, not Mr. Heathcliff, but a goblin' (*WH*, 329). Just a little later, after further consideration of Heathcliff's behaviour, his 'bloodless hue' and his unusually visible teeth (*WH*, 328), Nelly's thoughts tend in a comparably supernatural direction: '"Is he a ghoul, or a vampire?" I mused. I had read of such hideous, incarnate demons' (*WH*, 330). These are in one sense innocuous observations. The novel certainly frames them as idle superstitions of a kind that are repeated by a large portion of the neighbouring community – though we should remember that such framing is carried out by Nelly herself. But yet, as we progress through key examples of the century's vampire fiction in the remainder of this chapter, Nelly's seemingly throw-away remarks will acquire a kind of power and purchase that a reader of *Wuthering Heights* alone would not be able to grasp. This is because intense, poetic, aesthetic contemplation of the kind practised by Heathcliff at the end of this novel features so consistently in the vampire fiction that emerges between 1845 and 1900 that the term 'vampire' becomes something of a byword for the idle contemplator, or for the devotee of aesthetic consciousness. In this sense, Nelly's observations are prescient. Or, alternatively, Brontë should be recognized as tapping in to a strain of thought about the vampire that can already be found in texts like Coleridge's unfinished 'Christabel' of 1798, and John Polidori's 1819 'The Vampyre'. Coleridge has his vampiric protagonist bring about a kind of aesthetic half-sleep in her victim that we will return to presently. Polidori aligns his vampire Lord Ruthven with Byron, and even publishes his short story in such a way that it was at first assumed to be authored by that poet.[4]

What Brontë's handling of these connections show us, therefore, is that in 1847 a Keatsian contemplator, in the popular imagination that Nelly represents, *is* a vampire. This can be taken two ways. Firstly, one might say that the solipsistic and otherworldly vampire-figure shares qualities in common with the aesthetic contemplator. The latter is of course the figure who strives to transcend quotidian life by focusing his or her energies on the spiritual and ideal realm. Or, secondly, one might use Nelly's connection to contend that the Romantic invention that is the vampire in its modern form has, since Coleridge and Polidori, been a way of characterizing, investigating and ultimately critiquing the intense, poetic contemplator, he or she who prioritizes aesthetic consciousness above all else. I would contend that both these statements are true, and that the significance of Nelly's idle rumination is that it allows Brontë to connect her portrayal of intense, Keatsian aesthetic consciousness to one of that act's known and powerful critiques. In other words, the suggestion that Heathcliff is a vampire is part of *Wuthering Heights*'s strategy of layering doubt and ambiguity around the Keatsian aesthetic consciousness that forms the penetralium – the inner heart – of the novel.

The conventional view of the novel's two narrators, as has been referred to above, is that they stand at some distance from the intellectual heart of Heathcliff and Catherine's narrative, that they are above all disbelieving and even closed-minded. Nelly's association of Heathcliff with the figure of the vampire, however, opens up a more positive and a more intellectually significant role for her in the final pages of the novel. In this case, for example, she intuits the otherworldly dimensions of Heathcliff's mental life in terms that directly anticipate the novel's conclusion. And she thereby invokes a world of local popular wisdom that is shown to hold its own in relation to Lockwood's orthodox rationality. This contrast is justified by the two descriptions of Heathcliff's death and burial with which the novel ends. Here first is Lockwood's:

> I lingered round them [the graves of Heathcliff, Catherine and Edgar Linton], under that benign sky; watched the moths fluttering among the heath, and hare-bells; listened to the soft wind breathing through the grass; and wondered how any one could ever imagine unquiet slumbers, for the sleepers in that quiet earth. (*WH*, 337)

And here is Nelly's:

> at present it [Heathcliff's grave] is as smooth and verdant as its companion mounds – and I hope its tenant sleeps as soundly. But the country folks, if you asked them, would swear on their Bible that he *walks*. There are those who speak to having met him near the church, and on the moor, and even within this house – Idle tales, you'll say, and so say I. Yet that old man by the kitchen fire affirms he has seen two on 'em, looking out of his chamber window, on every rainy night, since his death – and an odd thing happened to me about a month ago [...] and [...] I don't like being out in the dark, now – and I don't like being left by myself in this grim house[.] (*WH*, 336)

Again here, with these two opposing passages, we are in the world of Romantic poetics, for the contrast between Lockwood's doggedly rational conception of death and Nelly's more flexible spirituality recalls a poem like Wordsworth's 'We Are Seven' (1798), with its opposition between an adult's received notion of 'heaven' and a child's more spontaneous conception of the permeable border between life and death. Brontë's version of this contrast even retains Wordsworth's original emphasis, whereby adult rationality is made to appear simplistic and defensive in comparison to the more intuitive popular imagination. The reason for this, in *Wuthering Heights*, is that the idea that Heathcliff and Catherine are revenants, that they are 'undead' (to use another contemporary term), and that they '*walk*', is only an extension of the apparent permeability between life and death that their Keatsian contemplative statements and actions have evoked throughout the novel. The episode following Lockwood's dream conjures exactly this idea. Heathcliff there addresses Catherine's ghost in imploring terms: '"Cathy, do come. Oh do – *once* more! Oh! my heart's darling, hear me *this* time – Catherine, at last!"' (*WH*, 28). Lockwood's opinion, in this case, is that Catherine's 'spectre' did not appear (*WH*, 28), even though Heathcliff's last words might be read rather differently. But either way, at the novel's end, in a mode of what Nelly describes as 'reverie' and what we have seen Heathcliff call his 'heaven', Heathcliff is heard to commune with Catherine 'as one would speak to a person present – low and earnest, and wrung from the depth of his soul' (*WH*, 332). It is in the context of these events, and of Catherine's suggestion that she would return from heaven were she to find herself there, that the popular superstitions surrounding the two protagonists' ghosts at the novel's conclusion must appear as a set of statements in complete accord with a significant strand of the novel's action.

We are now in a position to recognize the subtle and complex manner in which Brontë handles idle aesthetic contemplation in *Wuthering Heights*. For the novel is in one sense a positive exploration of the powers and significance of aesthetic consciousness that might be aligned with Keats or Shelley's accounts of that state. Heathcliff and Catherine in this view would be read as embodying a profound and primitive mode of being in the world that enriches and goes beyond quotidian reality. They are, in this line of reasoning, something like exemplars of Keatsian aesthetic democracy, or of the 'gipsy' life in Arnold's nearly contemporary 'Scholar-Gipsy'. But there is also a highly significant dark side to Brontë's novel, and to its protagonists' role in it, that makes *Wuthering Heights* a fitting starting point for the present chapter. In this strand to the novel one must observe the manner in which Heathcliff plays the role of villain, the extent to which he is not only the cuckoo that stays around to seize its guardians' property, but also the single-minded destroyer of earthly pleasures for all those around him. It is in this sense that Brontë's novel associates the concentration on aesthetic consciousness with an aggressive disregard for material existence in a conventional manner, and in this sense that it portrays Keatsian existence as a solipsistic, selfish and damaging mode of being in the world. To view the novel in these terms is to read Heathcliff's many bestial associations not as the purity of primitive consciousness but as a subrational distaste for, or incomprehension of, civilization and its attendant norms. Structurally, it is the notion that Heathcliff eventually becomes a vampire, a revenant, one who '*walks*', that Brontë positions as the final and most suggestive possibility of the novel. And because this judgement aligns most fully with the darker side to the novel's politics, because it brings out and plays up the extent to which aesthetic consciousness stands at a distance from the interactions of conventional society, it is hard not to take *Wuthering Heights*, ultimately, as a text in agreement with Tennyson's 'Lotos-Eaters', for example. Aesthetic consciousness, that is, is villainized and condemned by its association with the vampiric Heathcliff. And the vampire, the figure who can pass the boundary between life and death and who has no concern for the quotidian materiality of human society, is thus shown to embody the problematic associations idle aesthetic contemplation has acquired by the midpoint of the nineteenth century.

We must now turn to vampire literature proper, a field in which the associations that are made at the end of *Wuthering Heights* are both repeated and significantly amplified. My treatment of this body of writing will concentrate on the two stand-out vampire texts of the last decades of the century – Sheridan Le Fanu's *Carmilla* of 1872 and Bram Stoker's *Dracula* of 1897 – because it is in these texts that the intellectual and social fate of idle aesthetic contemplation in nineteenth-century culture as a whole is most clearly reflected.[5] But it will be necessary to contextualize these texts' handling of the ideas of repose and aesthetic consciousness by offering a brief tour through the whole century's vampire trope.

First then, we must look back to Coleridge's unfinished poem 'Christabel' which, as I have already mentioned, founds post-Enlightenment vampire discourse on the complexities and problems of aesthetic consciousness. 'Christabel' was begun in 1798, expanded in 1800, but not published until 1816, when Byron's financial assistance and warm praise for the poem helped Coleridge to bring it to public attention. The central moment of Coleridge's poem, in which the Lamia- or vampire-figure Geraldine holds Christabel in her quasi-maternal embrace, is one in which Christabel experiences an involuntary trance-like state:

> With open eyes (ah woe is me!)
> Asleep, and dreaming fearfully,
> Fearfully dreaming, yet I wis,

Dreaming that alone, which is—
O sorrow and shame!   ('Christabel', 280–4)

In these lines there is the germ of a whole century's vampire discourse. This is because they associate being a victim of a vampire with being cast, unwillingly, into a world of troubled and problematic aesthetic consciousness. As we saw in Chapter 1 of this study, for the first generation of Romantic writers, aesthetic contemplation was repeatedly and consistently conceived as a powerful but dangerous state that could either be engendered and practised deliberately, or could be thrust upon the individual without his or her consent or foreknowledge. Wordsworth's description of practised aesthetic consciousness in the Preface to *Lyrical Ballads* is an example of the former, while his account of a 'strange fit of passion' in 'Strange Fits of Passion Have I Known' (1798) is a direct portrayal of the latter.[6] Here in the central lines of 'Christabel', therefore, Coleridge describes being a victim of a vampire as having a trance-like state of consciousness involuntarily thrust upon one. To sleep with one's eyes open, to dream, but to dream 'that alone, which is': this is the same type of experience that is described in 'The Eolian Harp' or in 'Frost at Midnight', only here the experience of transcendent, otherworldly insight is rendered synonymous with a kind of nightmarish control by an external figure. As Coleridge goes on to clarify, 'the worker of these harms, / That holds the maiden in her arms' ('Christabel', 286–7) is none other than Geraldine. The experience at the centre of this poem then, the result of the embrace of its vampire figure, is thus simultaneously 'harm' and a 'dream', both insight into the truthful knowledge – into 'that alone, which is' – and a 'fearful' experience from which Christabel wakes in 'tears' ('Christabel', 303). In other words, Coleridge's extremely influential poem is marked by a significant ambiguity around its central event. Upon waking, Christabel 'doth smile, and she doth weep' ('Christabel', 308), because the narrative is simultaneously one of her victimhood and one of her coming of age, of being born into worldly – and both sexual and demonic – knowledge.

From this moment on, across the whole of the nineteenth century, to be a victim of a vampire is to be cast into a world of half-sleep that stands somewhere between nightmare and intense aesthetic contemplation. The flexible and protean genre of vampire fiction might sometimes appear to oscillate between these two poles of victimhood. But in fact, as we shall see, as the century progresses there is a very marked transition from Coleridgean poetic and intellectual ambivalence around vampiric victimhood to a strong consensus that the aesthetic consciousness at the heart of the vampire trope is to be regretted, to be avoided, and indeed to be purged from the world with violent and total means if at all possible. We will also see that, even in vampire texts less interested in the precise parameters of aesthetic consciousness than Coleridge's, the notion of transcendent non-rational experience is indicated by postures of involuntary inertia, sustained idleness, or extreme physical and mental lassitude. Polidori's 'The Vampyre' of 1819 is an example of the latter that nevertheless stands quite close to Coleridge's poem. Polidori's male protagonist is so persecuted by the text's eponymous villain that he eventually sinks below rational consciousness and the ability to do anything other than repose. Towards the novella's conclusion, for example, the protagonist Aubrey is rendered literarily insensible:

> He hardly appeared to notice [the physician hired to care for him], so completely was his mind absorbed by one terrible subject. His incoherence became at last so great, that he was confined to his chamber. There he would often lie for days, incapable of being roused. He had become emaciated, his eyes had attained a glassy lustre [. . .][7]

The 'glassy lustre' of Aubrey's eyes here, together with the sustained, Keatsian posture of intense idleness, serve to invoke poetic concentration and a neglect of social responsibilities in this late Romantic context. For to be inert in this manner, with eyes open but sealed off, directly echoes Coleridge's formulation. We can also see here an anticipation of the manner in which *Wuthering Heights* closes, because Aubrey's 'emaciated' form and disregard for society or quotidian concerns parallel Heathcliff's half-voluntary withdrawal into contemplative inertia.

The persistence and sustained popularity of vampire fiction throughout the century means that Brontë's allusions to vampiric states do not require her readers to have knowledge of Coleridge or Polidori specifically, however. Because in the three years immediately prior to the publication of *Wuthering Heights*, one of the century's most popular vampire narratives was published in serial form as part of the mid-nineteenth century's 'penny bloods' phenomenon. This was James Malcolm Rymer's *Varney the Vampyre* of 1845–7, which was also published in book form between 1847 and 1850. Rymer's melodramatic and voluminous narrative – it comprises over 660,000 words in total – maintains the connection between being the victim of a vampire and the involuntary experience of sustained repose and lassitude, even though Rymer seems only barely concerned with the philosophical or spiritual associations of these states. What this shows us is that this clustering of ideas was so commonplace by the mid-nineteenth

century that it even occurs in a largely unphilosophical, 'pulp' text.
Vampire-induced lassitude appears several times and, in many closely
connected forms, in *Varney*. Following the narrative's opening depiction
of a vampire attack, for instance, the text's initial victim, Flora
Bannerworth, describes how 'a strange drowsiness at time creeps over'
her (*Varney*, 38), including at the very moment when she describes this
sensation. The text's medical authority, Mr. Chillingworth, confirms the
simultaneously mental and physical reality of this involuntary idleness by
suggesting that Flora is 'labouring under the effect of some narcotic'
(*Varney*, 39), even though Rymer makes clear that there is no way Flora
could have ingested such a substance. Later in the narrative, several more
pronounced versions of this 'drowsiness' are engendered by subsequent
visitations of Varney. In one instance, Flora is cast into a 'death-like trance'
(*Varney*, 84), but is soon revived. In another her repeated bouts of lassitude
and their attendant altered states of consciousness culminate in her sleep-
walking into the arms of Varney himself:

> How strange and spectral-like she moves along; there seems no speculation
> in her countenance but with a strange and gliding step, she walks like some
> dim shadow of the past in that ancient garden. She is very pale, and on her
> brow there is the stamp of suffering[.] [. . .] Does she now walk forth with
> a disordered intellect, the queen of some fantastic realm, viewing the
> material world with eyes that are not of earth[?] [. . .] No; thank Heaven,
> such is not the case. Flora Bannerworth is not mad, but under the strong
> influence of some eccentric dream, which has pictured to her mind images
> which have no home but in the airy realms of imagination. (*Varney*, 270–1)

Rymer's exposition may be clunky and melodramatic, but a passage such as
this makes a set of assertions about vampiric victimhood that correspond
exactly with what we saw of Coleridge's 'Christabel', or indeed of Brontë's
Wuthering Heights. The mental state into which Flora sinks throughout
Rymer's narrative is one that stands extremely close to the world of
'spectres', ghosts and fantasies. It is one that seems to close the gap between
the living and the dead (it is for this reason that Flora appears as 'some dim
shadow of the past' in her 'ancient garden'). And it is one utterly distinct
from 'speculation', that same term that Keats used to describe the opposite
of aesthetic consciousness. Again here too, we should note the 'paleness' of
the victim figure and the association of her imaginative, dream-like, subrational state with 'suffering'. What we are witnessing here, in other words,
is the same cluster of ideas that Coleridge, Polidori and Brontë associate
with the vampire, and the same cluster of ideas that mark both Romantic
and mid-century accounts of aesthetic consciousness. Flora views 'the

material world with eyes that are not of earth', simultaneously enchanted and suffering, just as Arnold's 'gipsy child' 'wears' the 'mood' of 'Some angel [. . .] in an alien planet born', or just as Tennyson's lotos-eaters are characterized by their unearthly, uncanny 'mild-eyed melancholy' ('LE', 27).

By the time Brontë writes *Wuthering Heights*, therefore, the figure of the vampire is very clearly associated with the closely connected states of pervasive inertia and aesthetic consciousness. Equally clearly, this very association is a means of casting doubt on the social and moral value of idle aesthetic contemplation as that state was outlined – and celebrated – by Romantic poetics. The tendency to think negatively about aesthetic consciousness in this manner is very probably augmented by the wide-spread popularity of the early and mid-century thought surrounding the 'gospel of work' that we examined in the Chapter 3 of this study, or by the closely connected negative portrayals of aesthetic idleness such as Tennyson's 'Lotos-Eaters' that bolster and complement the 'gospel of work'. The years after Romanticism up until 1848 are in this sense quite firmly set against any positive conception of idle aesthetic contemplation. And Brontë's *Wuthering Heights* and Rymer's *Varney the Vampyre* can now be added to that broad sweep of antagonism. As we turn now to examples of vampire literature from the 1870s and 90s, however, we might expect to observe something of a rapprochement between this genre and positive conceptions of aesthetic consciousness. After all, as we have seen at some length, the years after 1847 are marked by a series of, in one sense, strikingly positive accounts human aesthetic capability. Mill's highly influential political economic thought from 1848 advocated a stationary state fostering aesthetic contemplation for all, and justified this contention through the individual and social health it would engender. Ruskin, Arnold and Pater's cultural and aesthetic theory from the 1850s and 1860s likewise celebrates human aesthetic powers of creation and contemplation and contends for the centrality of these to any successful society. Strikingly, however, there is no such change of tack in the field of vampire literature. On the contrary, the genre's discomfort with aesthetic consciousness in fact increases mark-edly across the second half of the century, to the extent that it becomes a convention to wage a kind of total war against a text's vampire antagonist. *Varney the Vampire* dramatized a frequently laughable oscillation between seeking to destroy the seemingly nocturnal, criminally active vampire, and then treating him utterly civilly and respectfully when he appeared in daylight, human, aristocratic form. In both Le Fanu and Stoker's handling of the vampire narrative, however, as soon as the vampire is revealed, it is

the unflinching duty of every character to purge the world of their existence. This heightening of antagonism against the world of aesthetic
consciousness that the vampire increasingly directly represents in the last
decades of the century is also the occasion for the repeated deployment of
the ethos of 'work' as the most potent counterforce to vampiric aesthetic
languor. In other words, neither Mill, Ruskin, Arnold nor Pater's positive
handling of aesthetic passivity would seem to be as powerful and influential, in the realm of late nineteenth-century vampire fiction, as the 'gospel
of work' itself. As we shall see, the vampire narrative becomes the occasion
to dramatize the triumph of diligent, social, moral labour over apparently
solipsistic and transcendent idleness.

Sheridan Le Fanu's short story 'Carmilla' was first serialized in John
Christian Freund's short-lived periodical *The Dark Blue* in 1871–2, and
then appeared in Le Fanu's famous collection *In a Glass Darkly* in 1872.
It holds several pertinences for the present analysis. It is firstly a partial
rewriting of Coleridge's 'Christabel': Le Fanu expands Coleridge's central
motif of the sexualized female vampire imposing troubled aesthetic consciousness on her also female victims into a more conventionally realist
narrative. Secondly, when 'Carmilla' appears as the final text of *In a Glass
Darkly*, Le Fanu casts it as another case study of his fictional scientist,
Dr Martin Hesselius. This framing device aligns the text with the supposed
scientific cataloguing and explaining of a large range of apparently occult and
spiritual phenomena. In this way, Le Fanu sets up a situation in which the
aesthetic consciousness at his narrative's heart is at least in part the matter of
pre-scientific superstition, implying that this state and anything that brings it
about could be inhibited and controlled with proper medical practice. This
is a subtle but important rebuttal of positive and creative conceptions of idle
consciousness such as those penned by Arnold and Pater, and one that also
anticipates the medicalization of aesthetic contemplation that takes place at
the beginning of the twentieth century. Thirdly, 'Carmilla' is also a direct
precursor to what becomes the most famous and the most influential of
vampire narratives, Stoker's *Dracula*, in that it dramatizes the purging of idle
aesthetic consciousness from polite society by the (primarily male) powers of
modern, scientific civilization. It is in this form that the fictionally dramatized argument against aesthetic consciousness will remain firmly lodged in
the public consciousness well beyond the nineteenth century.

　　Le Fanu's text, then, combines extended reference to its protagonists'
physical idleness with detailed attention to the altered states of consciousness that attend on that idleness. And more clearly than any vampire text

before it, 'Carmilla' makes these states of being and states of mind the shared property of both the vampire and her victims. Le Fanu's eponymous vampire, for example, is repeatedly characterized by her physical inactivity. Her first full description in the narrative has it that she 'was slender, and wonderfully graceful', '[e]xcept that her movements were languid – *very* languid' ('Carmilla', 262). Carmilla's repeated victimization of young girls in the narrative – including of the text's narrator, Laura – also engenders in these victims a kind of physical and mental paralysis, and a posture of languor, that parallels her own habit of sleeping every day until noon. In terms of the states of consciousness that accompany this physical idleness, there are several occasions in her narrative where Laura records Carmilla's discourse with her, and its effect upon her. Here is the first of those descriptions:

> She used to place her pretty arms about my neck, draw me to her, and laying her cheek to mine, murmur with her lips near my ear, '[. . .] In the rapture of my enormous humiliation I live in your warm life, and you shall die – die, sweetly die – into mine. I cannot help it; as I draw near to you, you, in your turn, will draw near to others, and learn the rapture of that cruelty, which yet is love [. . .]'.
> [. . .] From these [. . .] embraces, [. . .] I used to wish to extricate myself; but my energies seemed to fail me. Her murmured words sounded like a lullaby in my ear, and soothed my resistance into a trance, from which I only seemed to recover myself when she withdrew her arms. ('Carmilla', 263–4)

Carmilla's embrace is frequently read as primarily sexual. Fred Botting, for example, considers 'contemporary visions of sexual, primitive regression and independent femininity' to be 'embodied in Carmilla's languor and fluidity'.[8] But Le Fanu here also renders this embrace a poetic seduction that 'soothes' its victim 'into a trance'. It is poetic because of the amplified and literary register of Carmilla's speech and because of Laura's characterization of it as 'like a lullaby'. A repetitive and highly rhetorical phrase such as 'you shall die – die, sweetly die – into mine' thus casts Carmilla as poetic seductress, and as one who can express the rapturous beauty and experiential world-unto-itself that is supposed to be found in aesthetic consciousness. This connection between Carmilla and rapturous, poetic eloquence is underlined at several other points in the narrative. A little later, for instance, the dichotomy between physical repose and intense intellectual activity that we have seen in Keats and Shelley (and that can be found in countless other early nineteenth-century expositions of aesthetic consciousness) is again made clear. Carmilla's physical indolence when walking with Laura's family is apparently 'a bodily languor in which her mind did not sympathize. She was always an animated talker, and very intelligent' ('Carmilla', 265).[9] Such qualifications are repeated so often in the narrative that it is no exaggeration to say that, in the scheme of Le Fanu's plot, it is poetic, mental activity that Carmilla represents. The very similarly named General Spielsdorf and Doctor Spielsberg both embody scientific knowledge and its moral, classless work ethic. It is they who bring about the text's dénouement and secure Carmilla's destruction by their hard work and steady application of knowledge. Mademoiselle De Lafontaine, meanwhile, acts as a Hesselius figure within the narrative itself, observing, for example, the supposed connection between intense moonlight and 'special spiritual activity' ('Carmilla', 251), and thereby keeping in view the wider significance Le Fanu instils into this vampire narrative. Laura serves as the innocent blank slate of a next generation, ready to be guided by correct authority (the work ethic of the older generation), or alternatively seduced by the negative possibilities of human experience (those exemplified by Carmilla). And Carmilla herself, in a scheme that we will see repeated very clearly in *Dracula*, therefore serves to denote an ancient, pre-scientific and aristocratic world that is characterized by its almost constant repose and by its indulgent and total participation in the aesthetic pleasures of the mind. Carmilla's aristocratic connection is made in the text by, amongst other things, her startling likeness to an ancient portrait belonging to Laura's household, and by the eventual revelation that she is in fact the same person as the subject of that painting. This is a motif Le Fanu borrows entirely – but considerably enhances – from Rymer.

In terms of the changing reputation of the categories of idleness and aesthetic consciousness across the century, this clustering of significances in the figure of Carmilla is very important. What we are seeing here is a synthesis of two separate intellectual and political stances on idleness that have developed in the decades leading up to the 1870s. On the one hand we have the notion that we first came across in Mill, that aristocratic leisure is morally wrong because it is entirely financed by the overwork of the lower classes. Marx's version of this idea has also been fully formulated by this moment. This is the notion that aristocratic leisure came into being following a series of legal thefts of communal and lower-class property by the aristocracy.[10] This conception of idleness, in other words, is one configured entirely as an issue of class politics, as a small group of immoral usurpers living parasitically on the intense toil of their downtrodden fellow citizens. To be aristocratic and from an ancient family, from this perspective, is to be immorally and brazenly idle. On the other hand, however, we have the notion of idleness that we have traced more precisely in this study and that is represented most clearly in a text like Tennyson's 'Lotos-Eaters'. This is the widespread conception of idleness as a problematic state of being in terms of its disconnection from the morality of action and responsibility, but also in terms of the solipsistic, troubled and troubling states of mind that state engenders. Idle contemplation, in other words, is conceived increasingly often, across the century, as a troubled encounter with self-consciousness – as it was in Arnold's 'Scholar-Gipsy', for instance – or as a wilful casting of oneself into the world of the ghostly and uncanny – as it was in *Wuthering Heights* or, briefly, in Shelley's 'Mont Blanc'. Thus, whereas Keats daringly celebrated the experience of metaphysical 'mysteries' and 'doubts' and the radically permeable identity politics of aesthetic consciousness, what we are seeing in the figure of Carmilla is that such experiences, and the posture of languor and listlessness that brings them about, have become potential synonyms for villainous immorality, and dangerous otherworldliness, by the early 1870s. The vampire, up until this moment, had frequently denoted the contemplative side of these issues. He or she had also been associated loosely with aristocratic privilege, in Rymer's *Varney* and Polidori's 'Vampyre', for example. But it is in Le Fanu's and then Stoker's hands that this clustering of ideas thoroughly fuses the immorality of class politics with the dangerous, otherworldly seductions of aesthetic consciousness to create a dangerous and multifaceted villain and criminal. What late-century vampire fiction effects, in other words, is the gothicization and villainization of any form of idleness, be it aristocratic or contemplative.

The central incident in Le Fanu's narrative is Carmilla's vampiric attack on Laura. In terms of Dr Hesselius's scientific methodology which frames the entire narrative, this event exemplifies the vampire's dual existence in both the material and the spiritual worlds. From our perspective, what this means is that Laura's victimhood plunges her into the transcendent world of aesthetic contemplation in such a manner that she has no control over her experiences. The attack takes the form a troubled half-sleep again reminiscent of 'Christabel'. Laura experiences something like 'a nightmare' but with full consciousness 'of being asleep', and witnesses a prowling 'monstrous cat' that then changes into a 'female figure' as still as 'a block of stone'. During this event she is also bitten 'deep into' her 'breast', 'as if' by 'two large needles [. . .] an inch or two apart' ('Carmilla', 278). We should note that these two manifestations of Carmilla during the attack follow the patterns we have already traced for aesthetic contemplation's depiction across contemporary gothic literature. The cat's bestial and primitive associations are the same as those found in Heathcliff's animality in *Wuthering Heights*, while the otherworldly stillness of the female figure amplifies Carmilla's connection with pervasive inertia and repose. It is this final quality that is the most lasting in Laura's victimization, because this attack gives rise to her own pervasive and persistent languor:

> For some nights I slept profoundly; but still every morning I felt the same lassitude, and a languor weighed upon me all day. I felt myself a changed girl. A strange melancholy was stealing over me, a melancholy that I would not have interrupted. Dim thoughts of death began to open, and an idea that I was slowly sinking took gentle, and, somehow, not unwelcome, possession of me. If it was sad, the tone of mind which this induced was also sweet. Whatever it might be, my soul acquiesced in it. [...] Certain vague and strange sensations visited me in my sleep. [...] This was soon accompanied by dreams that seemed interminable, and were so vague that I could never recollect their scenery and persons, or any one connected portion of their action. But they left an awful impression, and a sense of exhaustion, as if I had passed through a long period of great mental exertion and danger. ('Carmilla', 281–2)

Once again, a passage like this must be read as an account of poetic, aesthetic consciousness. Laura's 'long period[s] of great mental exertion and danger' parallel the elongated experience described in Shelley's 'Mont Blanc', for instance. Both are periods of paralysis that promote heightened intellectual and spiritual activity. Laura's 'sweet' but 'melancholy' tone of mind and '[d]im thoughts of death' likewise encapsulate the experience of 'mysteries' and 'doubts' to be found in Keats, in Shelley and in many of their contemporaries. That these thoughts and experiences take 'gentle' but 'not unwelcome [...] possession' of Laura thus recalls the involuntary or half-involuntary experiences of aesthetic consciousness recorded, and alluded to so frequently, around the turn of the nineteenth century. This is therefore a portrait of Laura's descent into an extended and sustained state of idle aesthetic contemplation, into a state comparable to the morbidly selfish consciousness of Tennyson's 'mild-eyed', 'melancholy' lotos-eaters. In Laura's case too, this pervasive state of mind is soon reflected in her external body. Invoking a movement towards Aubrey or Flora's insensibility (in Polidori and Rymer's texts), Laura records how she 'had grown pale', with eyes 'dilated and darkened underneath', and how the 'languor which' she 'had long felt began to display itself in' her 'countenance' ('Carmilla', 282).

To purge the world of the vampiric Carmilla, as Laura's father and his accomplices do in the final stages of Le Fanu's narrative, is therefore to rid the world of the instigator of poetic melancholy and its troubling, absorbing otherworldliness. It is also to destroy the embodiment of contemplative idleness and the historical class that supposedly enshrines that activity as the pinnacle of human engagements. In place of this prioritization of aesthetic consciousness, Le Fanu's scheme positions diligent work and the collation of verifiable, scientific knowledge. In other words, it is as if Keats's negative capability, the capacity for ignoring facts and clarity and for immersing oneself in the complex possibilities of contemplative uncertainty, had been configured as the ultimate enemy to all polite civilization. Logically, therefore, we must note that, while Le Fanu's narrative dramatizes the undesirability of aesthetic consciousness in contemporary social life, it also thereby demonstrates the success and abundance of Keatsian and other contemplative models of being throughout the century. Vampire literature would surely have no need to enact the overthrow of aesthetic consciousness in this heightened and almost apocalyptic manner, were Keatsian thought only a marginal and derivative presence in the period's culture. 'Carmilla' show us, consequently, that the aesthetic and cultural projects of Mill, of Ruskin, of Arnold and of Pater are the collective target of vampire literature by this moment. Aesthetic consciousness may have been championed in problematic form by the cultural theorists we examined in Chapter 4, but their central contention, that idle contemplation and the experience of beauty hold a central role in human life, is clearly one worth attacking.

This contextualization, moreover, also works the other way around. 'Carmilla' is first published just a couple of years after Pater pens the essay that becomes the 'Conclusion' to his *Renaissance,* and Le Fanu's text is republished in *In a Glass Darkly* just one year before *Studies in the History of the Renaissance* is first published. When the controversy surrounding the 'Conclusion' breaks, therefore, we might say that 'Carmilla' exemplifies the negativity with which aesthetic consciousness can be conceived at this precise historical moment. A text like Pater's 'Conclusion' is therefore diametrically opposed to the popular conception of aesthetic contemplation to be found in the period's vampire fiction. We can now see, therefore, that to cast human life as primarily of value for the complexity and depth of its aesthetic experience (as Pater's essay does very dramatically) is to align oneself in all seriousness with exactly the set of priorities associated with vampiric evil in Le Fanu's text. But Pater should not be considered at all naïve, or unfortunate, in this gesture. *The Renaissance* might be said consciously to throw its lot in with the vampire herself. For in a passage we did not have occasion to consider in Chapter 4, Pater even goes so far as to contend that the *Mona Lisa* is itself an embodiment of vampiric knowledge in a positive sense:

> Hers [. . .] is a beauty wrought out from within upon the flesh, the deposit, little cell by cell, of strange thoughts and fantastic reveries and exquisite passions. Set it for a moment beside one of those white Greek goddesses or beautiful women of antiquity, and how would they be troubled by this beauty, into which the soul with all its maladies has passed! All the thoughts and experience of the world have etched and moulded there, in that which they have of power to refine and make expressive the outward form, the animalism of Greece, the lust of Rome, the reverie of the middle age with its spiritual ambition and imaginative loves, the return of the Pagan world, the sins of the Borgias. She is older than the rocks among which she sits; like the vampire, she has been dead many times, and learned the secrets of the grave; and has been a diver in deep seas, and keeps their fallen day about her[.]
> (*Renaissance*, 98–9)

This is a portrait of aesthetic and experiential complexity that would align well with Ruskin's notion of the northern 'feverish' imagination, or with Keats's revelling in 'uncertainties, mysteries' and 'doubts'. Pater celebrates Leonardo's painting for its 'strange thoughts and fantastic reveries', terms that would not be out of place in 'Carmilla' itself, or in *Wuthering Heights*. In other words, Pater's conception of aesthetic consciousness is overtly and unashamedly of a piece with that of Heathcliff, of Carmilla, and of the countless victims of vampiric aestheticism in the period's popular literature. Pater's Mona Lisa thus shares the vampiric melancholy that Rymer begins to explore in her sense of the 'fallen day',[11] and Carmilla's centuries-long knowledge of 'sin' and 'love'. To contend for the complex aesthetic capabilities of man at this historical moment is thus to take issue with the intensely conservative gothic imagination, and with its repeated homage to polite society and its Carlylean gospel of work. For vampire literature's advocacy of these dutiful and virtuous aspects of human life is a consistent feature of its narratives from Polidori through to Brontë, Rymer, Le Fanu and, as we shall see in a moment, Stoker as well. What we are seeing in this chapter, therefore, is the deeply reactionary case against contemplative idleness and aesthetic consciousness that has its roots in early nineteenth-century aesthetic discourse, but that finds its fullest and most developed form in the final decades of that century. It is most probably this context that also explains the pronounced and dangerous homosexuality of Le Fanu's vampiric antagonist, going as it does beyond the maternal connotations of Coleridge's Geraldine. This feature of 'Carmilla' invokes Pater's own homosexuality and the dangerous influence he therefore represents to contemporary norms. As Franco Moretti outlines, contemporary gothic literature is '[i]lliberal in a deep sense': '[t]o think for oneself, to follow one's own interests: these are the real dangers that this literature wants to exorcise'.[12] Le Fanu and Stoker thus make the case against individualistic, original, idle contemplation, and against Pater and his liberal aesthetic colleagues, in a complex and fully realized form that had not been seen until this precise historical moment. And by doing so they launch a powerful attack against the logic and appeal of passivity, repose and their attendant state of aesthetic consciousness.

In terms of its handling of idle aesthetic contemplation, Bram Stoker's *Dracula*, which was published in 1897, largely follows the pattern laid down by Le Fanu's 'Carmilla'. But because Stoker's novel is considerably longer, considerably more in-depth and because it amplifies and enhances Le Fanu's depictions of both aesthetic consciousness and that state's supposed alternatives, *Dracula* must be seen as an even more dramatic and urgent attempt to rebut the logic of texts like Pater's *Renaissance*. The very existence of Stoker's novel – ignoring for the moment its success and longevity – might thus be said to demonstrate the continued pertinence and allure of positive conceptions of idleness right up until the end of the century. As with earlier vampire literature, however, it is remarkable that the abundance of recent criticism of Stoker's novel has not had much to say about the contemplative inertia central to the text. All of the vampire figures described in the narrative cast their many victims into cataleptic, contemplative and other-worldly states (which the novel's various narrators describe at length), and all are intimately associated with landscapes and scenes that are the typical instigators of the poetic reverie throughout the nineteenth century. And yet when the vampiric victims' passivity is mentioned in scholarly commentary, it is in order to invoke some other idea entirely. David Glover, for example, refers to the novel's 'frequent evocation of states of reverie, unconsciousness, dream, and daydream' only as a means to discuss the genre of 'fantasy'.[13] Moretti, comparably, in his in many ways masterful treatment of the novel in *Signs Taken for Wonders*, renders Stoker's victims' passivity a comment not on those states themselves but on the condition of capitalist exploitation.[14] As was the case above with Tennyson's 'Lotos-Eaters', therefore, the present study allows for a direct consideration of what is in many ways *Dracula*'s central subject matter.

The numerous vampiric attacks in Stoker's novel – those carried out on Jonathan and Mina Harker and Lucy Westenra, for example – all share some very direct similarities, many of which will recall features of vampire literature from across the century. Any consideration of these incidents must begin with the ultimately abortive attack on Jonathan Harker that occurs at the beginning of the novel in 'Castle Dracula' itself. This is because Stoker uses this episode to set up the parameters of his vampiric attacks in thorough detail, so that in the remainder of the novel he can simply refer back to this primary event in a kind of symbolic shorthand. The first thing to note of this episode is the role Stoker gives to the beautiful scenery visible from the seemingly long-disused rooms that Jonathan has discovered. At the scene's opening, this scenery is described at some length:

> To the west was a great valley, and then, rising far away, great jagged mountain fastnesses, rising peak on peak, the sheer rock studded with mountain ash and thorn, whose roots clung in cracks and crevices and crannies of the stone. [...] The windows were curtainless, and the yellow moonlight, flooding in through the diamond panes, enabled one to see even colours [...]. The soft moonlight soothed, and the wide expanse without gave a sense of freedom which refreshed me. (*Dracula*, 40–1)

One might consider these details incidental, or as simply following the strand of the gothic tradition that includes frequent loco-description as a respite from its relentless action. Anne Radcliffe is perhaps the fullest exponent of this latter strategy, but Mary Shelley's *Frankenstein* (1818) also has passages that could be described in this way. But Stoker's deployment of this conventionally sublime scene and its attendant moonlight holds a different role here. This role is hinted at in the final line of my quotation, and is thoroughly confirmed at the episode's end. There, the three young female vampires depart from the scene (with their horrific repast) by 'fad[ing] into the rays of moonlight and pass[ing] out through the window'. Jonathan's final glimpse of them is 'outside', 'for a moment', 'before they entirely faded away' (*Dracula*, 44). At their entrance, likewise, the female figures are also associated with the 'yellow moonlight'. Not only are they first seen '[i]n the moonlight', but their existence appears to be an extension of that phenomenon: 'though the moonlight was behind them, they threw no shadow on the floor' (*Dracula*, 41–2). Now, if we add to these details the fact that the effect of these vampiric figures on Jonathan is to subdue, to relax and to pacify him, into what he describes – familiarly to us from Le Fanu – as 'a languorous ecstasy', in which he simply 'wait[s] with beating heart' (*Dracula*, 43), then we will see that Stoker's association of his vampire figures with the moonlit night is extremely thorough. The final line of my quotation above in fact anticipates the very experiential details of the vampires' appearance, and in this manner renders the female vampires of a piece with the striking natural phenomena outside the room's window. 'The soft moonlight soothed' Jonathan, with this 'soothing' serving to anticipate the vampires' casting of him into a mode of involuntary repose, of languor and 'ecstasy'. Similarly, 'the wide expanse without gave a sense of freedom' to the scene's protagonist, just as the vampires' appearance brings with it a sense of sexual freedom that Jonathan considers ignoble and inappropriate. The moonlit scene is thus expressed as casting Jonathan into the same sort of half-consciousness that the female vampires engender, the same half-voluntary repose that we have seen throughout this chapter, and into the same kind of inert 'stupor' (*Dracula*, 247) that Dracula himself casts Jonathan later in the narrative (in the attack where he has Mina feed on his own blood).

What these details amount to, therefore, is a situation in which vampiric attack is extremely closely associated with the states of trance-like, idle but intense, aesthetic contemplation that are brought about, in the century's literature, through landscape contemplation. Recall, for instance, Tennyson's mariners' celebration of their constant state of 'Falling asleep in a half-dream' ('LE', 101) that comes from 'watch[ing] the crisping ripples on the beach' and the 'tender curving lines of creamy spray'. Or the equivalent scene in Shelley's 'Mont Blanc', where the poet's 'trance' is engendered and sustained by the same sort of sublime mountain scenery that Stoker deploys at Dracula's castle. In this key scene from *Dracula*, therefore, as in its many recurrences throughout Stoker's novel, the vampire figure personifies and embodies the dangerous potential of such apparently indulgent states of contemplative repose. The female vampires that attack Jonathan, and Dracula himself throughout the remainder of the narrative, thus connote poetic consciousness and its problematic withdrawal from social virtues in a manner highly comparable to Le Fanu's handling of these ideas in 'Carmilla'. Stoker's portrayal of these ideas might even be described as more connected to earlier depictions of aesthetic consciousness than Le Fanu's, because he includes in the Jonathan Harker scene the same troubling possibility that haunted Shelley and Tennyson's accounts of idle contemplation. This is the apparent danger of mentally and spiritually leaving one's body so thoroughly, and surrendering oneself to the physical complexity of the landscape one is contemplating to such an extent, that the contemplator is unable to return to quotidian physicality and rationality. In the Jonathan Harker scene such a fate would seem to befall one who is successfully preyed upon by the female vampires, because the repast they are given by Dracula – the 'half-smothered child' in its 'dreadful bag' (*Dracula*, 44) – is carried away with the vampire figures as they fade back into the moonlight. The contemplative self might be annihilated by its radical aesthetic consciousness, in other words. To fall prey to the vampire would be to leave the human, quotidian world and to be cast into the intense and otherworldly physicality of the landscape. This is the exact danger we saw Shelley court when his 'spirit' seemed to 'fail' in his mountain's gothic intricacies.

This female vampire scene is so structurally and thematically important to *Dracula* that its details, its dangers and its connotations are invoked again and again throughout Stoker's novel. Let us look, for example, at Dracula's attack on Lucy Westenra that takes place once the narrative has moved to England, and to Whitby. The outline of this episode, which is narrated by Jonathan's then fiancée Mina, directly echoes Flora Bannerworth's sleep-walking towards her vampiric persecutor in Rymer's *Varney*. In both Rymer and Stoker's hands, in other words, trance-like sleep is shown to have a strong affinity with vampiric consciousness. Where Stoker's scene departs from Rymer's, however, is in the dramatic realization of the vampire's potential, and in its subtle layering of contemporary intellectual and cultural resonances.[15] Here is Mina's account of what takes place once Lucy has reached her unconscious goal:

> There was a bright full moon, with heavy black, driving clouds, which threw the whole scene into a fleeting diorama of light and shade as they sailed across. For a moment or two I could see nothing, as the shadow of a cloud obscured St Mary's Church and all around it. Then as the cloud passed I could see the ruins of the Abbey coming into view; and as the edge of a narrow band of light as sharp as a sword-cut moved along, the church and the churchyard became gradually visible. [. . .] [T]here, on our favourite seat, the silver light of the moon struck a half-reclining figure, snowy white. [. . .] [I]t seemed to me as though something dark stood behind the seat where the white figure shone, and bent over it. What it was, whether man or beast, I could not tell [. . .]. When I got almost to the top I could see the seat and the white figure, for I was now close enough to distinguish it even through the spells of shadow. There was undoubtedly something, long and black, bending over the half-reclining white figure. (*Dracula*, 87–8)

Just before this scene, Dracula's arrival in England involves his supernatural control over mist and clouds, as he uses these to shroud the ship that is under his control. This scene's combination of 'a bright full moon' and 'heavy black, driving clouds' thus represents the vampiric state of being both as it was introduced in the Jonathan Harker scene and as it has recently been expressed in Stoker's narrative. Once again, in other words, it is implied that the landscape and atmospheric conditions surrounding Lucy's victimization contain, denote or are to some extent synonymous with its vampire antagonist. In accordance with this scheme, we should note here too how the victim's interaction with these atmospheric light conditions anticipates and encapsulates the interaction that will subsequently take place between that victim and the vampire itself. In the Jonathan Harker scene, the protagonist was first 'soothed' and given the experience of 'freedom'. Here, Lucy is 'struck' by the 'sliver light of the moon' in a direct foreshadowing of Dracula subsequently bending over and biting her. There is also another echo of the details of the Jonathan Harker scene that should be observed in this passage. That is the reference to Lucy's semi-consciousness, to her being under the vampire's control and therefore somewhere intermediate between the physical and spiritual realms. Of course, the fact that Lucy has arrived on her and Mina's 'favourite seat' by means of trance-like sleep-walking serves to throw the veil of dreamlike half-knowledge over the scene as a whole. But in this passage Stoker exemplifies his strategy of referring in shorthand to the parameters of the Jonathan Harker scene in order to allude to the fuller account of troubled, otherworldly consciousness he developed there. Here, then, in a term that invokes the half-sleep related to aesthetic repose since the 1780s, and Jonathan Harker's half-consciousness during his attack, Stoker twice describes Lucy as 'half-reclining'. This term is noteworthy, not only because the posture it refers to is not precisely imaginable. Stoker's term, rather, has the effect of rendering Lucy a half-participant in the erotic drama of her attack, but also half-reposed, half-inert and, because of what was at stake in the Jonathan Harker scene, half in this world and half somewhere else.

Once again, therefore, the vampiric attack, in Stoker's hands, invokes the troubled aesthetic contemplation that was previously invoked by landscapes of sublime beauty. Dracula thus emerges from the mist in his arrival in England, and attacks from the moonlight in this Whitby scene, because he is the embodiment of the aesthetic consciousness that such phenomena traditionally bring about. And in this instance, his largely successful, though interrupted attack does indeed cast Lucy to a large extent out of the mortal, quotidian world and into a troubled, otherworldly state of being that is synonymous with the landscape and its atmospheric conditions. Stoker makes this explicit just a few pages after the attack itself, when he has Lucy recount her own experience of that night:

> '[. . .] Then I have a vague memory of something long and dark with red eyes, just as we saw in the sunset, and something very sweet and very bitter all around me at once; and then I seemed sinking into deep green water, and there was a singing in my ears, as I have heard there is to drowning men; and then everything seemed passing away from me; my soul seemed to go out from my body and float about the air. I seem to remember that once the West Lighthouse was right under me, and then there was some sort of agonizing feeling, as if I were in an earthquake, and I came back and found you shaking my body. I saw you do it before I felt you.' (*Dracula*, 94)

This account stands so close to the tradition of positive conceptions of aesthetic consciousness with which we began this study that it could be read as a rewriting of the central incident in Shelley's 'Mont Blanc', for example. This is a real possibility, furthermore, because, as Glover records, Stoker lectured on Shelley and other Romantic authors while an undergraduate at Trinity College, Dublin.[16] Lucy's experience of Dracula's attack here is one of being plunged into the physicality of the Whitby scene. Thus, she at first 'seemed' to be 'sinking into' the adjacent sea's 'deep green water', and is then cast 'out from' her 'body' to 'float about in the air'. The logic of this movement follows both Shelley's poem and the earlier details of Stoker's own narrative. It directly evokes 'Mont Blanc' because in that poem too, to contemplate the scene around the poet was to 'go out from' one's 'body', to 'float about' and to get experientially involved in its physical parameters. It follows Stoker's narrative up until this point because the recent association of Dracula with clouds themselves means that for Lucy to find herself right above the 'West Lighthouse' is for her to move like, or behave in accordance with, the fast-moving clouds in the windy moonlit scene. What Lucy's short narrative invokes, therefore, is exactly the same fate that befell the smothered infant in the Jonathan Harker scene. Lucy is carried off into the natural physicality that Dracula represents, and is only rescued, and returned to her mortal body, by the interruption and intervention of Mina. Mina's shaking of Lucy is registered negatively first, as an 'agonizing feeling', because the experience of aesthetic contemplation is so seductive, consuming and pleasurable that it represents a world unto itself. But in now speaking from her rational, quotidian perspective, such intervention must be a source of gratitude and self-completion: 'I came back'. Such a sentiment might be paraphrased by the Cowperian phrase we saw Keats allude to throughout his account of poetic self-annihilation: Lucy is 'restored to herself' following a contemplative departure from the confines of her physical body.

The striking similarity between this account of Dracula's attack and the many positive conceptions of aesthetic consciousness from earlier in the century should not for a moment lead us to think that Stoker's novel is significantly ambivalent in its handling of idle contemplation and its transcendent potential, however. On the contrary, Dracula is so firmly the villain in Stoker's scheme that Lucy's experience is unanimously understood, by her and by the text's other characters, as one of extreme and horrendous victimhood. Moreover, Stoker utilizes the now longstanding connection in vampire discourse between victimhood and deathly lassitude in order to cast Lucy's state as one deserving extreme pity. From the night of the attack until her death, Lucy's languor and passivity augments in the same manner as that of Carmilla's victims. She is at first often 'in a half-dreamy state, with an odd look on her face that' Mina cannot 'make out'. But this quickly changes to a 'drawn, haggard look under her eyes', and to her being constantly 'languid and tired' (*Dracula*, 91). Before her death, her existence is characterized by 'long spells of oblivion' (*Dracula*, 124), as if again her passivity connotes periods of absence from her physical body and existence elsewhere. In Stoker's hands this slow decline into another world is primarily the occasion for diligent pity and the exercise of an intense scientific work ethic by Van Helsing, Seward and his other cast of characters. At Van Helsing's instruction, for example, Lucy's life is prolonged several times by blood transfusions. Structurally, moreover, the fact that, following Lucy's attack, Stoker's entire plot takes place against a background of intense female suffering – first Lucy's then Mina's – means that neither readers nor characters are allowed to forget the regrettable and tragic effects of Dracula's attacks.

This emphasis on vampiric victimhood in *Dracula* means that there is an almost constant reference to states of contemplative and deathly inertia throughout the text, as well as to what Nina Auerbach and David Skal call the 'sleep that may not be sleep' that brings 'dreams that may not be dreams'.[17] Renfield, for instance, Dr Seward's psychiatric patient who is somehow psychically connected to Dracula, is frequently shown to be intellectually elsewhere in the many reports we are given of his, at times vampiric, and at times victim-like behaviour. A characteristic instance of the latter is when Seward describes him as 'look[ing] into space with lacklustre eyes' (*Dracula*, 96), again recalling Tennyson's lotos-eaters or the protagonists of Polidori and Rymer's narratives. Jonathan Harker is also thrown into a kind of intellectual and physical paralysis on several occasions after his initial involvement with the female vampires. When he coincidentally glimpses Dracula on the streets of London, for example, he is at once effectively insensible and quickly slips into an odd, 'quiet' sleep (*Dracula*, 156). When Mina is later attacked in his company, likewise, on the occasion that Dracula has her feed on his own blood, Jonathan is described by Seward as 'flushed and breathing heavily as though in a stupor' (*Dracula*, 246). This, according to Van Helsing in Stoker's next paragraph, is the 'stupor [. . .] we know the Vampire can produce' (*Dracula*, 247). This attack is also the beginning of the long sections of Stoker's narrative in which Mina is subject to several sustained periods of the same languor and lassitude that afflicted Lucy. Several weeks after the attack (in Stoker's meticulous plotting), for example, Seward describes how she is now 'greatly changed'. His simple expansion on this statement is that '[t]he lethargy grows upon her' (*Dracula*, 291). Mina's victimization by Dracula also gives Stoker the chance to allude, yet again, to Jonathan Harker's female vampire scene in order to keep Dracula's relation to aesthetic contemplation in constant view. When Mina is first attacked she herself makes the connection explicitly, because by this point in the narrative Stoker's characters have shared their experiences in the form of the casebook that effectively becomes the novel:

> I closed my eyes, but could still see through my eyelids. [. . .] The mist grew thicker and thicker, and I could see now how it came in, for I could see it like smoke – or with the white energy of boiling water – pouring in, not through the window, but through the joinings of the door. [. . .] Suddenly the horror burst upon me that it was thus that Jonathan had seen those awful women growing into reality through the whirling mist in the moonlight, and in my dream I must have fainted, for all became black darkness. (*Dracula*, 227–8)

Again here, Dracula is strongly associated with cloud, smoke and mist; all three terms are used by Mina several times during the episode. And while Stoker's allusion to his earlier scene is slightly inaccurate – adding a 'whirling mist' to the original 'yellow moonlight' – the effect is nevertheless to invoke the fuller scene of aesthetic, landscape contemplation and therefore to associate vampiric evil with the contemplative experience of the natural world. Stoker's slip also supports the readings of vampiric influence developed above, because it demonstrates the extent to which he conceives his vampire antagonists as being embodiments of the natural environment. The female vampires apparently grew 'into reality' out of the 'mist in the moonlight'.

We must now turn to *Dracula*'s portrayal of the counterforce to this deathly aesthetic passivity and vampiric otherworldliness, Stoker's version of the 'gospel of work'. For the very significant proportion of *Dracula* that is devoted to the portrayal and exploration of contemplative inertia is ultimately overshadowed by the novel's thorough dramatization of a moral work ethic that Stoker intimately associates with Britain's pre-eminent commercial modernity. This is to say that the cast of characters that band together in Stoker's novel to pursue and destroy Dracula and the pervasive passivity he engenders are characterized above all by their diligent, informed and collective work ethic. And this group's array of social positions and particular skills provides coverage, and therefore clear representation, of the features of contemporary British economy. This is one of the ways in which Stoker synthesizes his well-documented portrayal of the 'new woman' with the strands of the novel that concern idleness and otherworldliness.[18] Because what Mina, a partial representative of this identity-type, brings to the aid of those seeking to purge the world of vampires, is her array of secretarial and analytic abilities, coupled with an energy and diligence that is almost absurdly frequently praised by Van Helsing. Alongside these skills, the novel's band of heroes possess Seward's medical knowledge and experience, Van Helsing's 'absolutely open mind' (*Dracula*, 106) and scientific knowledge of the occult, Quincey Morris's hunting abilities and loyalty, and Jonathan Harker's property and legal knowledge. In each case, however, it is a restless work ethic and willingness to do whatever is necessary that Stoker's narrative stresses. I have left out of this list Arthur Holmwood, because his role in the novel is not simply to contribute to the diligent pursuit and destruction of Dracula, but also to contrast Dracula in more direct terms. This is because Holmwood's aristocratic title – he becomes Lord Godalming during the narrative – parallels Dracula's own status as a 'Count' and a member of an ancient family. Stoker's contrast is striking primarily because it is Holmwood's money that bankrolls the activities of the band of heroes in pursuit of Dracula and his fellow vampires. Dracula, by contrast, hoards money for hundreds of years at a time, and thereby removes it from various nations' economies, only to then use it in the most immoral of possible ways. The contrast is thus between the active, moral and energetic use of money – Holmwood enables his fellow protagonists to use their professional and personal skills for the direct and immediate benefit of their society as a whole – and the solipsistic, selfish hoarding of money as a means to destroy and consume the lives of others and to infiltrate a society by criminal and violent means. In this manner, Stoker's moral scheme makes use of the same get-out clause to be found in 'Carmilla'. In that text, General Spielsdorf and Laura's father were also partially aristocratic, but their arduous pursuit of Carmilla aligned them with a belief in virtuous and upstanding 'work'. In both texts, in other words, the association of aristocracy with idleness – and thus with selfish, contemplative otherworldliness – can be erased by an individual's diligent and sincere participation in the prevailing ideology of work.

This model of work is quite clearly a focus of Stoker's novel from early in the narrative, and it is quite clearly deployed as a counterforce to contemplative inertia. Seward, in many ways the prime instigator of the hunt against Dracula, is the first to give voice to what Auerbach and Skal also recognize as the orthodox Carlylean celebration of 'work'.[19] In Seward's first diary entry in the novel, following Lucy's refusal of his offer of marriage, he describes his response to his lack of appetite and general low state as follows: 'I have a sort of empty feeling; nothing in the world seems of sufficient importance to be worth the doing ... As I knew that the only cure for this sort of thing was work, I went down among the patients' (Dracula, 61). This turn to 'work' is not only a cure for distress, here, because Seward's low mood is also one of idleness, lethargy and despondency. In other words, this brief moment pits diligent labour against solipsistic and immoral passivity in a manner reminiscent of the lotos-eaters, and in a manner that anticipates the struggle against vampiric repose that will fill the entire novel. In plot terms, Stoker also has this opposition lead here to Seward's particular attention to Renfield, and thus directly into the pursuit of Dracula himself. Stoker's narrative should also be understood to showcase and promote the products of the contemporary British work-ethic through its foregrounding of various recent and state-of-the-art technologies. The phonograph, for example, which Thomas Edison had invented in 1877, had only been conceived as a possible receptacle for an audio diary as recently as March 1896 by Cecil Wray,[20] but Stoker's band of heroes use it with ease and effectiveness. The activities of this group are also marked by fluent navigation of the various nineteenth-century technologies that had become a central part of British life by the 1890s. The telegraph, the typewriter, steamships, trains and the complex and detailed timetabling of these last two modes of transport, are all essential components of Stoker's entire plot, but are used in an integrated and natural manner by his band of heroes in particular. Again, therefore, this aspect of Stoker's novel seems designed to demonstrate the power, and the countless positive outcomes, of a nation's commitment to diligent and arduous productive labour.

Even more clearly and thoroughly than 'Carmilla', then, *Dracula* opposes a supposedly old world of aristocratic, contemplative and spiritual passivity against one of commercial modernity and diligent, ethical work. And since Stoker's narrative concludes when Dracula has been destroyed by the band of heroes that represent the latter elements of this opposition, it is also extremely clear that the novel demonizes and villainizes the attributes it associates with its eponymous antagonist. To purge the world of the qualities that Dracula embodies and represents is thus both to restore order and to clear the path for Britain's further development along the lines of diligent labour, technological advancement and the moral use of capital. Stoker's novel is in this sense a celebration of Britain's commercial modernity, and a warning that any predominance of aesthetic consciousness and contemplative inertia in an individual, or in a group of individuals, marks those figures out as pariahs, and as enemies of national progress. Yes, there may be a small chink in the armour of this total warfare against idle aesthetic consciousness in that the text's many vampiric victims find their experiences at least momentarily seductive, pleasurable and connected to the apparently 'free' realm of sexual desire. But again the Jonathan Harker episode with which we began our analysis of *Dracula* sets the novel's tone for dealing with this inconvenient fact. Sexual seduction by a stranger is very clearly immoral, and to enjoy it even momentarily is something to be deeply ashamed of. In other words, Stoker's repeated association of aesthetic consciousness with sexual freedom casts both states as immoral and as at odds with the novel's celebration of ethical, upstanding, public-spirited labour.

Having considered Stoker's intellectual scheme in its entirety, we are now in a position to stand back from *Dracula* and to consider nineteenth-century vampire fiction as a whole. For what we have seen across this chapter enables us to make a number of judgements about the associations, and the changing significances, of idle aesthetic contemplation across the century. The first thing to note of this field is that each vampire text considered in this chapter has invoked a slightly different version of poetic or more general aesthetic consciousness. Stoker's association of his vampiric antagonists with the kind of landscape contemplation found in Shelley or in Tennyson is thus not identical with the more Coleridgean flavour of Le Fanu's poetically talkative vampire, or the Keatsian frame of reference in Brontë's partially vampiric narrative. In addition to these models, we have also had occasion to refer to Cowper, to Byron, as well as to Arnold, and it would have been possible to perform the analysis of this literature in reference to a host of other contemporary authors and texts as well.

What this variation shows us, importantly, is that the century-long association between the figure of the vampire and the poetic instigator or exemplar of aesthetic consciousness is by no means fixed or narrow. It is not the case that Byron and Coleridge alone, for example, become associated with problematic aesthetic consciousness, and thus that the figure of the vampire is a means of critiquing their particular bodies or styles of thought. On the contrary, the wide range of associations for nineteenth-century vampires demonstrates the solidity of the connection between the figure of the vampire and the category of aesthetic consciousness itself. It is idle contemplation and its associated spiritual otherworldliness that is the constant target of this intensely conservative field of literary discourse. And this conceptual and categorical focus itself allows for the proliferation of subtly varied – though thematically consistent – vampire narratives across the century.

The second thing we are now in a position to note concerns the type of progression, or development, that takes place across nineteenth-century vampire fiction. What we have seen in this chapter is a very dramatic augmentation of the case against the vampiric representative of idle aesthetic consciousness as the century develops. Around 1845 to 1847, for instance, Rymer and Brontë's narratives handle their vampire figures with considerable ambivalence. Heathcliff, for example, is the villain of his narrative in many respects, but his and Catherine's shared, Keatsian consciousness is also the inner heart and the alluring, interesting lifeblood, of Brontë's narrative. *Wuthering Heights* also concludes by imaginatively setting its otherworldly protagonists free to wander the space between the physical and spiritual worlds together, and one would misread Brontë's novel if one were to fail to notice that this final union takes the place that the hero and heroine's marriage would normally occupy in a romance's dénouement. *Varney the Vampire* is also marked by a comparable ambiguity surrounding its central vampiric figure. It eventually endows that figure with a troubled, suffering and therefore pitiable consciousness and also repeatedly dramatizes treating him with civil respect.[21] Le Fanu's *Carmilla*, in contrast to these ambivalent models, represents the raising of the intellectual stakes that takes place in the late century's vampire fiction. The chronology sketched out in the rest of this study would seem to suggest that this change should be aligned with the string of celebrations of aesthetic consciousness that we examined in Chapter 4, clustering as they do in the 1850s and 1860s. That is to say that once Ruskin, Arnold and Pater have made their very public and well-advertised cases for the centrality of idle aesthetic contemplation to contemporary life, the gothic case against these systems of thought seems to insist not on the vampire's troubling presence (as Brontë and Rymer might be said to do), but upon his or her total destruction and very graphic assassination. The fact that Stoker's text renders the narrative of the vampire's destruction a matter of national and broad social concern – by its association of the band of heroes with Britain's commercial modernity – demonstrates that by the end of the century what is at stake in the figure of the vampire has been augmented even further. It is tempting to connect this final heightening of vampiric drama with the considerably increased visibility of Paterian aestheticism in British society in the 1890s. Oscar Wilde's dandyish, aesthetically hedonist persona had borne the fruit, during this period, of his 1890 novel, *The Picture of Dorian Gray* and of his sensational and unsuccessful libel case against the Marquess of Queensbury in 1895. *Dorian Gray* has been very plausibly read as an attack on the Paterian figure of Lord Henry Wotton at its narrative's centre, and the approach to life that character largely borrows from Pater's 'Conclusion'.[22] But Wilde himself of course also famously embodied many of Wotton's – and thus Pater's – ideas and paradoxes himself. Stoker's friendship with fellow Irishman Wilde makes a final link in this chain.

We can conclude, finally, by noting that it has become something of a critical commonplace to think of the late nineteenth century as hosting a resurgence in gothic fiction, but one that is marked by a variety of different associations and preoccupations from the previous flowerings of this mode. Botting, for example, asserts that 'familiar Gothic figures' such as 'the double and the vampire [. . .] re-emerge [. . .] in new shapes' at the end of the century.[23] David Punter, similarly, denominates late-century writing in this mode as 'decadent Gothic' and again considers it as a significant reformulation of earlier tropes and narratives.[24] What we have seen in this chapter, by contrast, is that there is in fact a very significant continuity lying at the heart of the entire century's vampire fiction. The vampire figure can now be understood as a symbolic representation of the aesthetic contemplator, or indeed of the aesthetic objects and phenomena that bring about the state of idle aesthetic contemplation. From Coleridge's 'Christabel', right through to Stoker's *Dracula*, therefore, vampire fiction represents a mode of commentary on more mainstream literary and theoretical accounts of aesthetic experience and spiritual awareness. As the century develops, the vampire narrative may become primarily a mode of conservative and traditional reaction against the liberal and radically individualistic associations of aesthetic consciousness. In this sense the tone and ambitions of late-century vampire narratives may seem to stand at some distance from Rymer's *Varney*, or Polidori's 'The Vampyre'. But this shift should be understood as a concentration of the already latent function of the vampire form since 1798, rather than as anything like a new departure. Stoker and Le Fanu thus build on, and enhance, one of the primary associations of the vampire figure throughout the century. And they focus this association with a new energy and vigour on the late nineteenth century's many positive examinations of aesthetic capability.

Conclusion

Dracula might be said to bring together all the currents of thought we have examined in this study in its vision of apparently correct British values and the engagements and capacities that threaten those values. The Romantic model of transcendent aesthetic consciousness figures as the shadow-world to which the vampire can transport his victims, and the immaterial realm to which he belongs. The 'gospel of work' provides the moral blueprint for that shadow-world's negation, as well as for the vampire's destruction. Stoker's vision of a technological future in which even those without the financial need to labour contribute to society's welfare recalls a key aspect of Mill's *Political Economy*. And the association of the vampire with Paterian aestheticism casts the cultural theory of the final decades of the century as a form of immoral solipsism. This alignment – or meeting – of the strands of thought that have formed the terrain of this study shows us a number of important things. First, the categories of idleness and aesthetic consciousness are central to several key and interconnected debates and discourses in Victorian political, intellectual and social life. The vampire novel's conservative vision of correct society must, therefore, be made through the categories of repose, contemplation and their apparent opposites. For these alternatives are writ large in the century's political economic debates over society's priorities, in Carlyle and Marx's attempts to formulate ideal labour, in cultural theory's case for aesthetic experience and in contemporary poetry's preoccupation with the apparent loss of innate sensibility.

Second, however, this alignment of the ideas considered across this study allows us to see that the consequence of repose and contemplation's centrality to these debates is in fact the quite thorough degradation of those categories. Because it is not just vampire literature that challenges the positivity surrounding idleness and aesthetic consciousness to be found in the Romantics or in Mill. What we have seen in this study should be understood as the gradual but thorough refutation of the frequent positive claims made for idle contemplation at the beginning of the century. This degradation begins in the early 1830s, with Carlyle's *Sartor Resartus*. Carlyle there builds on, but also actively covers over and conceals, early century claims for idleness and the types of consciousness that it engenders. In so doing, he takes the positive effects of aesthetic contemplation but divorces them from repose, and associates them instead with fully realized labour. This hugely influential 'gospel of work' (that is also espoused by many of Carlyle's contemporaries) plays a significant part, amongst its many other effects, in the reformulation of the positive case for idle aesthetic contemplation from mid-century onwards. Whereas Schiller and Coleridge had proposed a society-wide fostering of aesthetic consciousness through the brief but powerful repose of contemplation, Ruskin, Arnold and Pater all configure aesthetic consciousness in such a manner as to require of the citizen an arduous and sustained work ethic, a lifelong attention to aesthetic objects and their contemplation. Even these attempted positive accounts of idle aesthetic contemplation therefore separate that engagement from spontaneous, natural life by negating the earlier widespread assumptions that aesthetic capability was innate to every individual and immediate in its effects. The individual who aspires to aesthetic consciousness, moreover, is now thought of as most likely to encounter failure, shame and disappointment, as Ruskin has it, or the intense experience of contingency and loss, in Pater's terms. Such pessimism around the ordinary citizen's encounter with idle contemplation is underlined by Pater himself, when in *Marius the Epicurean* he has the relentless quest for aesthetic culture experienced as an immovable barrier between the novel's protagonist and the physical and emotional contents of that protagonist's life.

In the early years of the nineteenth century, idleness and aesthetic consciousness were frequently described as the central categories in human life. They were conceived of as engendering the full realization of an individual's moral and social capability. They promised to solve the problems of mental stultification that attend on advanced commercial society. And they were consequently put forward as necessary experiences for every citizen. This case was made, we should remember, not simply by the Romantics, but by several systems of thought, including Benthamite Utilitarianism. As late as 1848, Mill's account of the stationary state represents a final instance of adherence to this pluralistic and egalitarian version of aesthetic consciousness, a partial anachronism that might be explained by Mill's idiosyncratic intellectual development, in which Bentham and the Romantics hold twin positions. By the end of the century, by contrast, idle contemplation is understood as beyond the attainment of the ordinary citizen; as a means of accessing loss, disappointment and repeated failure, rather than transcendent and life-affirming morality; and as a thorough withdrawal from quotidian life into a realm of morbid self-consciousness. At their extreme, these negative conceptions of idleness and aesthetic consciousness tip over into the comprehensive demonization and villainization of the idle contemplator. Tennyson's 'Lotos-Eaters', with its vision of benighted, intoxicated and wrong-headed human life is in this sense in the same line of thought as late-century vampire fiction's monstrous rendering of aesthetic consciousness and its devotees. Thus, even for overt proponents of aesthetic consciousness at the end of the century, idle contemplation cannot be described as a state that could bring about an immediate and positive moral awareness. When even Pater turns against his own earlier high-toned positivity regarding aesthetic potential – as we have seen him do in 1885 – one must conclude that the late-century climate is significantly at odds with any claim for the centrality and positive influence of aesthetic contemplation within social or individual life.

This dramatic transformation in the perception of idle contemplation can be explained in two ways, one of which we began to consider earlier. In Chapter 4 of this study, we saw how accounts of aesthetic consciousness's utility seemed to be transformed during periods of marked tension surrounding democratic reform. What were formerly arguments for every citizen's innate aesthetic potential, and therefore for the accessibility and power of idle contemplation, became – around the climax of Chartism in 1848 and at the moment of the Second Reform Act in 1867, for instance – authoritarian statements of the lifelong, professional and therefore elite commitment aesthetic contemplation necessitated. It would seem, from this repeated pattern, that the notion of unleashing the opinions and ideas of a relatively large proportion of the population tested the mettle of the proponents of aesthetic consciousness – and specifically tested their commitment to the innate and egalitarian model of aesthetic capability – and found them wanting. If aesthetic consciousness brings with it the experience of moral and philosophical expansion, and of liberation from 'codes of fraud and woe', then such liberty might combine with the liberty to participate in the political process to produce dramatic, far-reaching and unwanted results. In other words, the Victorian proponents of aesthetic consciousness were so integrated into elite and mainstream culture that they understood the unleashing of working-class contemplative liberty in entirely negative terms. In comparison to the Romantic model of the poet who is in rebellion and exile from – or simply on the outside of – mainstream society and its power structures, the Victorian intellectuals and artists who inherit the subject of aesthetic consciousness should thus be understood as belonging – ideologically and imaginatively, as well as professionally – to the establishment.

It is for this reason, indeed, that high Victorian cultural theory stands at such distance – generically and stylistically speaking – from earlier positive accounts of idle contemplation. The Romantic mode of seizing the knowledge only available to the aesthetic contemplator stressed its poet-figure's distance from society, or his or her marginality in some other sense. Shelley's 'Mont Blanc', for instance, is entirely structured by its remoteness from British – but indeed any other – society, and in this the poem follows comparable postures in Cowper, Coleridge, Byron, Wordsworth and Wollstonecraft. Keats, likewise, announces his distance from mainstream culture through his very passivity, through his non-participation in society's 'bee-like buzzing'. As I have argued elsewhere, in this sense, the Romantic analysis of aesthetic contemplation holds much in common with the pastoral, in which rural distance from society provides an opportunity to reconsider that society's priorities.[1] The Victorian poetic accounts of idle contemplation we considered in Chapter 3 of this study stand in contrast to these Romantic models. They either allude to the pastoral mode only in order to expose its irrelevance to the present (Arnold's 'Scholar-Gipsy' and Hopkins's 'Spring and Fall' do this, for instance), or they reconfigure the poem of idle contemplation as one taking place in a mythic nowhere (this is what 'The Strayed Reveller' and Tennyson's 'Lotos-Eaters' do). The genre of writing that becomes most associated with the exploration of aesthetic consciousness in Victorian society, then, is very definitely the kind of cultural theory written by the mature Arnold, by Ruskin and by Pater. The authoritative, donnish treatises of these figures are fundamentally opposed, however, to the writing of their marginal and oppositional Romantic forebears. For these 'high Victorians' not only belong to the establishment and to elite intellectual culture in no uncertain terms. They also write for the educated, leisured man of letters, he who can visit Venice, who has encountered Renaissance sculpture, and who has the time and freedom to pursue a course of reading 'the best that has been thought and said'. Idle contemplation is thus comprehensively institutionalized, and rendered elite, rather than radical or revolutionary, from the late 1840s onwards.

The second and indeed connected force driving the transformation of idle contemplation we have witnessed in this study lies in the changing significance of 'class' across the century. In comparison to the late eighteenth century, or the very first years of the nineteenth century, for instance, it is striking the extent to which nineteenth-century culture after Ricardo, and certainly after Carlyle and Marx, is preoccupied with questions of class. This increased awareness of the issues surrounding social stratification no doubt follows the introduction of the concept of 'capital' into political economy, which Ricardo effects, as well as early- to mid-century Chartist activity and contemporary schemes for communist societies, such as those penned by Owen and Fourier. The rise of class as a central issue in political and intellectual life, which these developments bring about, inflects contemporary conceptions of repose and passivity to the extent that the capitalized term 'Idleness' becomes, in the second half of the century, an oft-repeated shorthand for the economic and social injustice the aristocracy apparently imposes upon the rest of society. Morris's *News from Nowhere* is one of a number of texts that refers to aristocratic repose in this manner. Here, for example, is the novella's primary guide to Nowhere, Dick Hammond, explaining this now historical occurrence:

> It is said that in the early days of our epoch there were a good many people who were hereditarily afflicted with a disease called Idleness, because they were the direct descendants of those who in the bad times used to force other people to work for them – the people, you know, who are called slave-holders or employers of labour in the history books.[2]

In this passage problematic class relations are cast as one of the primary features of Victorian culture, and 'Idleness' is expressed as a class-specific 'disease'. It is this association of idleness with problematic class privilege – with the idea of aristocratic repose engendered by other classes' intense toil – that grows significantly across the century. This growth also explains the vampire figure's increasingly remarked-upon aristocratic status from Polidori onwards. Polidori's 'The Vampyre' is published just two years after Ricardo's *Principles of Political Economy*, and thus relatively early on in the century's analysis of class. By the publication of Rymer's *Varney the Vampyre* in 1845 and Le Fanu's 'Carmilla' in 1872, by contrast, idleness's association with the problem of class is more marked, and these narratives thus make significantly more out of their antagonists' apparently aristocratic tendencies to repose.

During the same years that the 'gospel of work' and the fraught climate of democratic reform render the category of idleness increasingly problematic, then, the growing political and intellectual focus on class inflects the category – in some contexts – with a kind of parasitical inertia. Idle

contemplation and its attendant state of aesthetic consciousness are therefore categorized more and more, as the century progresses, as the exclusive
possessions of the rich. Furthermore, the fact that these categories' primary
advocates belong – unashamedly and unquestionably – to the establishment, and that the writing of these figures argues consistently against the
innateness of aesthetic consciousness, means that this association of idleness with class theft is, from the writing of Ruskin onwards, increasingly
compelling. We should note too, in this context, that the association of
aesthetic repose with class privilege demonstrates – somewhat paradoxically – the extent to which Victorian debates around idleness are not
confined to elite intellectual culture. Vampire literature is intensely popular, and populist, across the nineteenth century, meaning that this genre's
preoccupation with questions of idleness and aesthetic consciousness indicates the visibility and pertinence of these issues across the social spectrum.
The terrain and issues this study has analysed are thus by no means
marginal or derivative. Aesthetic repose holds a central role in debates
over social and individual priorities across the century.

We can now turn, finally, to those critics who have touched on aspects
or features of the transformation this study describes, and to the manner in
which this detailed examination of the changing significances of idle
contemplation across the nineteenth century opens up ways of reconsider-
ing Victorian cultural politics. The first critical account to consider is
Linda Dowling's analysis of contemporary 'aesthetic democracy', which
we briefly considered in Chapter 4 of the study. Dowling's analysis of those
figures who explore the socially transformative potential of aesthetic consciousness concludes, as we saw, that such systems of thought are undermined by their ultimate dislocation from material reality. They are
eventually exposed, in other words, as the 'insubstantial dream' of the
'nobleman' who has never fully encountered the problems of the real
world. After considering Ruskin, Arnold and Pater's thought in detail,
we were able to observe the significance of the 'gospel of work' in these
figures' systems of thought, and therefore the extent to which Dowling's
analysis had no way of recognizing the dramatically increased profession-
alism, and also elitism, of aesthetic culture in the second half of the
century. We can now add several layers to this judgement, because we
have now identified the changing faces of democracy and class across the
nineteenth century that also have a pronounced effect on the Victorian
ability to cast aesthetic consciousness in socially and individually positive
terms. While Dowling therefore identifies something extremely important
about Victorian aesthetic thought's aristocratic lineage, the present study

positions Ruskin, Arnold, Pater, Morris and their many followers within a series of significantly broader currents of thought. From this perspective the thought surrounding aesthetic democracy must itself be seen as a problematic institutionalizing, and hardening, of what was previously a more flexible and protean phenomenon. Early-century thought – and Mill's political economy – considered aesthetic consciousness central to human life, innate to every individual, and able to flourish when society simply allowed the space for undirected repose. High Victorian cultural theory, by contrast, represents a complex apparatus of thought, and a thorough and laborious set of instructions in how to arrive at a state that is no longer considered innate and that is no longer considered transformative in either a social or a moral sense. Where Dowling stresses the immateriality of aesthetic democracy, therefore, what we have seen in the present study might lead us to see the over-determined materiality of such thought as one of its main problems. Were we to add to this study's analysis a more concrete history of the many educational and cultural institutions that are physically or metaphorically built in the wake of Ruskin, Arnold and Morris's principles, one might be led to see Victorian society as one both literally and metaphorically hardening – indeed setting in stone – what the early decades of the century saw as a matter of innate, protean and unproblematic existence. The most striking feature of Victorian considerations of aesthetic consciousness should thus be understood to be its rejection of the hypothesis that such a state is straightforwardly and unproblematically innate to every individual. It was the innateness of aesthetic capability that Keats contends for in his intensely democratic letters. It was this same innateness that Mill stressed both in his accounts of working-class consciousness and of pre-civilized life across the globe. It is the innateness of aesthetic capability that is mourned in Hopkins's 'Spring and Fall' and in Arnold's 'Gipsy Child by the Sea Shore'. But the only states that are innate for Ruskin and Arnold, for example, are failure and rioting. Idle aesthetic contemplation thus loses its democratic and pluralistic politics in the powerful currents of nineteenth-century industrialism and reform.

Significantly longer ago that Dowling's analysis, Raymond Williams also considered several aspects of the transformation described in this study in *Culture and Society*. The conclusion of that work that has most pertinence for the field of idle contemplation was that, by the mid-nineteenth century, aesthetic experience is reduced to the 'saving clause in a bad treaty', meaning that the realm of art is specialized into a 'reserve area in which feeling can be tended and organized'.[3] The present study, by contrast, has demonstrated the extent to which the ideology of labour is in fact thrown over the category of aesthetic repose itself, meaning that Victorian conceptions of aesthetic consciousness very often fuse that state with the arduous processes of contemporary work, rather than fence it off as an alternative type of mental reality. It is also important to note that these particular conclusions of Williams's are formed primarily in response to John Stuart Mill's account of his own intellectual history. The present study has demonstrated the extent to which Mill's intensely positive account of aesthetic capability is something of an anomaly – and an anachronism – in the arena of Victorian culture. One must look outside of Mill's thought, it seems, in order accurately to measure Victorian conceptions of human contemplative power. And when one does so, one finds a set of conceptions that often stand significantly closer to the vampiric demonizing of aesthetic consciousness than its Romantic celebration. Where Williams sees the field of art to be itself 'specialized' and fenced off around mid-century, then, the present study has demonstrated the extent to which the realm of aesthetic capability is far from immune to the wider pressures surrounding rapid industrialization and political reform.

What this study has produced, therefore, is a portrait of nineteenth-century culture preoccupied with, and troubled by, the categories of idleness, repose and aesthetic contemplation. The melancholy of the period's contemplative poetry, for instance, seems frequently to refer to the transcendent and reformative model of passivity lauded by the Romantics but that is considered lost to the Victorians. The political economy of the first half of the century should be understood to struggle with man's tendency towards complex passivity, and to eventually enshrine such states as contemplation and aesthetic consciousness as central to human progress, but to do so in a highly controversial manner – by equating aesthetic passivity with the cessation of economic and technological progress. The early and mid-century's powerful 'gospel of work' aggressively villainizes idleness, but is also intimately tied to that category and entirely constructed on a previous generation's aesthetics of passivity. And of course the second half of the century's rhetorically powerful and far-reaching models of aesthetic culture institutionalize and harden human contemplative potential, and dramatically elongate the aesthetic moment, so that the man of culture becomes an elite exception, rather than a representative everyman. It is no surprise, given this sustained preoccupation, that the period's most popular and repeated model of monstrosity, the vampire, would encapsulate and embody the many faces aesthetic passivity has taken since the 1790s. For aesthetic consciousness represents – to the Victorian mind – a powerful threat to democratic reform, to technological progress, and to social cohesion, precisely because it was consistently and compellingly conceived of, around the turn of the nineteenth century, as man's primary, fundamental nature. The complex social and industrial infrastructure of Victorian culture must be sustained and supported, in other words, by the repeated negation of aesthetic passivity – across the whole length of the century – because of the radical and revolutionary potential of that state. Such priorities are so urgent, so powerful and so central to Victorian consciousness that even the century's overt advocates of aesthetic culture – Ruskin, Arnold, Pater and Morris, for instance – render aesthetic contemplation a field for diligent, lifelong, never-ceasing labour. What this study has uncovered and reconstructed, therefore, is the dependence of a number of interconnected Victorian ideologies on the suppression of the categories of repose and aesthetic passivity. But to suppress and oppose something in this manner is also to acknowledge its power and its pertinence. Thus, even though by the end of the century there exist a range of complex and well-wrought ideologies and apparatuses of thought designed to negate the relevance of idle contemplation, this category, and the aesthetic consciousness that is still seen to attend on it, remain fraught and troubling presences for the late Victorian mind. *Dracula*'s subtly ambivalent portrayal of aesthetic consciousness's power, whereby the vampire's victim is seduced into a world of pleasurable, engrossing contemplative sensuality, is therefore a precise and visceral encapsulation of the status idle contemplation holds at the turn of the twentieth century. Idle aesthetic consciousness is simultaneously demonic and transcendent. It is the state that must be purged from diligent, ethical, work-based Victorian society at almost all costs. But it also contains – thanks to its trace of Romantic poetics and their revolutionary conception of human capability – the germ of the possibility of radical otherness, in both a personal and a social sense.

Substitutive Satisfaction

I want to end this study by briefly considering Sigmund Freud's conceptions of aesthetic consciousness and contemplative power, specifically as those are expressed in his 1930 work *Das Unbehagen in der Kultur*, which was published in English in the same year as *Civilization and Its Discontents*. Freud may lie in a very different tradition of thought from the trans-cultural preoccupation with idleness and aesthetic consciousness this study has reconstructed. But the nineteenth-century British debates over these categories in fact anticipate and foreshadow the psychoanalytic interpretation of aesthetic thought that Freud develops – and that is thrust upon British intellectual life – early in the twentieth century. While Matt Ffytche and others have shown that Freud's reading did not extend to nineteenth-century British literature or cultural analysis, then, many of the conceptions of aesthetic consciousness we have encountered in this study nevertheless hold surprising affinities with this aspect of Freud's thought.[1] This brief epilogue will therefore both analyse Freud's account of aesthetic consciousness in *Civilization and Its Discontents* – demonstrating the extent to which it represents something of a nadir of fortunes for that category – and pick out the many echoes of nineteenth-century British thought to be found in that account. This consideration of Freud will allow us to see something of the afterlife of the debates this study has focused on, three decades in to the twentieth century. But it will also illustrate very clearly why the nineteenth century's handling of the categories of idleness and aesthetic consciousness must be understood as a systematic destruction of the earlier positivity around those terms.

Freud's consideration of aesthetic consciousness in *Civilization and Its Discontents* comes out of his earlier examination, in *Die Zukunft einer Illusion* or *The Future of an Illusion* of 1927, of religious thought and religious impulses. Following that work, Freud's friend and correspondent Romain Rolland had suggested that 'die eigentliche Quelle der Reliogiosität', 'the real source of religiosity' was in fact 'das „ozeanische"

Gefühl', the '"oceanic" feeling' shared, Rolland assumed, 'bei Millionen Menschen', 'by millions'.[2] This feeling, or intellectual intuition, is, in Freud's terms, 'a sense of "eternity", a feeling of something limitless, unbounded – [...] a feeling [...] of being indissolubly bound up with and belonging to the whole of the world outside oneself[3] ('[D]ie Empfindung der "Ewigkeit" [...], 'ein Gefühl wie von etwas Unbegrenztem, Schrankenlosem [...] ein Gefühl [...] der Zusammengehörigkeit mit dem Ganzen der Außenwelt'[4]).The opening sections of *Civilization and Its Discontents* are devoted to this topic, which Freud uses as a way into his discussion of the many renunciations civilization requires of the individual. Already in Freud's elaboration of the '"oceanic" feeling' we should note an echo of the English Romantic conception of man's sublime encounter with the physical landscape. Shelley's 'Mont Blanc', for example, dramatized an attempt at grasping something very like the 'sense of "eternity"' conveyed by – and contained in – that text's eponymous mountain. Wordsworth's epiphanic vision of 'a silent sea of hoary mist' atop Snowden in the last book of *The Prelude* is an even more direct foreshadowing of this sense of man's place within a vast world of companionable, equal presences. For Wordsworth found in that 'still ocean' 'the emblem of a mind / That feeds upon infinity' and used it as evidence of man's place within a vast chain of being.[5]

Freud's handling of the 'oceanic feeling' after this initial definition and description is not at all celebratory, or even sympathetic, however. On the contrary, Freud comprehensively deconstructs – and indeed pathologizes – this version of human spirituality. This process begins with Freud's admission that he 'can discover no trace of this "oceanic" feeling in' himself[6] ('Ich selbst kann dies „ozeanische" Gefühl nicht in mir entdecken'[7]). Very soon in his analysis any experience of such shared identity with the world beyond the self becomes a psychically problematic occurrence:

> Die Pathologie lehrt uns eine große Anzahl von Zuständen kennen, in denen die Abgrenzung des Ichs gegen die Außenwelt unsicher wird, oder die Grenzen wirklich unrichtig gezogen werden; Fälle, in denen uns Teile des eigenen Körpers, ja Stücke des eigenen Seelenlebens, Wahrnehmungen, Gedanken, Gefühle wie fremd und dem Ich nicht zugehörig erscheinen, andere, in denen man der Außenwelt zuschiebt, was offenbar im Ich entstanden ist und von ihm anerkannt werden sollte. Also ist auch das Ichgefühl Störungen unterworfen und die Ichgrenzen sind nicht beständig.[8]

> Pathology acquaints us with a great many conditions in which the boundary between the ego and the external world becomes uncertain or the border-lines are actually wrongly drawn. There are cases in which parts of a person's

own body, indeed parts of his mental life – perceptions, thoughts, feelings – seem alien, divorced from the ego, and others in which he attributes to the external world what has clearly arisen in the ego and ought to be recognized by it. Hence, even the sense of self is subject to disturbances, and the limits of the self are not constant.[9]

Again, this passage can be understood, from the perspective we have taken up in this study, to invoke earlier British ideas of aesthetic consciousness and its philosophical possibilities. The notion that the ego's boundaries might be blurred, or disturbed, recalls Shelley, Wordsworth and Keats, but also Brontë. *Wuthering Heights*, for instance, explored what Freud terms the ego's 'uncertain' boundaries through the radically shared sense of self between Heathcliff and Catherine, as well as through those characters' closely connected conceptions of the passable border between life and death. Freud, however, renders these possibilities not transcendent insights into the real conditions of human life, but examples of pathological, diseased consciousness. Individuals who experience reality in these types of ways are, for Freud, in need of treatment in order to restore their egos to normal parameters. In other words, Freud's analysis renders the strand of Keatsian thought we traced through Brontë's novel and on to the late nineteenth century a series of illusions prompted by several faulty and diseased minds. If the 'boundary between the ego and the external world' can be 'wrongly drawn', or if the 'sense of self' can be radically 'disturb[ed]' and distorted, then occurrences of this sort are to be distrusted – and treated – not lauded and celebrated as transcendent insights. Freud's rhetoric turns from the wide-ranging terms of the 'oceanic feeling' to the particular patient, then, and does not use this analysis as an occasion for considering the historical development of transcendental thought. But his approach nevertheless serves to cast a powerful and much developed line of enquiry – from across the long nineteenth century – as itself carried out by figures suffering from pathologically malfunctioning egos.

We should remember at this point, of course, that Brontë, Rymer, Le Fanu and Stoker were all engaged, in their vampire narratives written during this period, in a process of problematizing – or casting as faulty, unworldly and wrong-headed – the aesthetic and 'oceanic' tendencies of several of their characters. The intense aesthetic consciousness of the vampire's victims, from *Varney* to *Dracula*, was overtly and repeatedly rendered a physiological and psychic disorder, one in need of treatment by the texts' embodiments of scientific and medical expertise. In this sense, Freudian psychoanalysis might be described a case of life imitating art. Alternatively, and more compellingly, one might connect this pathologization of aesthetic consciousness within vampire literature with the nineteenth century's growing distrust for that category, and celebration instead of solid, upstanding, public-spirited rationality. Freud, in this picture, is very much of his time insofar as he continues the process of castigating aesthetic consciousness and of lauding in its stead upstanding conventional rationality. For *Civilization and Its Discontents* does this not simply by its pathologization of aesthetic consciousness. It also equates the highly permeable ego-boundaries of the 'oceanic feeling' with the state of childhood:

> Ursprünglich enthält das Ich alles, später scheidet es eine Außenwelt von sich ab. Unser heutiges Ichgefühl ist also nu rein eingeschrumpfter Rest eines weitumfassenderen, ja – eines allumfassenden Gefühls, welches einer innigeren Verbundheit des Ichs mit der Umwelt entsprach. Wenn wir annehmen dürfen, daß dieses primäre Ichgefühl sich im Seelenleben vieler Menschen – in größeren oder geringerem Ausmaße – erhalten hat, so würde es sich dem enger und schärfer umgrentzen Ichgefühl der Reifezeit wie eine Art Gegenstück an die Seite stellen, und die zu ihm passenden Vorstellungsinhalte wären gerade die der Unbegrenztheit und der Verbundenheit mit dem All, dieselben, mit denen mein Freund das „ozeanische" Gefühl erläutert.[10]

> the ego is originally [in a state of early childhood] all-inclusive, but later it separates off an external world from itself. Our present [adult] sense of self is thus only a shrunken residue of a far more comprehensive, indeed all-embracing feeling, which corresponded to a more intimate bond between the ego and the world around it. If we may assume that this primary sense of self has survived, to a greater or lesser extent, in the mental life of many people, it would coexist, as a kind of counterpart, with the narrower, more sharply defined sense of self belonging to the years of maturity, and the ideational content appropriate to it would be precisely those notions of limitlessness and oneness with the universe – the very notions used by my friend to elucidate the 'oceanic' feeling.[11]

This stance echoes Hopkins's 'Spring and Fall' and Arnold's 'Gipsy Child by the Sea-Shore' in its categorization of the sense of 'limitlessness' and 'oneness' as the effect of an infantile, undeveloped – and soon to be erased – mental propensity. Hopkins's poem very clearly identified an 'intimate bond between the ego and the world around it', though the poem has a different flavour to Freud's analysis because its speaker's primary function was to mourn the inevitable loss of such childlike consciousness. Despite this difference, both Freud and Hopkins cast the intense connection with the physical world that characterizes aesthetic consciousness as initially innate in human development, but as soon to be surpassed. In this sense,

Freud's position here also aligns with an influential and highly representative text like Tennyson's 'Lotos-Eaters', therefore. That poem cast giving in to the selfish, solipsistic urges of the aesthetic reverie as a state of unmanly sensuous indulgence, as if something approximating the childlike ego also survived into adult life for Tennyson and was ready to accommodate the weak, undisciplined or seduced adult. Tennyson's conception of idleness in the 'Lotos-Eaters' might thus be described – in loosely Freudian terms that are also quite close to Tennyson's own frame of reference – as a giving in to one's least developed, most irrational self.[12]

This parallel between Tennyson's poem and Freud's analysis in *Civilization and Its Discontents* also means that Freud's final judgement on the '"oceanic" feeling' usefully sums up that poem's – and a large part of the nineteenth century's – perspective on aesthetic consciousness. As he reasserts the judgement of *The Future of an Illusion* – that religiosity stems 'from the helplessness of the child and a longing for its father',[13] 'der infantilen Hilflosigkeit und der durch sie geweckten Vatersehnsucht'[14] – Freud summarizes the '"oceanic" feeling' as a force that seeks 'to restore unlimited narcissism',[15] 'die Wiederherstellung des uneingeschränkten Narzißmus anstreben'.[16] Such 'unlimited narcissism' is in one sense a technical psychoanalytic term describing the ultimate object of the unrestricted ego. But the term also functions in a non-technical sense, as a categorization of transcendent contemplation's narrow and selfish individualism. In this manner, Freud's analysis encapsulates – and imbues with a new kind of scientific and medical authority – Victorian thought's opposition between the social and moral duties and intense contemplative individualism. Again, in other words, *Civilization and Its Discontents* aligns clearly not just with Tennyson's 'Lotos-Eaters' but with the vampire fiction of Le Fanu and Stoker. Those figures' narratives also dramatized and explored the complexities of aesthetic contemplation as a preparation for that state's problematization and a celebration instead of conventional morality and rationality.

While Freud's account of the '"oceanic" feeling' does not announce that state's connection to the category we have been calling aesthetic consciousness, the proximity between these terms means that *Civilization and Its Discontents* also makes some closely connected pronouncements on art itself, and on the states of mind that attend on both artistic creativity and receptivity. These elements of Freud's analysis follow his rejection of Rolland's thesis about the '"oceanic" feeling', and form part of his attempt to explain religiosity as a kind of defence mechanism against life's hardship. Civilized life is characterized by three sets of 'measures' for dealing with hardship, for Freud. These are 'powerful distractions, which cause us to make light of our misery, substitutive satisfactions, which diminish it, and intoxicants, which anaesthetize us to it'[17] ('mächtige Ablenkungen, die uns unser Elend gering schätzen lassen, Ersatzbefriedigungen, die es verringern, Rauchstoffe, die uns für dasselbe unempfindlich machen'[18]). Art and the thinking associated with it are apparently 'substitutive satisfactions' in this categorization: they are 'illusions that contrast with reality, but they are not, for this reason, any less effectively psychically, thanks to the role that the imagination has assumed in mental life'[19] ('sie [. . .] sind gegen die Realität Illusionen, darum nicht minder psychisch wirksam dank der Rolle, die die Phantasie im Seelenleben behauptet hat'[20]). This summary of art's place in human life is obviously in one sense deeply reductive, especially in comparison to the high-flung tenor of early nineteenth-century thought surrounding aesthetic consciousness. Art is only a 'substitute' for genuine satisfaction, not the real thing. It is an 'illusion' that takes us, temporarily, away from the painfulness of existence, but that does seem to be powerful enough to merit those earlier terms for the aesthetic journey, 'transport' or 'transcendence'. It can 'diminish' but not fundamentally alter life's difficulty. At first glance, Freud's radically utilitarian assessment of art might also seem to be opposed, on a fundamental level, to later nineteenth-century celebrators of aesthetic thought like Ruskin, Arnold and Pater. These aesthetic philosophers all placed art-experience as the central element in human life – and not just intellectual life – because of the heightened consciousness and breadth of intellectual and moral development it engendered in the individual contemplator. But we should recall, here, that Pater's 'Conclusion', in many ways the culmination of nineteenth-century aesthetic theory, was also a deeply pessimistic document in its account of the human position in a contingent and decaying world. Pater justified aesthetic consciousness and the repeated experience of art, moreover, as the only avenues of human experience that might keep that contingency, flux and profound sense of loss at bay. Art's 'transport' was for Pater thus also temporary, and fundamentally weaker than the negativity of experience as a whole. It is striking that in this sense Freud might again be described as encapsulating and taking the measure of – but also as expressing in unashamedly direct terms – the fundamental gist of British nineteenth-century thought surrounding aesthetic consciousness. It is not that he alludes to, quotes from or refers to a figure like Pater at all; and as already mentioned there is no evidence in all the work that has been done on Freud's reading and influences that he was even aware of Pater, of Arnold or of any of their British contemporaries.

But *Civilization and Its Discontents* nevertheless distils the developments in nineteenth-century aesthetic consciousness that this study has traced in a concise and telling manner.

This encapsulation of earlier thought regarding aesthetic consciousness in the opening sections of *Civilization and Its Discontents* is not the end of the story of Freud's analysis of human contemplative capability, however. For Freud goes significantly further than Pater's opposition between art and flux, and develops a comprehensive and overt deconstruction of the aesthetic impulse. This position is foreshadowed in the idea that we have already considered – that art is a 'substitutive satisfaction' – and is a result of Freud's account of how aesthetic experience fits into the process of 'sublimation' which civilized life promotes. *Civilization and Its Discontents* addresses this issue soon after its categorization of the measures that counteract life's hardship:

> Eine andere Technik der Leidabwehr bedient sich der Libidoverschiebungen, welche unser seelischer Apparat gestattet, durch die seine Funktion so viel an Geschmeidigkeit gewinnt. Die zu lösende Aufgabe ist, die Triebziele solcherart zu verlegen, daß sie von der Versagung der Außenwelt nicht getroffen werden können. Die Sublimierung der Triebe leiht dazu ihre Hilfe. Am meisten erreicht man, wenn man den Lustgewinn aus den Quellen psychischer und intellektueller Arbeit genügend zu erhöhen versteht. Das Schiksal kann einem dann wenig anhaben. Die Befriedigung solcher Art, wie die Freude des Künstlers am Schaffen, an der Verkörperung seiner Phantasiegebilde, die des Forschers an der Lösung von Problemen und am Erkennen der Wahrheit, haben eine besondere Qualität [...]. [...] [S]ie erscheinen uns „feiner und höher", aber ihre Intensität ist im Vergleich mit der aus der Sättigung grober, primärer Triebregungen gedämpft; sie erschüttern nicht unsere Lieblichkeit.[21]

> Another technique for avoiding suffering makes use of the displacements of the libido that are permitted by our psychical apparatus and lend its functioning so much flexibility. Here the task is to displace the aims of the drives in such a way that they cannot be frustrated by the external world. Sublimation of the drives plays a part in this. We achieve most if we can sufficiently heighten the pleasure derived from mental and intellectual work. Fate can then do little to harm us. This kind of satisfaction – the artist's joy in creating, in fashioning forth the products of his imagination, or the scientist's in solving problems and discovering truths – has a special quality [...]. [Such engagements] seem to us 'finer and higher', but their intensity is restrained when compared with that which results from the sating of crude, primary drives: they do not convulse our physical constitution.[22]

This passage should be recognized as a devastating deconstruction of earlier positive accounts of the centrality of aesthetic experience to human life, because it positions aesthetic consciousness as a comprehensive dilution of the physical – sexual – 'drive' that underlies and motivates that activity. The 'artist's joy in creating' may appear 'special', then, but it is in fact thoroughly 'restrained' and removed from its fundamental, non-sublimated impulse. Further, as Freud goes on to suggest, the sublimation that leads to aesthetic experience is especially 'weak' in terms of its effect on a whole community, because 'it cannot be employed universally, as it is accessible only to the few' in possession of 'special aptitudes and gifts'[23] ('sie nicht allgemein verwendbar, nur wenigen Menschen zugänglich ist. Sie setzt besondere, im wirksamenen Ausmaß nicht gerade häufige Anlagen und Begabungen voraus'[24]).

Countless figures across the eighteenth and nineteenth centuries may have theorized the deep, fundamental, essential experiences and modes of being they found in aesthetic consciousness and contemplative creativity, then, and may have done so in a manner that contended for the applicability of such experiences to whole communities, or to large swathes of a particular class. But Freud's observation that such engagements 'do not convulse our physical constitution' renders such aesthetic engagements faint, ineffectual echoes with no hope of really satisfying their individual artists, authors or contemplators. What Freud casts as the 'special' feature of aesthetic consciousness, that which makes it feel 'finer and higher', and which connotes 'special aptitudes and gifts', might thus be more properly described as a more advanced capacity for self-deception, or for surviving through weak iterations and faint impressions of one's primal, fundamental urges. Such a position might be thought of as recalling – but as also again extending – Ruskin's comprehensive account of the moral and technical failure encountered by the workman when he tries to engage with his work aesthetically. For both Freud and Ruskin's models of aesthetic activity position that act at a considerable distance from rounded, complete wholeness, and from the perfection of one's nature. Freud's aesthete can thus only encounter shadows and weak reflections of his whole self, and can never be 'convulsed' in his entire being. Ruskin's worker, likewise, finds aesthetic activity to reflect his failings, his incompleteness and his limitations. For both, in other words, aesthetic consciousness is primarily unsatisfying and incomplete, especially in comparison to the celebratory earlier accounts of that state both figures are aware of.[25]

Aesthetic consciousness is therefore fundamentally weak and artificial, and to a large extent socially irrelevant, for Freud. It induces what he goes on to describe as 'die milde Narkose',[26] a 'mild narcosis' that can 'free us only temporarily from the hardships of life',[27] that 'nicht mehr als eine flüchtige Entrückung aus den Nöten des Lebens herbeizuführen'.[28] This is an observation that was foreshadowed in Rymer's depiction of vampiric aesthetic consciousness, which also appeared to his narrative's physician to be the effect of a 'narcotic'. The weakness of aesthetic consciousness, meanwhile, might be said to recall *Middlemarch*'s rather lightweight Ladislaw and the marginal and derivative pursuits Eliot had him represent for large sections of that novel. For Freud, the object of art experience, 'Schönheit' or 'beauty', is likewise only 'mildly intoxicating':[29] it has a 'milde berauschenden Empfindungscharakter'.[30] In these senses, *Civilization and Its Discontents* renders explicit – and casts as scientifically factual – the pessimistic conception of aesthetic consciousness that was constructed across the second half of the nineteenth century. Freud's stance on contemplative spirituality and aesthetic capability summarizes and encapsulates the developments and intellectual positions this study has reconstructed, therefore. But he also builds on that negativity by delivering an overt castigation of aesthetic repose's flimsiness, frailty and distance from the primary impulsions of human psychic and physical life. Like many of the texts and discourses considered in this study, then, *Civilization and Its Discontents* entertains the arguments for aesthetic consciousness's transcendence, immanent morality and connection with the most valuable aspects of human existence. But these claims are ultimately unjustified and unsustainable, from Freud's perspective. Aesthetic consciousness becomes a kind of false category in Freud's thought, a useless sublimation that blights contemporary culture. High Victorian cultural theory struggled to deal with the discrepancy between its high-flung aesthetic terms and ambitions and the material conditions of life and labour for the majority of the contemporary population. Freud takes this problem a step further by thoroughly undermining, and indeed pathologizing, the aesthete who believes that aesthetic experience can be anything other than a negligible narcotic applicable to a small number of votaries. The story this study has told, of the decay of early-century positive conceptions of aesthetic consciousness in the currents of Victorian political and intellectual life, is thus completed by the extreme negativity with which Freudian thought handles idle contemplation and aesthetic capability.

Notes

Introduction

1. George Eliot, *Middlemarch*, ed. D. Carroll (Oxford: Oxford University Press, 1996), p. 202.
2. Ibid.
3. Ibid., pp. 74, 75, 76.
4. Ibid., p. 75.
5. See ibid., p. 194.
6. Ibid., p. 263.
7. Ibid., p. 337.
8. Ibid.
9. Percy Shelley, 'A Defence of Poetry', in *The Major Works*, eds. Z. Leader and M. O'Neill (Oxford: Oxford University Press, 2009), p. 701.
10. Ibid., p. 675.
11. Eliot, *Middlemarch*, p. 74.
12. Ibid., p. 433.
13. Ibid., p. 782.
14. Ibid., p. 777.
15. Donald Stone, 'Matthew Arnold and the Pragmatics of Hebraism and Hellenism', *Poetics Today*, 19:2 (Summer, 1998): 183–4.
16. Henry Staten, 'Is *Middlemarch* Ahistorical?', *PMLA*, 115:5 (October, 2000): 991–1005 (991).
17. Eliot, *Middlemarch*, p. 357.
18. Felicia Bonaparte, 'Introduction', in George Eliot, *Middlemarch*, ed. D. Carroll (Oxford: Oxford University Press, 1996), p. xviii.
19. Joseph Wiesenfarth, '*Middlemarch*: The Language of Art', *PMLA*, 97:3 (May, 1982): 363–77 (371).
20. Despite this proviso, Schiller does in fact appear in the analysis that follows, because he is invoked directly by both Carlyle and Marx; the overall plan of the study, though, remains the exploration of British thought.
21. Jacques Rancière, *The Politics of Aesthetics*, ed. and trans. Gabriel Rockhill (London: Bloomsbury, 2004), p. 40.
22. Ibid., p. 41.
23. Ibid.

Chapter 1
Idleness, Moral Consciousness and Sociability

1. My focus on Shelley and Keats in this chapter does not mean that the reputation and status of contemporary idle contemplation rests on their works alone. In fact, as I have shown at length in *Idleness, Contemplation and the Aesthetic* (Cambridge: Cambridge University Press, 2011), the years between 1784 and 1830 are marked by a widespread conception of idle contemplation as a positive, powerful and intensely active state, across a broad spectrum of writers. For a reconstruction of this position in the thought of John Howard, Jeremy Bentham and Friedrich Schiller, see *Idleness, Contemplation and the Aesthetic*, pp. 38–67; for a full account of first-generation Romanticism's positive exploration of idle contemplation, see pp. 68–101 and 102–32; and for an analysis of Wordsworth's adherence to this pattern of thought, see my 'Idle Thought in Wordsworth's Lucy Cycle', *Romanticism*, 17:1 (April 2011), 94–105.

2. Mary Shelley and Percy Bysshe Shelley, *History of a Six Weeks' Tour*, ed. J. Wordsworth (Oxford: Woodstock Books, 1991), p. vi.

3. Ibid., pp. 150–1.

4. Mary and Percy Shelley, *History*, p. 167.

5. See Hugo Donnelly, 'Beyond Rational Discourse: The "Mysterious Tongue" of "Mont Blanc"', *Studies in Romanticism*, 29:4 (winter 1990), 571–81; and Frances Ferguson, 'Shelley's *Mont Blanc*: What the Mountain Said', in *Coleridge, Keats and Shelley*, ed. P. Kitson (Basingstoke: Macmillan, 1996), pp. 172–85.

6. Mary and Percy Shelley, *History*, pp. 110–12.

7. Samuel Taylor Coleridge, 'Frost at Midnight', in *Coleridge's Poetry and Prose*, eds. N. Halmi, P. Magnuson and R. Modiano (London: W. W. Norton, 2004), pp. 120–3; ll. 18, 20–5.

8. Ibid., l. 19.

9. Jerrold Hogle, 'Shelley as Revisionist: Power and Belief in *Mont Blanc*', in *The New Shelley*, ed. G. K. Blank (New York: St Martin's Press, 1991), pp. 108, 115.

10. John Rieder, 'Shelley's "Mont Blanc": Landscape and the Ideology of the Sacred Text', *ELH*, 48:4 (winter 1981), 790. For examples of readings of the poem more in line with the present essay, see Judith Chernaik, *The Lyrics of Shelley* (Cleveland: Press of Case Western Reserve University, 1972), pp. 40–52; Gerald McNiece, 'The Poet as Ironist in "Mont Blanc" and "Hymn to Intellectual Beauty"', *Studies in Romanticism*, 14:4 (fall 1975), 311–36; and Sally West, *Coleridge and Shelley: Textual Engagement* (Aldershot: Ashgate, 2007), pp. 73–98. Chernaik's reading of the poem is similar to my own in its observation that the metaphor of section I 'anticipates' section II 'point for

point' (p. 41), and in its reading of the phrase 'thou art there!' as a 'recall[ing]' of the self once the poet's 'trance' is 'broken' (p. 42). McNiece reads the poem as 'resembling' canonical 'Romantic irony' (p. 311) in a comparable manner to my drawing out of the scepticism of Coleridge's 'Eolian Harp' and 'Frost at Midnight'. West, meanwhile, also treats Shelley's second section as coloured by the metaphor of the poem's opening (p. 80). The present account seeks to extend, and add detail to, these various observations by explaining them as parts of Shelley's poem's generic consanguinity with Coleridge's 'Eolian Harp' and 'Frost at Midnight'.

11. For an example of a reading of 'Mont Blanc' alongside Coleridge's 'Hymn', see West, *Coleridge and Shelley*, pp. 73–98.

12. Coleridge, 'The Eolian Harp', in *The Complete Poems*, ed. W. Keach (London: Penguin, 1997), pp. 87–8, ll. 38, 40–3, 47.

13. Hogle, 'Shelley as Revisionist', pp. 108–9.

14. Ferguson, 'Shelley's *Mont Blanc*', p. 175.

15. Coleridge, 'Eolian Harp', ll. 44–8.

16. Ibid., ll. 55–7.

17. The poem was published as 'Effusion XXXV' in 1796; see Jack Stillinger, *Coleridge and Textual Instability* (Oxford: Oxford University Press, 1994), pp. 27–35.

18. Coleridge, 'Eolian Harp', l. 39.

19. See Ferguson, 'Shelley's *Mont Blanc*: What the Mountain Said', and Donnelly, 'Beyond Rational Discourse: The "Mysterious Tongue" of "Mont Blanc"'.

20. Coleridge, 'Frost at Midnight', 1812–1817, ll. 28–30; again, a detailed account of the different versions of 'Frost at Midnight' can be found in Stillinger, *Coleridge and Textual Instability*, pp. 52–6.

21. Ibid., ll. 65–7.

22. Shelley, *A Defence of Poetry*, p. 675.

23. Ibid., pp. 696–7.

24. Ibid., p. 675.

25. Coleridge, 'Eolian Harp', ll. 26–7.

26. See, for instance, p. 699, where we find the observation that poetry 'is not subject to the control of the active powers of the mind, [. . .] that its birth and recurrence has no necessary connection with consciousness or will'. Again, this statement could be read as attempting to render the tentative musings of 'The Eolian Harp' factual.

27. Shelley, 'Hymn to Intellectual Beauty', *The Major Works*, pp. 114–17, ll. 1–2.

28. Shelley, 'Ode to the West Wind', *The Major Works*, pp. 412–14, l. 57.

29. James Sambrook, *William Cowper: The Task, and Selected Other Poems* (London: Longman, 1994), IV, 286–7, 303–7.

30. Ibid., IV, 287.

31. William Shakespeare, *Troilus and Cressida*, in *The Complete Works*, ed. W. J. Craig (Oxford: Oxford University Press, 1949), pp. 667–700, I.ii.15–16.

32. Ibid., III.iii.103–8.

33. Further evidence for Keats's knowledge of and engagement with this passage of Cowper is to be found in a letter to Charles Dilke dated 31 July 1819, where Keats describes the 'cruelty' of forcing a man out of his 'idleness' in terms that recall Cowper's 'snapping short / The glassy threads': 'you cut the thread of his existence'; see I, 134.

34. Woodhouse, for instance, uses the term 'fit' in this sense in a letter to John Taylor from October 1818, which reports and agrees with Keats's 'poetical character' letter: '– and it is the excess of this power that I suppose Keats to speaks [sic], when he says he has no identity – As a poet, and when the fit is upon him, this is true' (*Letters*, I, 389).

35. Jacques Rancière, 'The Politics of the Spider', *Studies in Romanticism,* 50:2 (summer 2011), p. 245.

36. Ibid., p. 244.

37. Ibid., p. 242.

38. See Adelman, *Idleness, Contemplation and the Aesthetic*, pp. 68–101.

39. See ibid., pp. 68–77.

40. David Bonnell Green, 'Keats, Swift, and Pliny the Elder', *Notes and Queries*, CXCV (11 November 1950), 499–501.

41. Li Ou, *Keats and Negative Capability* (London: Continuum, 2009), p. 2.

42. Walter Jackson Bate, *John Keats* (London: The Hogarth Press, 1992), p. 249.

43. Steven Knapp, *Literary Interest: The Limits of Anti-Formalism* (Cambridge: Harvard, 1993), p. 32.

44. Margaret Ann Fitzpatrick, 'The Problem of Identity in Keats's "Negative Capability"', *Dalhousie Review*, 61 (spring 1981), p. 41; quoted in Knapp, *Literary Interest*, p. 149, n. 2.

45. Knapp, *Literary Interest*, p. 40.

46. Ibid., p. 36.

47. See Adelman, *Idleness, Contemplation and the Aesthetic*, pp. 94–101.

48. Keats, *Letters*, I, 191, n. 1; cf. Li, *Keats and Negative Capability*, pp. 1–2.

49. Cowper, *Task*, IV, 288–9.

50. Kevis Goodman, *Georgic Modernity and British Romanticism* (Cambridge: Cambridge University Press, 2004), pp. 89–90.

51. Cowper, *Task*, IV, 296, 298.

52. Adelman, 'Idle Thought in Wordsworth's Lucy Cycle', 94–105.

53. John Keats, 'Ode on Indolence', in *The Complete Poems*, ed. J. Barnard (London: Penguin, 1988), pp. 349–51, ll. 25, 26&30; as the 'Ode on Indolence' does not contain concentrated reference to the sociability of idle

contemplation, and thus does not extend first-generation Romantic thought on aesthetic consciousness in the same manner as Keats's correspondence, I have chosen to mention it only in passing in this analysis. The poem nevertheless exemplifies the attention Keats devotes to the subject of idleness.

54. For an example of a contemporary account of Coleridge's work that sees his poetry as intensely, and indeed problematically, interested in 'mysteries' and 'doubts', see Anna Letitia Barbauld 'To Mr S. T. Coleridge', in *Selected Poetry and Prose*, eds. W. McCarthy and E. Kraft (Ormskirk: Broadview, 2002), pp. 142–3.

55. Bate, *John Keats*, p. 249, n. 16.

56. Adelman, *Idleness, Contemplation and the Aesthetic*, pp. 38–101.

57. Li, *Keats and Negative Capability*, pp. 62–107.

58. See note 1, above.

Chapter 2
Political Economy and the Logic of Idleness

1. The present chapter's attempt to complicate the politics and provenance of nineteenth-century political economy should thus be seen as a complementary project to Philip Connell's reconsideration of 'the historical identity of Romanticism'. Connell goes beyond the often simplistic opposition between Romanticism and a 'liberal ideology, identified above all with the reductive, calculating rationality of utilitarianism and economic science'. The present analysis reads nineteenth-century political economy up until mid-century as taking very seriously the Romantic analysis of idleness and its individual and social benefits. See Philip Connell, *Romanticism, Economics and the Question of 'Culture'* (Oxford: Oxford University Press, 2001), p. vii.

2. Catherine Gallagher, *The Body Economic: Life, Death, and Sensation in Political Economy and the Victorian Novel* (Princeton, NJ: Princeton University Press, 2006), p. 60.

3. Connell, *Romanticism*, p. 84.

4. Abstraction from the contingency of life is of course central to political economy's very identity. Simon Dentith, for instance, asserts that '[t]he founding gesture of Political Economy [. . .] can be seen as an abstraction to the economic', and that this gesture 'is accompanied by a further abstraction, within the economic itself, from the level of multifarious and particular facts to the more certain knowledge of economic laws'. See Simon Dentith, 'Political Economy, Fiction and the Language of Practical Ideology in Nineteenth-Century England', *Social History*, 8:2 (May 1983): 183–99 (esp. p. 186). My point is that Ricardo's work is a high point in this trend of abstraction, and that his contemporaries and followers in fact try and offer

much more space to human contingency even while they write political economy.

5. Maxine Berg, *The Machinery Question and the Making of Political Economy: 1815–1848* (Cambridge: Cambridge University Press, 1980), pp. 45–6.

6. Pedro Schwartz, *The New Political Economy of J. S. Mill* (London: Weidenfeld and Nicholson, 1972), p. 10.

7. Adam Ferguson, *Essay on the History of Civil Society*, ed. D. Forbes (Edinburgh: Edinburgh University Press, 1966), p. 37.

8. Berg, *The Machinery Question*, p. 47.

9. Ibid., pp. 46–7.

10. Berg summarizes these readings in *The Machinery Question*, pp. 47–8.

11. See Schwartz, *J. S. Mill*, pp. 13–14.

12. Both Adam Smith and Adam Ferguson draw heavily on the proto-anthropological writing of figures like Joseph-François Lafitau in their nascent political economy, and refer to primitive societies from across the globe almost as often as they reference classical antiquity. For more on this subject, see J. G. A. Pocock, *Barbarism and Religion*, 4 vols. (Cambridge: Cambridge University Press, 1999), vol. II, p. 336, and for an account of 'stadial history', see H. M. Hopfl, 'From Savage to Scotsman: Conjectural History in the Scottish Enlightenment', *Journal of British Studies*, 17:2 (spring 1978): 19–40.

13. Schwartz, *J. S. Mill*, p. 12.

14. I am indebted to Norman Vance for this observation. For more on *The Anti-Jacobin* in this context, see John Halliwell, 'Loyalist Satire, Parody, and *The Anti-Jacobin*', in *The British Periodical Text, 1797–1835*, ed. Simon Hull (Penrith: Humanities-Ebooks, 2008), pp. 35–67 (45).

15. Berg, *The Machinery Question*, p. 142.

16. My previous work on Smith and Ferguson traced this logic in detail in their political economy and other writing; see Adelman, *Idleness, Contemplation and the Aesthetic*, pp. 10–37.

17. As Piero Sraffa notes, the South Seas passage was 'rewritten as a result of criticisms by George Ensor in his *Inquiry Concerning the Population of Nations: Containing a Refutation of Mr. Malthus's Essay on Population* ((London: E. Wilson, 1818), pp. 264–50'. See Ricardo, *Principles*, I, 100, n. 1.

18. For an excellent account of Malthus's *Essay on Population* together with its changing argument that I referred to above, see Hans E. Jensen, 'The Development of T. R. Malthus's Institutionalist Approach to the Cure of Poverty: From Punishment of the Poor to Investment in Their Human Capital', *Review of Social Economy*, 57:4 (December 1999): 450–65. Schwartz's also very useful account of Malthus's *Essay* can be found in *J. S. Mill*, pp. 10–12.

19. John Pullen, 'Introduction', in Malthus, *Principles*, I, xxvi. This plan was unsuccessful because of David Buchanan's very similar work, which was published in 1814.

20. Ibid., p. xxviii.

21. For an account of this correspondence, see Pullen, 'Introduction', pp. xx–xxi.

22. Ibid., p. xxi.

23. See Pullen, 'Introduction', pp. xxx–xxxiv for an account of Malthus's final stages of writing his *Principles*. While the publication was delayed several times, there is no evidence to suggest that the published version of Malthus's work engages with an outdated text of Ricardo's.

24. While Smith's *Wealth of Nations* considered the moral and martial health of a community in detail, and therefore addressed the stultifying effects of manual labour, his observations do not position the worker's life outside of labour as the decisive factor in his wellbeing. See Smith, *An Inquiry into the Nature and Causes of the Wealth of Nations*, eds. R. H. Campbell and A. S. Skinner, 2 vols. (Indianapolis: Liberty Fund, 1976), pp. 781–2.

25. This idea obviously foreshadows the rise of trade union movement, which was soon attempting to perform exactly the feat that Malthus considers impossible. Schwartz offers a comprehensive account of the rise of trade unions: see *J. S. Mill*, pp. 67–104.

26. See Jeremy Bentham, *Chrestomathia*, eds. M. J. Smith and W. H. Burston (Oxford: Clarendon Press, 1984), pp. 20–3. I offer a full treatment of this aspect of Bentham's thought in *Idleness, Contemplation and the Aesthetic*, pp. 46–52.

27. Schwartz, *J. S. Mill*, p. 63. Rudi Verburg also records the extent to which Mill's political economy was indebted to Smith: 'he designed the book after Adam Smith's *Wealth of Nations* and its attempt to associate [. . .] principles with their applications, filling the gap that had grown with the advances made in both political economy and the philosophy of society since Smith's days'. See Rudi Verburg, 'John Stuart Mill's Political Economy: Educational Means to Moral Progress', *Review of Social Economy*, 64:2 (June 2006): 225–46 (p. 238).

28. Ibid., p. 61. Evidence for a mode of cultural relativism in Mill's text similar to that of Smith and Ferguson is to be found in *Principles* I, 205: 'Mankind are capable of a far greater amount of public spirit than the present age is accustomed to suppose possible.'

29. Ibid., p. 59.

30. For Schwartz, Mill's 'authority as an economist was unrivalled in his own country' – and one should therefore talk of a 'Millian orthodoxy' – for 'twenty-five years' after the publication of his *Principles*. Further, for Schwartz, this dominance in fact 'paralysed the development of economic

science in Great Britain'; see Schwartz, *J. S. Mill*, pp. 1 and 17. For Berg, similarly, Mill 'was to dominate' political economy 'until the 1890s'; see Berg, *The Machinery Question*, p. 316.

31. Donald Winch, *Wealth and Life* (Cambridge: Cambridge University Press, 2009), p. 7.

32. For a slightly different reading of Mill's emphasis on 'custom', especially in relation to economic practices in England, see Dentith, 'Ideological Language', p. 187.

33. Schwartz, *J. S. Mill*, p. 60.

34. J. S. Mill, *Autobiography*, ed. J. Stillinger (Oxford: Oxford University Press, 1971), p. 86.

35. Ibid., p. 92.

36. Ibid., pp. 89–90. The details of Mill's 1826 crisis and the manner in which he expresses it in the *Autobiography* have more relevance for the present study than this brief summary allows. But as the companion piece to this book, my *Idleness, Contemplation and the Aesthetic, 1750–1830*, treats this aspect of Mill's thought at length in its epilogue (see pp. 158–70), further treatment of this subject here would be repetitive.

37. I will not focus heavily on the moral philosophy implied in passages of Mill's writing such as this; for a focused analysis of this aspect of Mill's system, see H. S. Jones, 'John Stuart Mill as Moralist', *Journal of the History of Ideas*, 53:2 (April–June, 1992): 287–308.

38. See Bentham, *Chrestomathia*, pp. 20–3.

39. T. W. Heyck, *The Transformation of Intellectual Life in Victorian England* (London: Croom Helm, 1982), p. 195.

40. This reading obviously opens up the complex field of Mill's relationship to imperialism. The present subject does not allow me to go into this issue in any detail, but for a thorough account of Mill's thinking and professional life in that context, see Beate Jahn, 'Barbarian Thoughts: Imperialism in the Philosophy of John Stuart Mill', *Review of International Studies*, 31 (2005): 599–618.

41. While highly interesting in the context of nineteenth-century political economy more generally, the thought of neither Robert Owen nor Charles Fourier hold relevance for the present study as their writing does not focus on the notions of passivity and idleness in any detail. For a concise summary of Owen's relationship to Mill's thought, see Schwartz, *J. S. Mill*, p. 31; and for an extended account of Mill's relationship to socialism before Marx (including Fourier), see Schwartz, *J. S. Mill*, pp. 153–92.

42. Mill's advocacy of population control through contraception was lifelong, though the precise reasons for this advocacy changed over time. On this subject, and on the eighteen-year-old Mill's arrest for distributing Francis

Place's 'diabolical handbills' which 'advis[ed] on methods of contraception', see Schwartz, *J. S. Mill*, pp. 28–9.

43. See *Principles*, II, 752–3.

44. V. W. Bladen, 'Introduction', in Mill, *Principles*, I, xxxix.

45. I say 'conventional' because of the utilitarian and reductive manner in which art-objects are handled in Smith's *Wealth of Nations*. His work's brief engagement with '[p]ublick diversions', for instance, simply notes how these 'have always been the objects of dread and hatred, to all the fanatical promoters of those popular frenzies. The gaiety and good humour which those diversions inspire were altogether inconsistent with that temper of mind, which was fittest for their purpose, or which they could best work upon'; see Smith, *Wealth of Nations*, pp. 796–7.

46. These are two of the many ways in which Mill's text anticipates Karl Marx's critique of political economy, and 'one of the great puzzles of the history of economic thought', as Bela Balassa expresses it, is why Marx treats Mill so scathingly throughout his oeuvre. For an excellent discussion of the relationship between these two figures that has not yet been surpassed, see Balassa's piece 'Karl Marx and John Stuart Mill', *Weltwirtschaftliches Archiv*, 83 (1959): 147–65.

47. Berg, *The Machinery Question*, p. 253.

48. Martin Wiener and Donald Winch both observe the extent to which this 'disdain' for material gain (Winch's term, quoted in Wiener) was influential on almost all 'economists in later-nineteenth- and twentieth-century England'. Again therefore, Mill's ideas should be seen as holding considerable authority. See Martin Wiener, *English Culture and the Decline of the Industrial Spirit, 1850–1980* (Cambridge: Cambridge University Press, 2004), p. 90.

49. Donald Winch, *Wealth and Life* (Cambridge: Cambridge University Press, 2009), p. 92.

50. Mill, 'The Negro Question', in *Essays on Equality, Law and Education, Collected Works of John Stuart Mill*, vol. XXI, ed. J. M. Robson (London: Routledge, 1984), pp. 85–96 (91).

Chapter 3
The 'Gospel of Work'

1. Samuel Smiles, *Self-Help* (London: John Murray, 1897), pp. v–vi.

2. See, for example, intellectual historians J. W. Burrow, *The Crisis of Reason: European Thought, 1848–1914* (New Haven: Yale University Press, 2000), p. 31, and Frederic Ewen, *A Half-Century of Greatness: The Creative Imagination of Europe, 1848–1884* (New York: New York University Press, 2007), pp. 27–32,

and literary critic Isobel Armstrong, *Victorian Poetry: Poetry, Poets and Politics* (London: Routledge, 1996).

3. Anne Mellor, *English Romantic Irony* (Cambridge: Harvard University Press, 1980), pp. 112–13.

4. Janice Haney, '"Shadow-Hunting": Romantic Irony, *Sartor Resartus*, and Victorian Romanticism', *Studies in Romanticism*, 17:3 (Summer, 1978): 307–33 (307).

5. Mellor, *English Romantic Irony*, p. 111.

6. S. T. Coleridge, *Biographia Literaria*, eds. J. Engell and W. J. Bate, 2 vols. (Princeton, NJ: Princeton University Press, 1983), I, p. 304.

7. For an account of Carlyle's extremely wide reading in German idealism, see Haney, 'Shadow-Hunting', p. 311.

8. See Friedrich Schiller, *On the Aesthetic Education of Man, in a Series of Letters*, eds. E. M. Wilkinson and L. A. Willoughby (Oxford: Clarendon Press, 1967), pp. 78–95.

9. The interrelations between Coleridge and Schiller around these terms are dealt with at length in Adelman, *Idleness, Contemplation and the Aesthetic* (Cambridge: Cambridge University Press, 2011), pp. 52–67, 108–32.

10. It should be noted, though, that aesthetic consciousness is, for Schiller, still a path towards correct moral and political behaviour, and that Coleridge's thought associates a comparable moral awareness with aesthetic contemplation.

11. I have written in more detail about political economy's 'stultification theory' in 'The "Desecrated Mind" and Its Alternatives: Dante Rossetti and Political Economy', *English Literary History*, 84:1 (2017): 195–222.

12. Coleridge, *Biographia*, II, pp. 15–16.

13. The shared ground between Carlyle, Schiller and Coleridge might be described as a Rousseauvian belief that the psychic wholeness of pre-industrial society can be re-established within commercial society (stemming from Jean-Jacques Rousseau's 'A Discourse on the Origin of Inequality', in, *The Social Contract and Discourses*, ed. G. D. H. Cole (London: Everyman, 2001), pp. 31–126).

14. Carlyle's notion that 'helldogs' of 'doubt', 'sorrow' and so on 'beleaguer' man until he sets himself to work could also be understood as a reformulation of the Romantic aesthetics of contemplation. William Cowper, for instance, in *The Task*, had attributed the same suspension of 'themes of sad import' and the 'anxieties of life' to the composition of poetry, contending that the quality of attention in aesthetic concentration outstripped that of manual or other forms of labour. See Cowper, *The Task*, II, 285–303.

15. See Ewen, *A Half-Century of Greatness*, pp. 23–5.

16. Michael John Kooy, *Coleridge, Schiller and Aesthetic Education* (Basingstoke: Palgrave, 2002), p. 111.

17. Jonathan Mendilow, 'Carlyle, Marx & the ILP: Alternative Routes to Socialism', *Polity*, 17:2 (winter 1984): 225–47 (241).

18. Ibid.

19. It is for this reason that Friedrich Engels's thought, in *The Condition of the Working Classes in England* (1845), for example, also shares affinities with Carlyle and Marx. See, for instance, his description of the arduous labour on which the factory system is built, which William Henderson and William Chaloner consider to be lacking in the 'inner spiritual satisfaction' of more aesthetic or rounded activity (Friedrich Engels, *The Condition of the Working Classes in England*, eds. W. O. Henderson & W. H. Chaloner (Oxford: Blackwell, 1971), p. 133).

20. Karl Marx, *Grundrisse*, in Karl Marx and Friedrich Engels, *Marx-Engels-Gesamtausgabe (MEGA)*, Section II: *Das Kapital und Vorarbeiten* (Berlin: Dietz, 1988), vol. 1.2, p. 499.

21. Karl Marx, *Grundrisse*, trans. Martin Nicolaus (London: Penguin, 1974), p. 611.

22. See below for more on the idea of the 'thirst for labour' in the thought of Adam Ferguson, who Marx refers to throughout his writings.

23. Karl Marx, *Das Kapital: Krtik der politischen Oekonomie*, in Karl Marx and Friedrich Engels, *Werke*, vol. 23 (Berlin: Dietz, 1962), p. 57.

24. Karl Marx, *Capital: A Critique of Political Economy*, eds. B. Fowkes, E. Mandel and D. Fernbach, 3 vols. (London: Penguin, 2006), I, p. 133.

25. Ibid., p. 667.

26. Marx, *Das Kapital*, p. 552.

27. Marx, *Grundrisse*, in *MEGA*, vol. 1.2, p. 392.

28. Marx, *Grundrisse*, p. 488.

29. Terry Eagleton, *The Ideology of the Aesthetic* (Oxford: Blackwell, 1990), p. 206.

30. Ibid.

31. Isobel Armstrong offers a set of more general analogies between Carlyle and Marx's projects, observing that the former developed a theory of commercial society's alienation a decade before the latter, for instance. See Isobel Armstrong, *Victorian Poetry: Poetry, Poetics and Politics* (London: Routledge, 1996), p. 4.

32. Gregory Dart, 'The Reworking of "Work"', *Victorian Literature & Culture*, 27:1 (1999): 69–96 (80).

33. Rob Breton, 'WorkPerfect: William Morris and the Gospel of Work', *Utopian Studies*, 13:1 (2002): 43–56 (43).

34. Francis O'Gorman, 'Tennyson's "The Lotos-Eaters" and the Politics of the 1830s', *Victorian Review*, 30:1 (2004): 1–20.

35. Armstrong, *Victorian Poetry*, pp. 86–94.

36. Ibid., pp. 87–8.

37. Eve Kosofsky Sedgwick, *Between Men: English Literature and Male Homosocial Desire* (New York: Columbia University Press, 1985), pp. 129–30.

38. Alan Sinfield, *Dramatic Monologue* (London: Methuen, 1977), p. 32.

39. I have analysed *The Castle of Indolence* in these terms in 'Idleness and Creativity: Between Neo-Classicism and Romanticism', in *Idleness, Indolence and Leisure in English Literature*, eds. M. Fludernik and M. Nandi (Basingstoke: Palgrave, 2014), pp. 174–94 (see especially 174–8).

40. In the 1842 edition of the poem.

41. Coleridge, 'Effusion' (the first version of 'The Eolian Harp'), ll. 28–9.

42. Samuel Taylor Coleridge, 'The Rime of the Ancient Mariner' (1834 text), in *The Complete Poems*, ed. William Keach (London: Penguin, 1997), pp. 167–86, ll. 270–1.

43. William A. Ulmer, 'The Human Seasons: Arnold, Keats, and "The Scholar-Gipsy"', *Victorian Poetry*, 22:3 (autumn 1984): 247–61 (247).

44. David Moldstat, 'The Imagination in *The Vanity of Dogmatizing* and "The Scholar-Gipsy": Arnold's Reversal of Glanvill', *Victorian Poetry*, 25:2 (summer 1987): 159–72 (160).

45. The present consideration of the wide influence of the 'gospel of work' necessitates dealing with Hopkins here, even though in Chapter 4 we will return to the period between 1850 and the 1880s. This approach, of course, obscures the extent to which Hopkins's writing builds on and develops from the thought of figures such as Ruskin and Arnold, considered in Chapter 4.

46. William Morris, *News from Nowhere and Other Writings*, ed. Clive Wilmer (London: Penguin, 2004), p. 204.

Chapter 4
Cultural Theory and Aesthetic Failure

1. See Peter Faulkner, 'Ruskin and Morris', *Journal of William Morris Studies*, 14:1 (autumn 2000): 6–17, who recounts Morris first encountering Ruskin in the 1850s and how this encounter (in J. W. Mackail's words) transformed a 'strong direction' into a 'true vocation' (6). Ruskin is of course also extremely influential on George Eliot, and specifically on her conception of 'realism', although the account of *Middlemarch* I gave in this study's 'Introduction' did not leave occasion to explore such a connection. For more on this, see

Darrel Mansell, Jr., 'Ruskin and George Eliot's "Realism"', *Criticism*, 7:3 (summer 1965): 203–16.

2. For a fuller account of political economy's mental stultification theory, see Adelman, 'The "Desecrated Mind" and Its Alternatives: Dante Rossetti and Political Economy', *ELH*, 84:1 (2017): 195–222 (195–206).

3. Schiller, *Aesthetic Education*, p. 35.

4. I am not meaning to imply, with these and other comments on the 'Lotos-Eaters', that Tennyson is himself ideologically aligned with the perspective of that poem. In this sense his 'Ulysses' of 1842 should be seen as an interesting and obviously connected counterpart to the 'Lotos-Eaters', for it challenges the applicability and power of its eponymous speaker's heroic and active impulses. For my purposes in this study, the 'Lotos-Eaters' nevertheless encapsulates an important strand of nineteenth-century thought, and an influential stance on the issue of human idleness.

5. Along with Arnold, Pater and Morris, Ruskin is one of the primary focal points of *The Vulgarization of Art: The Victorians and Aesthetic Democracy*.

6. See Morris, *News from Nowhere*, p. 66.

7. It is for this reason that Ruskin is conventionally described, like Carlyle, as an advocate of the 'gospel of work'; see, for instance, Breton, 'WorkPerfect', p. 43.

8. 'The Strayed Reveller' and 'The Scholar-Gipsy' are even more contemporary with *The Stones of Venice* than 'The Lotos-Eaters'. The first was published in 1849; the second the same year as 'The Nature of Gothic', 1853.

9. George Gordon Lord Byron, 'Manfred', in *The Major Works*, ed. Jerome J. McGann (Oxford: Oxford University Press, 2000), pp. 274–314, I.ii.40–3.

10. Dowling, *Vulgarization*, p. 35.

11. Ibid., pp. 31–2; cf. Elizabeth K. Helsinger, *Ruskin and the Art of the Beholder* (Cambridge: Harvard University Press, 1982), p. 206.

12. Kenneth Daley, *The Rescue of Romanticism* (Athens: Ohio University Press, 2001), pp. 6–7.

13. See Francis O'Gorman, 'Ruskin's Aesthetic of Failure in *The Stones of Venice*', *The Review of English Studies*, 55:220 (June 2004): 374–91.

14. Dowling, *Vulgarization*, p. 1; for a more detailed and textual account of the work's genesis, see R. H. Super, 'Culture and Anarchy' in his *Culture and Anarchy*, pp. 408–17.

15. William Wordsworth, *The Prelude, 1799, 1805, 1850*, eds. J. Wordsworth, M. H. Abrams and S. Gill (London: Norton, 1979), 1850, XIII, ll. 71, 76–8, 80–81. Wordsworth's hostility to political economy, and especially to Malthus, is discussed in Winch, *Riches and Poverty*, pp. 318–20.

16. Contemporary critics certainly picked up on this issue. Henry Sidgwick, for example, described Arnold as separating off the claims of 'harmonious self-

development' from the 'cries of struggling humanity'; see 'The Prophet of Culture', *Macmillan's Magazine*, 1867: xvi, *Matthew Arnold Prose Writings: the Critical Heritage*, eds. C. Dawson and J. Pfordresher (London: Routledge, 1979), pp. 209–24 (p. 213). Sidgwick's tone of studied disbelief reflects the incompatibility between Arnold's essentially idealist project and the beliefs of contemporary utilitarian thought: 'if it were possible that all men, under all circumstances, should feel what some men, in some fortunate spheres, may truly feel – that there is no conflict, no antagonism, between the full development of the individual and the progress of the world – I should be loth [sic] to hint at any jar or discord in this harmonious movement' (p. 213). This stance also prefigures Dowling's take on aesthetic democracy, which will be considered at the end of this chapter.

17. Dowling, *Vulgarization*, pp. 20–2.
18. See, for example, Mill, *Principles*, II, 761–2.
19. See, for example, Dowling, *Vulgarization*, p. 28.
20. See Adelman, *Idleness, Contemplation and the Aesthetic*, pp. 141–58.
21. Stefan Collini, *Arnold* (Oxford: Oxford University Press, 1988), p. 85; Collini's italics.
22. See *Culture*, 191, where Arnold takes issue with contemporary 'earnest lovers of action'.
23. Collini offers an excellent treatment of this important Arnoldian catchphrase, observing how these terms have taken on an 'unctuous, almost genteel [and] even anaemic air' when in fact they were chosen 'to stand for gaiety rather than solemnity, for knowledge rather than righteousness, for pure, useless self-exploration rather than corrective, functional, self-improvement'; see Collini, *Arnold*, pp. 83–4. This unfortunate transformation is evidence of the degradation of aesthetic consciousness between 1850 and 1885 that the present chapter is analysing.
24. While Keats's correspondence stresses the transformative effect of a 'page full of poesy', the 1818 letter to Reynolds that explains this phenomenon also makes clear that it is the beauty of 'the Morning and the Thrush' that initially inspired these thoughts; see Keats, *Letters*, I, 232–3.
25. See Coleridge, 'Frost at Midnight', ll. 56–8.
26. Dowling, *Vulgarization*, p. 76.
27. In 1873, Pater retitled his work *The Renaissance: Studies in Art and Poetry*, in part in response to criticism (by figures such as Emilia Frances Strong) that it did not contain much actual history (see Jeffrey Wallen, 'Alive in the Grave: Walter Pater's Renaissance', *ELH*, 66:4 (winter 1999): 1033–51 (1033)); for ease of reference, I will use the shortened form of this second title.

28. Pater, 'Wordsworth', in *Appreciations, with an Essay on Style* (Rockville, Maryland: Arc Manor, 2008), pp. 26–39 (p. 37).

29. Ibid., p. 38.

30. Matthew Potolsky, 'Fear of Falling: Walter Pater's *Marius the Epicurean* as a Dangerous Influence', *ELH*, 65:3 (fall 1998): 701–29 (701).

31. Wallen, 'Alive in the Grave', p. 1036.

32. Pater makes the comparison with Keats explicit slightly later in the 'Winckelmann' essay; see *Renaissance*, 177.

33. Laurel Brake, 'Pater, Walter Horatio (1839–1894)', *Oxford Dictionary of National Biography* (Oxford: Oxford University Press, 2004), accessed 25 February 2015, www.oxforddnb.com/view/article/21525?docPos=1.

34. Jonathan Wordsworth, 'Letter dated 17 March 1873', in *Walter Pater: The Critical Heritage*, ed. R. M. Seiler (London: Routledge, 1995), pp. 61–3 (pp. 61–2); Jonathan Wordsworth's father was William Wordsworth's nephew.

35. I will refer to some of these below.

36. Indeed, in 1868, Pater even included a short paragraph admitting that this outlook 'seem[s] desolate', and that 'all the bitterness of life seems concentrated in' these words; see Pater, 'Poems by William Morris', *Westminster Review*, XC (October 1868): 300–312 (p. 311).

37. Dowling notes that Pater's *Renaissance* is part of a distinctly 'liberalist' agenda, meaning that the work aligns with the energies of contemporary 'republicanism and reform' (see *Vulgarization*, pp. 75–6). What we are seeing here, by contrast, are the metaphysical and psychic conditions that necessitate aesthetic consciousness.

38. Wolfgang Iser, *Walter Pater: The Aesthetic Moment*, trans. David H. Wilson (Cambridge: Cambridge University Press, 2011), p. 31.

39. In 1868, this phrase was a clarification of the famous formulation 'art for art's sake' (see Pater, 'Poems by William Morris', p. 312). As Iser summarizes, the rationale of this idea is that art 'can transcend the fleeting experience and offer its devotee a feeling of detachment from the ravages of time' (Iser, *The Aesthetic Moment*, p. 31). Note here that it is logically the 'devotee' who can feel this effect, not any untutored citizen, as it was in previous versions of this argument.

40. Dowling, *Vulgarization*, p. 75.

41. Ibid., p. xii.

42. Ibid., p. 24.

43. In *News from Nowhere*, this dissipation is represented by Ellen's grandfather, 'the old grumbler' (see Morris, *News*, p. 173).

44. Iser, *The Aesthetic Moment*, pp. 131–2.

45. Ibid., p. 141.

46. It is presumably the pervasive scepticism of *Marius* that motivated Pater's reinstatement of the 'Conclusion' in the 1888 *Renaissance*; the novel radically sours – and might even be said to negate – that essay's claims.

47. Pater, *Marius the Epicurean*, ed. Michael Levey (London: Penguin, 1985), p. 211.

48. See ibid., p. 117.

49. Ibid., p. 118.

50. Ibid., p. 241.

51. Iser, *The Aesthetic Moment*, p. 151.

Chapter 5
The Gothicization of Idleness

1. See Anne Williams, 'Natural Supernaturalism in *Wuthering Heights*', *Studies in Philology*, 82:1 (winter 1985): 104–27, Anne K. Mellor, *Romanticism & Gender* (London: Routledge, 1993) and Michael S. Macovski, '*Wuthering Heights* and the Rhetoric of Interpretation', *ELH*, 54:2 (summer 1987): 363–84. Williams convincingly explores the extent to which Brontë's novel shares Wordsworth's conviction that 'the natural and supernatural provide the complementary contexts for the revelation of [. . .] "the primary laws of our nature"' (105); Mellor argues for *Wuthering Heights*' inheritance of 'a masculine Romanticism' from Shelley, Byron and Wordsworth (191); and Macovski, standing closest to the concerns of the present chapter, explores the notions of 'the externally-defined self' and 'plural self-consciousness' in the novel (377), doing so with reference to a wide range of Romantic concerns.

2. See, for example, Joseph Holt Ingraham's American travelogue, *The South-West* (New York: Harper & Brothers, 1835), I, p. 126, and James Tod's *Travels in Western India* (London: W. H. Allen & Co., 1839), p. 384.

3. On Lockwood's status within Brontë's scheme, see Williams, 'Natural Supernaturalism', p. 110.

4. For a detailed account of Polidori's text's conception and publication, see Patricia L. Skarda, 'Vampirism and Plagiarism: Byron's Influence and Polidori's Practice, *Studies in Romanticism*, 28:2 (summer 1989): 249–69 (especially 250–1).

5. It is worth noting that Le Fanu and Stoker – and indeed Oscar Wilde, who will briefly appear in my analysis of *Dracula* – are all Irish and therefore might all be seen as sharing a kind of marginality within British literary culture. There will not be occasion to consider this shared position in detail in the present study, or its connection to gothic writing and the sideways look at a society that discourse promotes, other than to quote Roy Foster on these issues: 'the line of Irish protestant supernatural fiction is an obvious one, though it has not been

analysed as such. It leads from [Charles] Maturin and Le Fanu to Bram Stoker and Elizabeth Bowen and [William Butler] Yeats – marginalized Irish protestants all, often living in England but regretting Ireland, stemming from families with strong clerical and professional colorations, whose occult preoccupations surely mirror a sense of displacement, a loss of social and psychological integration, and an escapism motivated by the threat of a takeover by the Catholic middle classes'. See Roy Foster, *Paddy and Mr Punch: Connections in Irish and English History* (London: Allen Lane, 1993), p. 220.

6. I have compared these two texts in these terms in 'Idle Thought in Wordsworth's Lucy Cycle'.

7. John Polidori, *'The Vampyre' and Other Tales of the Macabre*, eds. R. Morrison and C. Baldick (Oxford: Oxford University Press, 1998), p. 20.

8. Fred Botting, *Gothic* (London: Routledge, 1996), p. 145.

9. This description might be read as recalling Coleridge's nineteenth-century reputation as a figure whose ability to talk beautifully and encyclopaedically was not matched by his actual productivity. See, for example, William Hazlitt's account, 'Mr. Coleridge' in *The Spirit of the Age*, in D. Wu (ed.), *Romanticism: An Anthology*, pp. 784–91, which begins 'The present is an age of talkers, and not of doers' (p. 784).

10. See, for example, Marx, *Capital*, I, 874: 'In actual history, it is a notorious fact that conquest, enslavement, robbery, murder, in short, force, play the greatest part [in the history of property]'.

11. See *Varney*, 277.

12. Franco Moretti, *Signs Taken for Wonders: On the Sociology of Literary Forms* (London: Verso, 2005), p. 107.

13. David Glover, *Vampires, Mummies, and Liberals: Bram Stoker and the Politics of Popular Fiction* (London: Duke University Press, 1996), p. 15.

14. Moretti, *Signs Taken for Wonders*, pp. 83–98.

15. Nina Auerbach and David Skal note that Stoker also partially borrows the outline of Dracula's arrival in England from Rymer. In their description, Rymer's story is one 'of a mysterious continental nobleman, Lord Francis Varney, who arrives in England by way of a shipwreck in a storm to vampirize young maidens'; see their headnote at *Dracula*, 335–6.

16. Glover, *Vampires, Mummies, and Liberals*, p. 6; no manuscripts of the Shelley lecture are extant, so it is not possible to pursue this connection further. It is also worth noting, in this connection, that Stoker's undergraduate studies were in mathematics and that his subsequent career as a Dublin civil servant and then business manager at the Lyceum Theatre mark him out as in one sense a model of Carlylean, or even Millite, professionalized virtue. *Dracula's* partisan exploration of the interconnections between aesthetic consciousness

and virtuous productivity is thus closely tied to the differing roles and worlds Stoker experienced in his professional and personal lives.

17. *Dracula*, 38, n. 8.

18. For a classic analysis of this subject, see for example Carol A. Senf, '*Dracula*: Stoker's Response to the New Woman', *Victorian Studies*, 26:1 (autumn 1982): 33–49.

19. See *Dracula*, 61, n. 7.

20. Keith Williams, *H. G. Wells, Modernity and the Movies* (Liverpool: *Liverpool University Press*, 2007), p. 55.

21. In Rymer's narrative, Flora's sleep-walking scene leads (somewhat absurdly) to a kind of 'heart-to-heart' between her and Varney in which the vampire explains how his existence oscillates between an irresistible thirst for blood and long periods of remorse, regret and melancholy; see *Varney*, 277.

22. There is a long history of reading Wilde's novel in this manner; the most appropriate for the present context is perhaps John Paul Riquelme's 'Oscar Wilde's Aesthetic Gothic: Walter Pater, Dark Enlightenment, and The Picture of Dorian Gray', *Modern Fiction Studies*, 46:3 (2000): 610–31, which has it that Wilde 'echoes Pater not in order to agree with the older [. . .] writer's views but to present them darkly, in shades of gray [sic], as at base contradictory in destructive and self-destructive ways' (617). Pater also reviewed Wilde's novel himself and stepped outside of the terms of his 'Conclusion' to criticize it for its disregard for conventional morality; see Pater, 'A Novel by Mr Oscar Wilde', *The Bookman*, 23 (November 1891), pp. 59–60.

23. Botting, *Gothic*, p. 135.

24. David Punter, *The Literature of Terror*, 2 vols. (London: Longman, 1996), II, p. 1.

Conclusion

1. See *Idleness, Contemplation and the Aesthetic*, pp. 138–9.

2. Morris, *News from Nowhere*, p. 75.

3. Raymond Williams, *Culture and Society* (London: Chatto & Windus, 1967), p. 67.

Epilogue: Substitutive Satisfaction

1. See Matt Ffytche, *The Foundation of the Unconscious: Schelling, Freud, and the Birth of the Modern Psyche* (Cambridge: CUP, 2012) and *Reading Freud's*

Reading, eds. S. L. Gilman, J. Birmele, J. Geller and V. D. Greenberg (New York: New York University Press, 1994).

2. Sigmund Freud, *Civilization and Its Discontents*, trans. D. McLintock (London: Penguin, 2004), p. 1; Freud, *Das Unbehagen in der Kultur*, *Gesammelte Werke*, vol. XIV (Frankfurt am Main: S. Fischer Verlag, 1976), pp. 419–506 (pp. 421 & 425).
3. Freud, *Civilization*, pp. 1–2.
4. Freud, *Kultur*, p. 422.
5. See Wordsworth, *Prelude*, 1850, XIV, ll. 42, 44 & 70–1.
6. Freud, *Civilization*, p. 2.
7. Freud, *Kultur*, p. 422.
8. Ibid., pp. 423–4.
9. Freud, *Civilization*, p. 4.
10. Freud, *Kultur*, p. 425.
11. Freud, *Civilization*, pp. 5–6.
12. It should be noted, at this point, that in Freud's other writing he often uses literary examples in order to demonstrate how aesthetic culture has anticipated or intuited his psychology (the use of E. T. A. Hoffman in the 1919 essay 'Das Unheimliche' – 'The Uncanny' – is a case in point). While *Civilization and Its Discontents* does not do this, the connections I am tracing here, such as this one to Tennyson's influential 'Lotos-Eaters', demonstrate that such a relationship between psychoanalytic theory and aesthetic writing could also be constructed for this work. In this case, however, this relationship is double-edged, for by making these connections, nineteenth-century English literary culture is put in the position of effectively confirming its own irrelevance.
13. Ibid., p. 11.
14. Freud, *Kultur*, p. 430.
15. Freud, *Civilization*, p. 11.
16. Freud, *Kultur*, p. 430.
17. Freud, *Civilization*, pp. 14–15.
18. Freud, *Kultur*, p. 432.
19. Freud, *Civilization*, p. 15.
20. Freud, *Kultur*, p. 433.
21. Ibid., pp. 437–8.
22. Freud, *Civilization*, p. 21.
23. Ibid.
24. Freud, *Kultur*, p. 438.
25. Freud may not be steeped in the English tradition of enquiry into these ideas, but he is certainly aware of a text like Schiller's *On the Aesthetic Education of*

Man and its argument for the wholeness and perfection the individual worker attains in aesthetic consciousness.

26. Freud, *Kultur*, p. 439.
27. Freud, *Civilization*, p. 23.
28. Freud, *Kultur*, p. 439.
29. Freud, *Civilization*, p. 25.
30. Freud, *Kultur*, p. 441.

Bibliography

Primary Sources

Barbauld, Anna Letitia. 'To Mr. S. T. Coleridge', in *Anna Letitia Barbauld: Selected Poetry and Prose*, eds. W. McCarthy & E. Kraft (Ormskirk: Broadview, 2002), pp. 142–3.

Bentham, Jeremy. *Chrestomathia*, eds. M. J. Smith & W. H. Burston (Oxford: Clarendon Press, 1984).

Braddon, Mary Elizabeth. 'Good Lady Ducayne', *The Strand Magazine*, XI (February, 1896): 185–99.

Byron, George Gordon Lord. 'Manfred', in *The Major Works*, ed. Jerome J. McGann (Oxford: Oxford University Press, 2000), pp. 274–314.

Carlyle, Thomas. *Selected Writings*, ed. A Shelston (London: Penguin, 1986).

Carlyle, Thomas & John Ruskin. *The Correspondence of Thomas Carlyle & John Ruskin*, ed. George Allen Cate (Stanford, CA: Stanford University Press, 1982).

Coleridge, Samuel Taylor. 'Frost at Midnight', in *Coleridge's Poetry and Prose*, eds. N. Halmi, P. Magnuson & R. Modiano (London: W. W. Norton, 2004), pp. 120–3.

'The Eolian Harp', in *The Complete Poems*, ed. W. Keach (London: Penguin, 1997), pp. 87–8.

'The Rime of the Ancient Mariner', in *The Complete Poems*, ed. W. Keach (London: Penguin, 1997), pp. 167–86.

Biographia Literaria, eds. J. Engell & W. J. Bate, 2 vols. (Princeton, NJ: Princeton University Press, 1983).

Cowper, William. *The Task, and Selected Other Poems*, ed. J. Sambrook (London: Longman, 1994).

Eliot, George. *Middlemarch*, eds. D. Carroll & F. Bonaparte (Oxford: Oxford University Press, 1998).

Engels, Friedrich. *The Condition of the Working Classes in England*, eds. W. O. Henderson & W. H. Chaloner (Oxford: Blackwell, 1971).

Die Lage der arbeitenden Klasse in England (Stuttgart: J. H. W. Diek, 1892).

Fourier, Charles. *The Theory of the Four Movements*, eds. G. S. Jones & I. Patterson (Cambridge: Cambridge University Press, 1996).

Freud, Sigmund. *Civilization and Its Discontents*, trans. D. McLintock (London: Penguin, 2004).

Das Unbehagen in der Kultur, Gesammelte Werke, vol. XIV (Frankfurt am Main: S. Fischer Verlag, 1976), pp. 419–506.

Hazlitt, William. 'Mr. Coleridge', in *Romanticism: An Anthology,* ed. D. Wu (Oxford: Blackwell, 1994), pp. 784–91.

Ingraham, Joseph Holt. *The South-West,* 2 vols. (New York: Harper & Brothers, 1835).

Jerome, Jerome K. *Three Men in a Boat* (London: Folio Society, 1964).

Idle Thoughts of an Idle Fellow, ed. S. Pile (London: Everyman, 1983).

The Second Thoughts of an Idle Fellow (London: Hurst & Blackett, 1898).

Kant, Immanuel. *Kritik der Urtheilskraft* (Berlin: Druck und Derlag von Georg Reimer, 1913).

The Critique of Judgement, ed. J. C. Meredith (Oxford: Clarendon Press, 1978).

Keats, John. 'Ode on Indolence', in *The Complete Poems,* ed. J. Barnard (London: Penguin, 1988), pp. 349–51.

Le Fanu, Sheridan. *In a Glass Darkly,* ed. R. Tracy (Oxford: Oxford University Press, 1993).

Malthus, Thomas. *An Essay on the Principle of Population,* ed. Patricia Hames, 2 vols. (Cambridge: Cambridge University Press, 1989).

Marx, Karl. *Capital: A Critique of Political Economy,* eds. B. Fowkes, E. Mandel & D. Fernbach, 3 vols. (London: Penguin, 2006).

'Das Kapital: Krtik der politischen Oekonomie', in *Werke,* eds. Karl Marx & Friedrich Engels, vol. 23 (Berlin: Dietz, 1962).

Grundrisse, trans. Martin Nicolaus (London: Penguin, 1974).

Grundrisse, in *Marx-Engels-Gesamtausgabe (MEGA), Section II: Das Kapital und Vorarbeiten,* eds. Karl Marx & Friedrich Engles (Berlin: Dietz, 1988), pp. 1–748.

Marx, Karl & Friedrich Engels. *The Marx-Engels Reader,* ed. Robert C. Tucker (London: Norton, 1978).

The Communist Manifesto, ed. Gareth Stedman Jones (London: Penguin, 2002).

Mayhew, Henry. *London Labour and the London Poor,* 4 vols. (London: Cass, 1967).

Mill, John Stuart. *Principles of Political Economy,* 2 vols. (London: Parker, 1852).

Selected Economic Writings, ed. D. Winch (London: Oliver, 1966).

Essays on Some Unsettled Questions of Political Economy (London: Kelley, 1968).

'The Negro Question', in *Essays on Equality, Law and Education, Collected Works of John Stuart Mill,* vol. XXI, ed. J. M. Robson (London: Routledge, 1984), pp. 85–96.

On Liberty, eds. John Gray & G. W. Smith (London: Routledge, 1991).

Morris, William. *News from Nowhere and Other Writings,* ed. Clive Wilmer (London: Penguin, 2004).

Owen, Robert. *A New View of Society and Other Writings,* ed. G. Claeys (London: Penguin, 1991).

Pater, Walter. *Marius the Epicurean,* ed. Michael Levey (London: Penguin, 1985).

'Wordsworth', in *Appreciations, with an Essay on Style* (Rockville, MD: Arc Manor, 2008), pp. 26–39.

'Poems by William Morris', *Westminster Review,* XC (October, 1868): 300–12.

'A Novel by Mr Oscar Wilde', *The Bookman*, 23 (November, 1891): 59–60.

Peacock, Thomas Love. '*The Four Ages of Poetry*', ed. H. F. B. Brett-Smith (Oxford: Basil Blackwell, 1953).

Polidori, John. *'The Vampyre' and Other Tales of the Macabre*, eds. R Morrison & C. Baldick (Oxford: Oxford University Press, 1998).

Ricardo, David. *Notes on Malthus's Principles of Political Economy*, ed. P. Sraffa (Cambridge: Cambridge University Press, 1951).

Rousseau, Jean-Jacques. 'A Discourse on the Origin of Inequality' in *The Social Contract and Discourses*, ed. G. D. H. Cole (London: Everyman, 2001), pp. 31–126.

Ruskin, John. '*A Joy For Ever*', *The Two Paths* (London: George Allen & Sons, 1911).
    Lectures on Art (London: George Allen, 1892).
    The Genius of John Ruskin, ed. John D. Rosenberg (London: George Allen & Unwin, 1964).
    Selected Writings, ed. Dinah Birch (Oxford: Oxford University Press, 2009).
    '*Unto This Last*': *Four Essays on the First Principles of Political Economy*, ed. P. M. Yarker (London: Collins, 1970).

Schiller, Friedrich. *On the Aesthetic Education of Man, in a Series of Letters*, eds. E. M. Wilkinson & L. A. Willoughby (Oxford: Clarendon Press, 1967).

Shakespeare, William. *Troilus and Cressida, The Complete Works*, ed. W. J. Craig (Oxford: Oxford University Press, 1949), pp. 667–700.

Shelley, Mary & Percy Bysshe Shelley. *History of a Six Weeks' Tour*, ed. J. Wordsworth (Oxford: Woodstock Books, 1991).

Shelley, Percy Bysshe. *A Defence of Poetry, The Major Works*, eds. Z. Leader & M. O'Neill (Oxford: Oxford University Press, 2003), pp. 674–701.
    'Hymn to Intellectual Beauty', *The Major Works*, eds. Z. Leader & M. O'Neill (Oxford: Oxford University Press, 2003), pp. 114–17.
    'Ode to the West Wind', *The Major Works*, eds. Z. Leader & M. O'Neill (Oxford: Oxford University Press, 2003), pp. 412–14.

Sidgwick, Henry. 'The Prophet of Culture', *Macmillan's Magazine*, 1867: xvi, *Matthew Arnold Prose Writings: The Critical Heritage*, eds. C. Dawson & J. Pfordresher (London: Routledge, 1979), pp. 209–24.

Smiles, Samuel. *Self-Help* (London: John Murray, 1897).

Smith, Adam. *An Inquiry into the Nature and Causes of the Wealth of Nations*, eds. R. H. Campbell & A. S. Skinner, 2 vols. (Indianapolis, IN: Liberty Fund, 1976).

Tennyson, Alfred. *Tennyson's Poetry*, ed. R. W. Hill Jr. (London: Norton, 1999).

Tod, James. *Travels in Western India* (London: W. H. Allen & Co., 1839).

Wilde, Oscar. *The Picture of Dorian Gray*, eds. M. P. Gillespie & D. L. Lawler (London: Norton, 2007).

Wollstonecraft, Mary. Letters Written during a Short Residence in Sweden, Norway and Denmark, in *The Complete Works*, eds. J. Todd & M. Butler, 7 vols. (New York, NY: New York University Press, 1989), vol. VI, pp. 237–348.

Wordsworth, William. *The Prelude, 1799, 1805, 1850*, eds. J. Wordsworth, M. H. Abrams & S. Gill (London: Norton, 1979).

Secondary Sources

Adelman, Richard. 'Idle Thought in Wordsworth's Lucy Cycle', *Romanticism*, 17:1 (April, 2011): 94–105.
    Idleness, Contemplation and the Aesthetic, 1750–1830 (Cambridge: Cambridge University Press, 2011).
    'The Desecrated Mind and Its Alternatives: Dante Rossetti and Political Economy', *ELH*, 84:1 (spring, 2017): 195–222.
Armstrong, Isobel. *Victorian Poetry: Poetry, Poets and Politics* (London: Routledge, 1996).
Balassa, Bela A. 'Karl Marx and John Stuart Mill', *Weltwirtschaftliches Archiv*, 83 (1959): 147–65.
Bate, Walter Jackson. *John Keats* (London: The Hogarth Press, 1992).
Berg, Maxine. *The Machinery Question and the Making of Political Economy* (Cambridge: Cambridge University Press, 1980).
    'Progress and Providence in Early Nineteenth-Century Political Economy', *Social History*, 15:3 (October, 1990): 365–75.
Bewell, Alan. 'The Political Implication of Keats's Classicist Aesthetics', *Studies in Romanticism*, 25:2 (summer, 1986): 220–9.
Bonnell Green, David. 'Keats, Swift, and Pliny the Elder', *Notes and Queries* CXCV (11 November 1950): 499–501.
Botting, Fred. *Gothic* (London: Routledge, 1996).
Brake, Laurel. 'Pater, Walter Horatio (1839–1894)', *Oxford Dictionary of National Biography* (Oxford: Oxford University Press, 2004), accessed 25 February 2015, http://www.oxforddnb.com/view/article/21525?docpos=1.
Breton, Rob. 'WorkPerfect: William Morris and the Gospel of Work', *Utopian Studies*, 13:1 (2002): 43–56.
Bromwich, David. 'Keats', *Critical Essays on John Keats*, ed. H. de Almeida (Boston: G. K. Hall and Co., 1990), pp. 222–60.
Burrow, J. W. *The Crisis of Reason: European Thought, 1848–1914* (London: Yale University Press, 2000).
Butler, Marilyn. *Romantics, Rebels & Reactionaries* (Oxford: Oxford University Press, 1981).
Carroll, Joseph. *The Cultural Theory of Matthew Arnold* (Berkeley: University of California Press, 1982).
Casaliggi, Carmen & Paul March-Russell (eds.). *Legacies of Romanticism: Literature, Culture, Aesthetics* (London: Routledge, 2012).
Charlton, John. *The Chartists* (London: Pluto, 1997).
Chernaik, Judith. *The Lyrics of Shelley* (Cleveland: Press of Case Western Reserve University, 1972).

Coleman, Dermot. *George Eliot and Money: Economics, Ethics and Literature* (Cambridge: Cambridge University Press, 2014).

Collini, Stefan. *Arnold* (Oxford: Oxford University Press, 1988).

Collini, Stefan, B. W. Young & Richard Whatmore (eds.). *Economy, Polity and Society: British Intellectual History, 1750–1950* (Cambridge: Cambridge University Press, 2000).

Connell, Philip. *Romanticism, Economics and the Question of Culture* (Oxford: Oxford University Press, 2001).

Cranston, Maurice. 'John Stuart Mill and Liberty', *The Wilson Quarterly*, 11:5 (winter 1987): 82–91.

Dart, Gregory. 'The Reworking of "Work"', *Victorian Literature & Culture*, 27:1 (1999): 69–96.

Daley, Kenneth. *The Rescue of Romanticism: Walter Pater and John Ruskin* (Athens: Ohio University Press, 2001).

De Almeida, Hermione (ed.). *Critical Essays on John Keats* (Boston, MA: G. K. Hall & Co., 1990).

Dentith, Simon. 'Political Economy, Fiction and the Language of Practical Ideology in Nineteenth-Century England', *Social History*, 8:2 (May, 1983): 183–99.

Donnelly, Hugo. 'Beyond Rational Discourse: The "Mysterious Tongue" of "Mont Blanc"', *Studies in Romanticism*, 29:4 (winter, 1990): 571–81.

Dowling, Linda. *The Vulgarization of Art: The Victorians and Aesthetic Democracy* (Charlottesville, VA: University Press of Virginia, 1996).

Eagleton, Terry. *The Ideology of the Aesthetic* (Oxford: Blackwell, 1990).

Ewen, Frederic. *A Half-Century of Greatness: The Creative Imagination of Europe, 1848–1884* (New York: New York University Press, 2007).

Faulkner, Peter. *Against the Age: An Introduction to William Morris* (London: George Allen & Unwin, 1980).

  'Ruskin and Morris', *Journal of William Morris Studies*, 14:1 (autumn, 2000): 6–17.

Ferguson, Frances. 'Shelley's *Mont Blanc*: What the Mountain Said', in *Coleridge, Keats and Shelley*, ed. P. Kitson (Basingstoke: Macmillan, 1996), pp. 172–85.

Fermanis, Porscha. *John Keats and the Ideas of Enlightenment* (Edinburgh: Edinburgh University Press, 2009).

Folbre, Nancy. '"The Improper Arts": Sex and Classical Political Economy', *Population and Development Review*, 18:1 (March, 1992): 105–21.

Foucault, Michel. *The Order of Things: An Archaeology of the Human Sciences* (London: Routledge, 2002).

  The Birth of Biopolitics: Lectures at the Collège de France, 1978–79, ed. Michel Senellart, trans. Graham Burchell (Basingstoke: Palgrave, 2008).

Ffytche, Matt. *The Foundation of the Unconscious: Schelling, Freud, and the Birth of the Modern Psyche* (Cambridge: Cambridge University Press, 2012).

Gagnier, Regenia. *The Insatiability of Human Wants* (Chicago: University of Chicago Press, 2000).

Gallagher, Catherine. *The Body Economic: Life, Death and Sensation in Political Economy and the Victorian Novel* (Oxford: Princeton University Press, 2008).

Gilman, S. L., J. Birmele, J. Geller & V. D. Greenberg (eds.). *Reading Freud's Reading* (New York: New York University Press, 1994).

Glover, David. *Vampires, Mummies and Liberals: Bram Stoker and the Politics of Popular Fiction* (London: Duke University Press, 1996).

Goodman, Kevis. *Georgic Modernity and British Romanticism* (Cambridge: Cambridge University Press, 2004).

Gray, Robert. *The Aristocracy of Labour in Nineteenth-Century Britain* (London: Macmillan, 1981).

Gribble, Barbara. 'William Morris's *News from Nowhere*: A Vision Impaired', *Journal of the William Morris Society*, 6 (1985): 16–22.

Halliwell, John. 'Loyalist Satire, Parody, and *The Anti-Jacobin*', in *The British Periodical Text, 1797–1835*, ed. Simon Hull (Penrith: Humanities-Ebooks, 2008), pp. 35–67 (45).

Haney, Janice L. '"Shadow-Hunting": Romantic Irony, *Sartor Resartus*, and Victorian Romanticism', *Studies in Romanticism*, 17:3 (summer, 1978): 307–33.

Hausman, Daniel M. 'John Stuart Mill's Philosophy of Economics', *Philosophy of Science*, 48:3 (September, 1981): 363–85.

Heinzelman, Kurt. *The Economics of the Imagination* (Amherst, MA: University of Massachusetts Press, 1980).

Helsinger, Elizabeth K. *Ruskin and the Art of the Beholder* (Cambridge: Harvard University Press, 1982).

Hewlett, Maurice. 'A Materialist's Paradise', in *William Morris: The Critical Heritage*, ed. P. Faulkner (London: Routledge, 1973), pp. 343–53.

Hillis Miller, J. '*Wuthering Heights* and the Ellipses of Interpretation', *Notre Dame English Journal*, 12:2 (April, 1980): 85–100.

Hogle, Jerrold. 'Shelley as Revisionist: Power and Belief in *Mont Blanc*', in *The New Shelley*, ed. G. K. Blank (New York, NY: St Martin's Press, 1991), pp. 108–27.

Holzman, Michael. 'Anarchism and Utopia: William Morris's *News from Nowhere*', *ELH*, 51:3 (autumn, 1984): 589–603.

Iser, Wolfgang. *Walter Pater: The Aesthetic Moment*, trans. David H. Wilson (Cambridge: Cambridge University Press, 2011).

Jack, Ian. *Keats and the Mirror of Art* (Oxford: Clarendon Press, 1967).

Jahn, Beate. 'Barbarian Thoughts: Imperialism in the Philosophy of John Stuart Mill', *Review of International Studies*, 31:3 (July, 2005): 599–618.

Janowitz, Anne. *Lyric and Labour in the Romantic Tradition* (Cambridge: Cambridge University Press, 1998).

Jay, Richard & Elisabeth Jay (eds.). *Critics of Capitalism: Victorian Reactions to Political Economy* (Cambridge: Cambridge University Press, 1986).

Jensen, Hans E. 'The Development of T. R. Malthus's Institutionalist Approach to the Cure of Poverty: From Punishment of the Poor to Investment in Their Human Capital', *Review of Social Economy*, 57:4 (December, 1999): 450–65.

Jones, H. S. 'John Stuart Mill as Moralist', *Journal of the History of Ideas*, 53:2 (April–June, 1992): 287–308.

Kirchhoff, Frederick. *William Morris: The Construction of a Male Self, 1856–72* (Athens: Ohio University Press, 1990).

Knapp, Steven. *Literary Interest: The Limits of Anti-Formalism* (Cambridge: Harvard University Press, 1993).

Kooy, Michael John. *Coleridge, Schiller and Aesthetic Education* (Basingstoke: Palgrave, 2002).

Krupat, Arnold. 'The Strangeness of *Wuthering Heights*', *Nineteenth-Century Fiction*, 25:3 (December, 1970): 269–80.

Ledger, Sally. 'Chartist Aesthetics in the Mid-Nineteenth Century: Ernest Jones, a Novelist of the People', *Nineteenth-Century Literature*, 57:1 (June, 2002): 31–63.

Lesser, Wendy, Millicent Dillon, Christopher Ricks, Deirdre Levinson, Diane Johnson, Alexander Nehemas, Stephen Greenblatt, Irene Oppenheim & Leonard Michaels. 'Symposium on *Culture and Anarchy*', *The Threepenny Review*, 59 (autumn, 1994): 10–13.

Li Ou. *Keats and Negative Capability* (London: Continuum, 2009).

Lipkes, Jeff. *Politics, Religion and Classical Political Economy in Britain* (Basingstoke: Macmillan, 1999).

Macovski, Michael S. '*Wuthering Heights* and the Rhetoric of Interpretation', *ELH*, 54:2 (summer, 1987): 363–84.

Manganiello, Dominic. 'Ethics and Aesthetics in *The Picture of Dorian Gray*', *The Canadian Journal of Irish Studies*, 9:2 (December, 1983): 25–33.

Mansell, Darrel Jr., 'Ruskin and George Eliot's "Realism"', *Criticism*, 7:3 (summer, 1965): 203–16.

Matthews, G. M. (ed.). *Keats: The Critical Heritage* (London: Routledge, 1971).

McFarland, Thomas, *The Masks of Keats* (Oxford: Oxford University Press, 2000).

McGowan, John. 'From Pater to Wilde to Joyce: Modernist Epiphany and the Soulful Self', *Texas Studies in Literature and Language*, 32:3 (fall, 1990): 417–45.

McMaster, Rowland. 'Tensions in Paradise: Anarchism, Civilization, and Pleasure in Morris's *News from Nowhere*', *English in Canada*, 17 (1991): 73–87.

McNiece, Gerald. 'The Poet as Ironist in "Mont Blanc" and "Hymn to Intellectual Beauty"', *Studies in Romanticism*, 14:4 (fall, 1975): 311–36.

Mellor, Anne K. *English Romantic Irony* (Cambridge: Harvard University Press, 1980).

    Romanticism & Gender (London: Routledge, 1993).

Mendilow, Jonathan. 'Carlyle, Marx & the ILP: Alternative Routes to Socialism', *Polity*, 17:2 (winter, 1984): 225–47.

Moldstat, David. 'The Imagination in *The Vanity of Dogmatizing* and "The Scholar-Gipsy": Arnold's Reversal of Glanvill', *Victorian Poetry*, 25:2 (summer, 1987): 159–72.

Moretti, Franco. *Signs Taken for Wonders: On the Sociology of Literary Forms* (London: Verso, 2005).

Morgan, Benjamin. 'Aesthetic Freedom: Walter Pater and the Politics of Autonomy', *ELH*, 77:3 (fall, 2010): 731–56.

Newey, Vincent. 'Keats, history and the poets', in *Keats and History*, ed. N. Roe (Cambridge: Cambridge University Press, 1995), pp. 165–93.

O'Gorman, Francis. '"Suppose It Were Your Own Father of Whom You Spoke:" Ruskin's *Unto This Last*', *The Review of English Studies*, 51: 202 (May, 2000): 230–47.

'Tennyson's "The Lotos-Eaters" and the Politics of the 1830s', *Victorian Review*, 30:1 (2004): 1–20.

'Ruskin's Aesthetic of Failure in *The Stones of Venice*', *The Review of English Studies*, 55:220 (June, 2004): 374–91.

O'Neill, Michael. *Percy Bysshe Shelley: A Literary Life* (Basingstoke: Palgrave, 1989).

O'Neill, Michael (ed.). *Keats: Bicentenary Readings* (Edinburgh: Edinburgh University Press, 1997).

Plotz, John. 'Crowd Power: Chartism, Carlyle, and the Victorian Public Sphere', *Representations*, 70 (spring, 2000): 87–114.

Poovey, Mary. *Genres of the Credit Economy: Mediating Value in Eighteenth- & Nineteenth-Century Britain* (Chicago, IL: University of Chicago Press, 2008).

Potolsky, Matthew. 'Fear of Falling: Walter Pater's *Marius the Epicurean* as a Dangerous Influence', *ELH*, 65:3 (fall, 1998): 701–29.

Punter, David. *The Literature of Terror*, 2 vols. (London: Longman, 1996).

Rancière, Jacques. 'The Politics of the Spider', *Studies in Romanticism*, 50:2 (summer, 2011): 239–50.

The Politics of Aesthetics, ed. and trans. Gabriel Rockhill (London: Bloomsbury, 2004).

Rena-Dozier, Emily. 'Gothic Criticisms: *Wuthering Heights* and Nineteenth-Century Literary History', *ELH*, 77:3 (fall, 2010): 757–75.

Rieder, John. 'Shelley's "Mont Blanc": Landscape and the Ideology of the Sacred Text', *ELH*, 48:4 (winter 1981): 778–98.

Ricks, Christopher. *Keats and Embarrassment* (Oxford: Clarendon Press, 1974).

Roe, Nicholas, *John Keats and the Culture of Dissent* (Oxford: Clarendon Press, 1997).

Roe, Nicholas (ed.). *Keats and History* (Cambridge: Cambridge University Press, 1995).

Roston, Murray. *Victorian Contexts* (London: Macmillan, 1996).

Schwarz, Pedro. *The New Political Economy of J. S. Mill* (London: Weidenfeld, 1972).

Searle, G. R. *Morality and the Market in Victorian Britain* (Oxford: Clarendon Press, 1998).

Sedgwick, Eve Kosofsky. *Between Men: English Literature and Male Homosocial Desire* (New York, NY: Columbia University Press, 1985).

Senf, Carol A. '*Dracula*: Stoker's Response to the New Woman', *Victorian Studies*, 26:1 (autumn, 1982): 33–49.

Shell, Marc. *The Economy of Literature* (Baltimore, MD: Johns Hopkins University Press, 1978).

Money, Language, and Thought: Literary and Philosophical Economies from the Medieval to the Modern Era (Berkeley, CA: University of California Press, 1982).

Shuter, William F. *Rereading Walter Pater* (Cambridge: Cambridge University Press, 1997).

Sinfield, Alan. *Dramatic Monologue* (London: Methuen, 1977).

Skarda, Patricia L. 'Vampirism and Plagiarism: Byron's Influence and Polidori's Practice, *Studies in Romanticism*, 28:2 (summer, 1989): 249–69.

Spiegelman, Willard. *Majestic Indolence* (Oxford: Oxford University Press, 1995).

Stillinger, Jack. *Coleridge and Textual Instability* (Oxford: Oxford University Press, 1994).

Stone, Donald D. 'Matthew Arnold and the Pragmatics of Hebraism and Hellenism', *Poetics Today*, 19:2 (summer, 1998): 179–98.

Swift, Roger. 'Thomas Carlyle, "Chartism", and the Irish in Early Victorian England', *Victorian Literature and Culture*, 29:1 (2001): 67–83.

Tambling, Jeremy. 'Carlyle Through Nietzsche: Reading *Sartor Resartus*', *The Modern Language Review*, 102:2 (April, 2007): 326–40.

Timko, Michael. *Carlyle & Tennyson* (London: Macmillan Press, 1988).

Trilling, Lionel. *The Opposing Self* (London: Secker and Warburg, 1955).

'Agression and Utopia: A Note on William Morris's *News from Nowhere*', in *The Last Decade: Essays and Reviews, 1965–75*, ed. Diana Trilling (New York: Harcourt Brace, 1979), pp. 148–59.

Turley, Richard Marggraf. *Keats's Boyish Imagination* (London: Routledge, 2004).

Ulmer, William A. 'The Human Seasons: Arnold, Keats, and "The Scholar-Gipsy"', *Victorian Poetry*, 22:3 (autumn, 1984): 247–61.

Verburg, Rudi. 'John Stuart Mill's Political Economy: Educational Means to Moral Progress', *Review of Social Economy*, 64:2 (June, 2006): 225–46.

Vine, Steven. 'The Wuther of the Other in *Wuthering Heights*', *Nineteenth-Century Literature*, 49:3 (December, 1994): 339–59.

Wallen, Jeffrey. 'Alive in the Grave: Walter Pater's Renaissance', *ELH*, 66:4 (winter, 1999): 1033–51.

Walters, Tim. 'The Question of Culture (and Anarchy)', *MLN*, 112 (1997): 349–65.

Waithe, Marcus. *William Morris's Utopia of Strangers: Victorian Medievalism and the Ideal of Hospitality* (Cambridge: D. S. Brewer, 2006).

Wasserman, Earl. *Shelley: A Critical Reading* (London: Johns Hopkins University Press, 1977).

Watkins, Daniel. *Keats's Poetry and the Politics of the Imagination* (London: Associated University Presses, 1989).

West, Sally. *Coleridge and Shelley: Textual Engagement* (Aldershot: Ashgate, 2007).

Wiener, Martin. *English Culture and the Decline of the Industrial Spirit, 1850–1980* (Cambridge: Cambridge University Press, 2004).

Wiles, Peter. 'The Necessity and Impossibility of Political Economy', *History and Theory*, 11:1 (1972): 3–14.

Williams, Anne. 'Natural Supernaturalism in *Wuthering Heights*', *Studies in Philology*, 82:1 (winter, 1985): 104–27.

Williams, Keith. *H. G. Wells, Modernity and the Movies* (Liverpool: Liverpool University Press, 2007).

Williams, Raymond. *Culture and Society* (London: Chatto & Windus, 1967).

Winders, James A. *European Culture Since 1848* (Basingstoke: Palgrave, 2001).

Winch, Donald. *Riches and Poverty* (Cambridge: Cambridge University Press, 1996).

  Wealth and Life (Cambridge: Cambridge University Press, 2009).

Wolfson, Susan. 'Feminizing Keats', in *Critical Essays on John Keats*, ed. H. de Almeida (Boston, MA: G. K. Hall and Co., 1990), pp. 317–56.

Index

aesthetic democracy, 7, 118, 123, 124, 144, 156, 188, 189, 214
Aristotle, 86, 93
Armstrong, Isobel, 100, 210, 211
Arnold, Matthew, 5, 7, 10, 100, 107–9, 114, 120, 122, 123, 134, 135, 136, 137, 138, 141, 142, 143, 144, 149, 156, 161, 162, 165, 167, 179, 184, 186, 195
  Culture & Anarchy, 124–33
Auerbach, Nina, 175, 178, 217

Balassa, Bela, 209
Barbauld, Anna Letitia, 45, 205
Bate, Walter Jackson, 39, 45
Bentham, Jeremy, 9, 12, 45, 63, 65, 66, 67, 184
Berg, Maxine, 49, 52, 59, 77, 208
Bladen, V. W., 73
Blaug, Mark, 50
Bonaparte, Felicia, 5
Botting, Fred, 163, 181
Bowen, Elizabeth, 217
Brake, Laurel, 140
Breton, Rob, 99
Brontë, Emily, 149–57, 159, 160, 161, 165, 168, 179, 180, 194
Burrow, J. W., 209
Byron, George Gordon, 5, 121, 122, 147, 150, 154, 157, 179, 186

Canning, George, 52
Carlyle, Thomas, 5, 6, 8, 78, 82–94, 96, 98–100, 112, 114, 116, 117, 119, 120, 124, 127, 133, 136, 137, 145, 149, 168, 178, 183, 184, 187, 217
  'Occasional Discourse on the Negro Question', 78
  Past & Present, 88–93, 96
  Sartor Resartus, 83–8, 89, 90, 91, 93, 101, 105
  Signs of the Times, 84
Chaloner, William, 211
Chernaik, Judith, 202

Coleridge, Samuel Taylor, 9, 11, 14, 15, 41, 44, 48, 64, 65, 85, 87, 89, 90, 91, 95, 96, 119, 127, 129, 132, 133, 145, 147, 153, 154, 158, 169, 179, 184, 186
  'Frost at Midnight', 24, 26, 27, 28, 102
  'Hymn before sunrise in the vale of Chamouni', 19
  'The Eolian Harp', 3, 5, 18, 20–2, 24, 26, 27, 36, 42, 103, 105
  Biographia Literaria, 85, 87, 90, 96
  'Christabel', 157–8, 160, 162, 181
  'Frost at Midnight', 17–18, 28
  On the Constitution of Church and State, 9
  Sibylline Leaves, 21, 30
Collini, Stefan, 131, 214
communism, 71, 94–9
Comte, Auguste, 64
Connell, Philip, 205
Cowper, William, 11, 14, 18, 26, 30–47, 48, 64, 153, 179, 186, 210

Daley, Kenneth, 123
Dart, Gregory, 99
democratic reform, 8, 125, 129–30, 185
Dentith, Simon, 205, 208
Dilke, Charles, 40, 41, 204
Dobb, Maurice, 50
Donnelly, Hugo, 202, 203
Dowling, Linda, 118, 122, 124, 125, 134, 143, 144–5, 188, 214, 215

Eagleton, Terry, 98
Eliot, George, 29, 200
  Middlemarch, 1–6
Engels, Friedrich, 116, 211
Ensor, George, 206
Ewen, Frederic, 92, 209

failure, 10, 107, 116–22, 123, 128, 146
Faulkner, Peter, 212

Ferguson, Adam, 9, 13, 50, 56, 64, 75, 88, 206, 206, 211
Ferguson, Frances, 21, 202, 203
Ffytche, Matt, 192
Fitzpatrick, Margaret Ann, 40
Flaubert, Gustave, 10, 12
Foster, Roy, 216
Fourier, Charles, 70, 75, 187
Freud, Sigmund, 8, 124, 192–200
Freund, John Christian, 162

Gallagher, Catherine, 49
Glanvill, Joseph, 105
Glover, David, 169, 174
Goethe, Johann Wolfgang, 65, 92, 139
Goodman, Kevis, 42
gospel of work, the, 5, 7, 12, 81–113, 114, 123, 128, 130, 131, 145, 149, 161, 162, 168, 177–9, 184, 188
gothic, 6, 26, 31, 114–24, 149–82
Green, David Bonnell, 38

Halliwell, John, 206
Haney, Janice, 83
Hazlitt, William, 217
Hegel, Georg Wilhelm Friedrich, 11
Hellenism, 134–48
Helsinger, Elizabeth, 123
Henderson, William, 211
Heyck, T. W., 67
Hogle, Jerrold, 19
Hopfl, H. M., 206
Hopkins, Gerard Manley, 100, 109–11, 122, 186, 195
Howard, John, 45
Hugo, Victor, 139

Inglis, H. D., 69
Iser, Wolfgang, 141, 146, 147

Jahn, Beate, 208
Jeffrey, John, 41
Jensen, Hans E., 206
Jones, H. S., 208

Kant, Immanuel, 11, 12, 35, 40
Keats, George, 40
Keats, John, 6, 11, 14, 30–47, 48, 51, 63, 66, 67, 68, 75, 76, 78, 80, 82, 101, 103, 109, 117, 122, 126, 131, 133, 136, 142, 145, 150–7, 159, 163, 165, 166, 168, 179, 186, 194
  'negative capability', 7, 39–47, 150, 167
Kingsley, Charles, 9, 129, 130, 133
Knapp, Steven, 40
Kooy, Michael John, 93

Lafitau, Joseph-François, 206
Le Fanu, Sheridan, 8, 157, 162–9, 171, 178, 179, 180, 187, 194
Locke, John, 42

Macovski, Michael, 150
Malthus, Thomas, 7, 49, 51, 53, 55–64, 66, 69, 72, 74, 79, 86, 88, 213
  Essay on Population, 51, 54, 55
  Principles of Political Economy, 55–64
Mansell, Darrel Jr, 213
Marx, Karl, 10, 12, 70, 82, 94–9, 112, 116, 164, 183, 187, 209
  Capital, 94, 96, 112
  Grundrisse, 95–6
  The Communist Manifesto, 94
Maturin, Charles, 217
McCulloch, John, 72
McNiece, Gerald, 202
Mellor, Anne, 83, 85, 150
Mendilow, Jonathan, 93
Mill, James, 58, 65, 66
Mill, John Stuart, 7, 9, 49, 51, 53, 55, 61, 63, 64–80, 81, 88, 92, 104, 108, 109, 111, 119, 120, 122, 126, 131, 133, 137, 142, 149, 161, 164, 167, 183, 184, 217
  'gospel of leisure', 78, 113
  Autobiography, 65–6
  Principles of Political Economy, 7, 64–80
Moretti, Franco, 169
Morris, William, 94, 99, 112, 115, 119, 122, 139, 144, 187

O'Gorman, Francis, 100, 123
Ou, Li, 39
Owen, Robert, 70, 75, 187

Pater, Walter, 7, 129, 133–48, 161, 162, 167–9, 181, 183, 184, 186, 197
Place, Francis, 209
Pocock, J. G. A., 206
Polidori, John, 154, 158–9, 165, 168, 175, 182, 187
political economy, 6, 7, 11, 12, 13, 37, 48–80, 81, 95, 96, 124, 161, 183
Potolsky, Matthew, 135
Pullen, John, 55
Punter, David, 181

Radcliffe, Anne, 170
Rancière, Jacques, 11–12, 35–6, 37, 40, 44, 99
Reynolds, John Hamilton, 34
Ricardo, David, 7, 48, 49–55, 56, 58, 59, 63, 65, 66, 68, 69, 72, 75, 79, 187
  'stationary state', 50, 72

On the Principles of Political Economy and Taxation, 49–55

Rieder, John, 19

Riquelme, John Paul, 218

Rollins, Hyder, 32

Romanticism, 6, 9, 10, 12, 46, 48, 63, 66, 67, 68, 70, 76, 78, 79, 81, 82, 85, 87, 89, 96, 97, 100, 101, 103, 105, 108, 111, 113, 117, 123, 124, 128, 135, 136, 144, 145, 147, 149, 153, 155, 158, 161, 174, 183, 184, 193

Rousseau, Jean-Jacques, 142, 210

Ruskin, John, 6, 7, 10, 94, 98, 114–24, 126, 127, 128, 133, 135, 144, 149, 161, 167, 168, 184, 186

Rymer, James Malcolm, 159–61, 164, 165, 168, 172, 175, 180, 182, 187, 194

Saint-Simonians, the, 64, 70

savagery, 52–3, 59, 68, 73, 77

Say, Jean-Baptiste, 58

Schiller, Friedrich, 9, 12, 35, 87, 90, 91, 93, 94, 95, 96, 98, 109, 116, 117, 119, 120, 122, 125, 129, 130, 131, 132, 139, 184, 219

Schopenhauer, Arthur, 10

Schwartz, Pedro, 50, 51, 64, 65, 66, 206, 206, 209

Sedgwick, Eve, 101

Senf, Carol, 218

Shakespeare, William, 41, 44, 45–6
    King Lear, 45
    Troilus and Cressida, 32

Shelley, Mary, 14, 170

Shelley, Percy Bysshe, 3, 5, 11, 14, 48, 63, 66, 75, 78, 80, 82, 95, 101, 105, 108, 109, 110, 114, 122, 133, 137, 145, 156, 163, 165, 166, 171, 174, 179, 186, 193, 194
    'Mont Blanc', 7, 14–30, 31, 32, 36, 42, 76, 85, 102
    Defence of Poetry, 3, 7, 29–30, 95

Sidgwick, Henry, 213

Sinfield, Alan, 102

Skal, David, 175, 178, 217

Skarda. Patricia, 216

Smiles, Samuel, 82

Smith, Adam, 9, 13, 48, 49, 55, 56, 57, 58, 60, 64, 70, 72, 79, 88, 95, 96, 206, 206, 209

Southey, Robert, 52

Sraffa, Piero, 206

stadial history, 51

Staten, Henry, 5

Sterne, Laurence, 83, 89

Stillinger, Jack, 203

Stoker, Bram, 8, 157, 162, 165, 168, 169–82, 183, 194

Stone, Donald, 5

Tennyson, Alfred, 100–5, 110, 114, 118, 120, 123, 128, 133, 143, 157, 161, 165, 166, 169, 171, 175, 179, 185, 186, 196

Thomson, James, 102

Ulmer, William, 105

Vance, Norman, 206

Voltaire, 142

West, Sally, 202

Wiener, Martin, 209

Wiesenfarth, Joseph, 5

Wilde, Oscar, 181, 216

Williams, Anne, 149

Williams, Keith, 218

Williams, Raymond, 77, 189

Winch, Donald, 77, 208, 209, 213

Winckelmann, Johann, 35, 134, 135

Wollstonecraft, Mary, 9, 45, 64, 186

Woodhouse, Richard, 31, 204

Wordsworth, William, 35, 43, 64, 65, 95, 108, 124, 129, 130, 131, 155, 158, 186, 193

Yeats, William Butler, 217

CAMBRIDGE STUDIES IN NINETEENTH-CENTURY LITERATURE AND CULTURE

GENERAL EDITOR: Gillian Beer, *University of Cambridge*

Titles published

1. The Sickroom in Victorian Fiction: The Art of Being Ill
   Miriam Bailin, *Washington University*
2. Muscular Christianity: Embodying the Victorian Age
   edited by Donald E. Hall, *California State University, Northridge*
3. Victorian Masculinities:
   Manhood and Masculine Poetics in Early Victorian Literature and Art
   Herbert Sussman, *Northeastern University, Boston*
4. Byron and the Victorians
   Andrew Elfenbein, *University of Minnesota*
5. Literature in the Marketplace:
   Nineteenth-Century British Publishing and the Circulation of Books
   edited by John O. Jordan, *University of California, Santa Cruz* and Robert
   L. Patten, *Rice University, Houston*
6. Victorian Photography, Painting and Poetry
   Lindsay Smith, *University of Sussex*
7. Charlotte Brontë and Victorian Psychology
   Sally Shuttleworth, *University of Sheffield*
8. The Gothic Body: Sexuality, Materialism and Degeneration at the
   Fin de Siècle
   Kelly Hurley, *University of Colorado at Boulder*
9. Rereading Walter Pater
   William F. Shuter, *Eastern Michigan University*
10. Remaking Queen Victoria
    edited by Margaret Homans, *Yale University* and Adrienne Munich, *State
    University of New York, Stony Brook*
11. Disease, Desire, and the Body in Victorian Women's Popular Novels
    Pamela K. Gilbert, *University of Florida*
12. Realism, Representation, and the Arts in Nineteenth-Century Literature
    Alison Byerly, *Middlebury College, Vermont*
13. Literary Culture and the Pacific
    Vanessa Smith, *University of Sydney*
14. Professional Domesticity in the Victorian Novel
    Women, Work and Home
    Monica F. Cohen
15. Victorian Renovations of the Novel:
    Narrative Annexes and the Boundaries of Representation
    Suzanne Keen, *Washington and Lee University, Virginia*

16. Actresses on the Victorian Stage:
    Feminine Performance and the Galatea Myth
    Gail Marshall, *University of Leeds*
17. Death and the Mother from Dickens to Freud:
    Victorian Fiction and the Anxiety of Origin
    Carolyn Dever, *Vanderbilt University, Tennessee*
18. Ancestry and Narrative in Nineteenth-Century British Literature: Blood
    Relations from Edgeworth to Hardy
    Sophie Gilmartin, *Royal Holloway, University of London*
19. Dickens, Novel Reading, and the Victorian Popular Theatre
    Deborah Vlock
20. After Dickens: Reading, Adaptation and Performance
    John Glavin, *Georgetown University, Washington D C*
21. Victorian Women Writers and the Woman Question
    edited by Nicola Diane Thompson, *Kingston University, London*
22. Rhythm and Will in Victorian Poetry
    Matthew Campbell, *University of Sheffield*
23. Gender, Race, and the Writing of Empire:
    Public Discourse and the Boer War
    Paula M. Krebs, *Wheaton College, Massachusetts*
24. Ruskin's God
    Michael Wheeler, *University of Southampton*
25. Dickens and the Daughter of the House
    Hilary M. Schor, *University of Southern California*
26. Detective Fiction and the Rise of Forensic Science
    Ronald R. Thomas, *Trinity College, Hartford, Connecticut*
27. Testimony and Advocacy in Victorian Law, Literature, and Theology
    Jan-Melissa Schramm, *Trinity Hall, Cambridge*
28. Victorian Writing about Risk:
    Imagining a Safe England in a Dangerous World
    Elaine Freedgood, *University of Pennsylvania*
29. Physiognomy and the Meaning of Expression
    in Nineteenth-Century Culture
    Lucy Hartley, *University of Southampton*
30. The Victorian Parlour: A Cultural Study
    Thad Logan, *Rice University, Houston*
31. Aestheticism and Sexual Parody 1840–1940
    Dennis Denisoff, *Ryerson University, Toronto*
32. Literature, Technology and Magical Thinking, 1880–1920
    Pamela Thurschwell, *University College London*
33. Fairies in Nineteenth-Century Art and Literature
    Nicola Bown, *Birkbeck, University of London*
34. George Eliot and the British Empire
    Nancy Henry *The State University of New York, Binghamton*

35. Women's Poetry and Religion in Victorian England:
    Jewish Identity and Christian Culture
    Cynthia Scheinberg, *Mills College, California*
36. Victorian Literature and the Anorexic Body
    Anna Krugovoy Silver, *Mercer University, Georgia*
37. Eavesdropping in the Novel from Austen to Proust
    Ann Gaylin, *Yale University*
38. Missionary Writing and Empire, 1800–1860
    Anna Johnston, *University of Tasmania*
39. London and the Culture of Homosexuality, 1885–1914
    Matt Cook, *Keele University*
40. Fiction, Famine, and the Rise of Economics in Victorian Britain and Ireland
    Gordon Bigelow, *Rhodes College, Tennessee*
41. Gender and the Victorian Periodical
    Hilary Fraser, *Birkbeck, University of London*
    Judith Johnston and Stephanie Green, *University of Western Australia*
42. The Victorian Supernatural
    edited by Nicola Bown, *Birkbeck College, London*
    Carolyn Burdett, *London Metropolitan University*
    and Pamela Thurschwell, *University College London*
43. The Indian Mutiny and the British Imagination
    Gautam Chakravarty, *University of Delhi*
44. The Revolution in Popular Literature: Print, Politics and the People
    Ian Haywood, *Roehampton University of Surrey*
45. Science in the Nineteenth-Century Periodical:
    Reading the Magazine of Nature
    Geoffrey Cantor, *University of Leeds*
    Gowan Dawson, *University of Leicester*
    Graeme Gooday, *University of Leeds*
    Richard Noakes, *University of Cambridge*
    Sally Shuttleworth, *University of Sheffield*
    and Jonathan R. Topham, *University of Leeds*
46. Literature and Medicine in Nineteenth-Century Britain
    from Mary Shelley to George Eliot
    Janis McLarren Caldwell, *Wake Forest University*
47. The Child Writer from Austen to Woolf
    edited by Christine Alexander, *University of New South Wales* and
    Juliet McMaster, *University of Alberta*
48. From Dickens to Dracula:
    Gothic, Economics, and Victorian Fiction
    Gail Turley Houston, *University of New Mexico*
49. Voice and the Victorian Storyteller
    Ivan Kreilkamp, *University of Indiana*
50. Charles Darwin and Victorian Visual Culture
    Jonathan Smith, *University of Michigan-Dearborn*

51. Catholicism, Sexual Deviance, and Victorian Gothic Culture
    Patrick R. O'Malley, *Georgetown University*
52. Epic and Empire in Nineteenth-Century Britain
    Simon Dentith, *University of Gloucestershire*
53. Victorian Honeymoons: Journeys to the Conjugal
    Helena Michie, *Rice University*
54. The Jewess in Nineteenth-Century British Literary Culture
    Nadia Valman, *University of Southampton*
55. Ireland, India and Nationalism in Nineteenth-Century Literature
    Julia Wright, *Dalhousie University*
56. Dickens and the Popular Radical Imagination
    Sally Ledger, *Birkbeck, University of London*
57. Darwin, Literature and Victorian Respectability
    Gowan Dawson, *University of Leicester*
58. 'Michael Field': Poetry, Aestheticism and the *Fin de Siècle*
    Marion Thain, *University of Birmingham*
59. Colonies, Cults and Evolution:
    Literature, Science and Culture in Nineteenth-Century Writing
    David Amigoni, *Keele University*
60. Realism, Photography and Nineteenth-Century Fiction
    Daniel A. Novak, *Lousiana State University*
61. Caribbean Culture and British Fiction in the Atlantic World, 1780–1870
    Tim Watson, *University of Miami*
62. The Poetry of Chartism: Aesthetics, Politics, History
    Michael Sanders, *University of Manchester*
63. Literature and Dance in Nineteenth-Century Britain:
    Jane Austen to the New Woman
    Cheryl Wilson, *Indiana University*
64. Shakespeare and Victorian Women
    Gail Marshall, *Oxford Brookes University*
65. The Tragi-Comedy of Victorian Fatherhood
    Valerie Sanders, *University of Hull*
66. Darwin and the Memory of the Human:
    Evolution, Savages, and South America
    Cannon Schmitt, *University of Toronto*
67. From Sketch to Novel:
    The Development of Victorian Fiction
    Amanpal Garcha, *Ohio State University*
68. The Crimean War and the British Imagination
    Stefanie Markovits, *Yale University*
69. Shock, Memory and the Unconscious in Victorian Fiction
    Jill L. Matus, *University of Toronto*
70. Sensation and Modernity in the 1860s
    Nicholas Daly, *University College Dublin*

71. Ghost-Seers, Detectives, and Spiritualists:
    Theories of Vision in Victorian Literature and Science
    Srdjan Smajić, *Furman University*
72. Satire in an Age of Realism
    Aaron Matz, *Scripps College, California*
73. Thinking About Other People in Nineteenth-Century British Writing
    Adela Pinch, *University of Michigan*
74. Tuberculosis and the Victorian Literary Imagination
    Katherine Byrne, *University of Ulster, Coleraine*
75. Urban Realism and the Cosmopolitan Imagination in the
    Nineteenth Century: Visible City, Invisible World
    Tanya Agathocleous, *Hunter College, City University of New York*
76. Women, Literature, and the Domesticated Landscape: England's Disciples
    of Flora, 1780–1870
    Judith W. Page, *University of Florida*
    Elise L. Smith, *Millsaps College, Mississippi*
77. Time and the Moment in Victorian Literature and Society
    Sue Zemka, *University of Colorado*
78. Popular Fiction and Brain Science in the Late Nineteenth Century
    Anne Stiles, *Washington State University*
79. Picturing Reform in Victorian Britain
    Janice Carlisle, *Yale University*
80. Atonement and Self-Sacrifice in Nineteenth-Century Narrative
    Jan-Melissa Schramm, *University of Cambridge*
81. The Silver Fork Novel: Fashionable Fiction in the Age of Reform
    Edward Copeland, *Pomona College, California*
82. Oscar Wilde and Ancient Greece
    Iain Ross, *Colchester Royal Grammar School*
83. The Poetry of Victorian Scientists: Style, Science and Nonsense
    Daniel Brown, *University of Southampton*
84. Moral Authority, Men of Science, and the Victorian Novel
    Anne DeWitt, *Princeton Writing Program*
85. China and the Victorian Imagination: Empires Entwined
    Ross G. Forman, *University of Warwick*
86. Dickens's Style
    Daniel Tyler, *University of Oxford*
87. The Formation of the Victorian Literary Profession
    Richard Salmon, *University of Leeds*
88. Before George Eliot: Marian Evans and the Periodical Press
    Fionnuala Dillane, *University College Dublin*
89. The Victorian Novel and the Space of Art: Fictional Form on Display
    Dehn Gilmore, *California Institute of Technology*
90. George Eliot and Money: Economics, Ethics and Literature
    Dermot Coleman, *Independent Scholar*

91. Masculinity and the New Imperialism: Rewriting Manhood in British Popular Literature, 1870–1914
Bradley Deane, *University of Minnesota*

92. Evolution and Victorian Culture
edited by Bernard Lightman, *York University, Toronto* and Bennett Zon, *University of Durham*

93. Victorian Literature, Energy, and the Ecological Imagination
Allen MacDuffie, *University of Texas, Austin*

94. Popular Literature, Authorship and the Occult in Late Victorian Britain
Andrew McCann, *Dartmouth College, New Hampshire*

95. Women Writing Art History in the Nineteenth Century: Looking Like a Woman
Hilary Fraser Birkbeck, *University of London*

96. Relics of Death in Victorian Literature and Culture
Deborah Lutz, *Long Island University, C. W. Post Campus*

97. The Demographic Imagination and the Nineteenth-Century City: Paris, London, New York .
Nicholas Daly, *University College Dublin*

98. Dickens and the Business of Death
Claire Wood, *University of York*

99. Translation as Transformation in Victorian Poetry
Annmarie Drury, *Queens College, City University of New York*

100. The Bigamy Plot: Sensation and Convention in the Victorian Novel
Maia McAleavey, *Boston College, Massachusetts*

101. English Fiction and the Evolution of Language, 1850–1914
Will Abberley, *University of Oxford*

102. The Racial Hand in the Victorian Imagination
Aviva Briefel, *Bowdoin College, Maine*

103. Evolution and Imagination in Victorian Children's Literature
Jessica Straley, *University of Utah*

104. Writing Arctic Disaster: Authorship and Exploration
Adriana Craciun, *University of California, Riverside*

105. Science, Fiction, and the *Fin-de-Siècle* Periodical Press
Will Tattersdill, *University of Birmingham*

106. Democratising Beauty in Nineteenth-Century Britain: Art and the Politics of Public Life
Lucy Hartley, *University of Michigan*

107. Everyday Words and the Character of Prose in Nineteenth-Century Britain
Jonathan Farina, *Seton Hall University, New Jersey*

108. Gerard Manley Hopkins and the Poetry of Religious Experience
Martin Dubois, *University of Newcastle upon Tyne*

109. Blindness and Writing: From Wordsworth to Gissing
Heather Tilley, *Birkbeck College, University of London*

110. An Underground History of Early Victorian Fiction:
     Chartism, Radical Print Culture, and the Social Problem Novel
     Gregory Vargo, *New York University*
111. Automatism and Creative Acts in the Age of New Psychology
     Linda M. Austin, *Oklahoma State University*
112. Idleness and Aesthetic Consciousness, 1815–1900
     Richard Adelman, *University of Sussex*